Golden Moments

A Treasure of Giesel Family Recipes

Compiled and Edited
by Arlene (Giesel) Koehn

GOLDEN MOMENTS PUBLISHING
WEST POINT, MISSISSIPPI

D1295360

Golden Moments
A *Treasure of Giesel Family Recipes*

Copyright © 1996 by Arlene Giesel Koehn

1st Printing - 1996
2nd Printing - 1998

Golden Moments Publishing

Printed in the United States of America
TOOF COOKBOOK DIVISION
STARR ★ TOOF
670 South Cooper Street
Memphis, TN 38104

Library of Congress Catalog Number: 96-77620

ISBN: 0-9653741-0-6

Grandmother Caroline

*"She looketh well to the ways of her household, and
eateth not the bread of idleness."*

A stirring of memories comes like a whisper, and we remember with fondness the character of this strong woman. Grandma Carrie was born August, 29, 1882, the daughter of Peter and Carolina (Jantz) Unruh. She and her parents were members of the Lonetree Mennonite Church near Galva, Kansas.

Grandfather John William Giesel was born April 15, 1875, near Wisner, Nebraska to August and Sophia (Obenauer) Giesel. At the age of twenty-four years, he and a friend traveled to Kansas by horse and buggy and train.

Grandpa John found employment with a threshing company in the Mennonite community near Galva, Kansas. He was invited to a church dinner where he met a young pretty girl and remarked, "This is the girl I am going to marry." John was later baptized in the Mennonite faith.

After their marriage in 1899, they purchased a house in Galva where he owned a repair shop. John was industrious and very inventive, working with new ideas in his shop. Six children were born to them: Mornie (Morna Jo), Freeman (my father) Nathan, Mable, Sophie, and Elma. Grandma Carrie always said, "John was the love of my life." She was a happy, contented wife and mother who loved to sew for her girls and cook for her family. On December 27, 1913, after eating lunch with his family, John hugged and kissed Carrie and said, "Carrie, the children are all yours." Grandpa John with his two sons went back to the shop to work on a new invention. Moments later, Grandpa was killed in a tragic accident. Fortunately, his sons were out of harm's way. Later the memory of his last words would return with poignant meaning.

It has been said that Grandma Carrie never recovered from her grief; however, she courageously went on with her life, caring for six children, ages one to twelve years, with a hope that conquered despair, in a world of turmoil and a devasted family. This was difficult, but she was determined to survive and provide for her family. She had no source of income but what she could earn. There was no time to sit idle; she was very industrious, often taking employment in the harvest fields shocking wheat bundles. Freeman and Nathan would help carry the bundles of wheat. One day a neighbor stopped by the field on his way to town and she gave him a nickel to buy a loaf of bread for her family.

Many times the children were home alone while she worked, going from place to place doing housework, laundry, ironing and baking bread. She would hang wallpaper for one dollar per room and could paper two rooms a day.

Her means of transportation was horse and buggy. One winter day her job took her ten miles from home. Darkness came early; a cold wind and snow forced her to spend the night. She slept very little thinking of her children at home. In the morning, snow and ice made the road impassable, and she traveled across the fields, thankful to find her children safe.

Later she was hired to cook for the Keener Threshing Company, sometimes traveling two hundred miles from home with her son Nathan. Freeman lived with the Dan Wiggers family; Mornie worked as a live in helper for near by families; and Mable, Sophie and Elma stayed with their grandmother. She was often weary, and yet there was much to do at home at the end of the day. Many were the sacrifices she made, and many were the comforts and dreams she gave up to make life better for her children.

Grandma Carrie was known for her cooking; often she was asked to prepare a wedding reception. She was appointed the first cook at Mercy Hospital when its doors opened in 1944.

During the years she worked hard to keep her family together and in school. She was very hospitable and loved people, and she especially enjoyed inviting and cooking for company.

She had no medical training in the accepted sense, yet for miles around people had faith in her skill and treatment. Often in illness, neighbors would call for her to care for a sick patient or a new mother and baby.

Grandma Carrie was a lover of song and during the long lonely evenings, when the amber glow of the kerosane lamps cast flickering shadows along the wall, she would gather her children around the table and together they would sing.

The courage that sustained her, along with the love for her children, helped her to triumph against the backdrop of heartache and loneliness. She knew God had not forsaken her and she remembered His goodness.

Christmas and birthdays were not forgotten; a small gift or a new dress for the girls were delightful presents. Christmas mornings were special times with a sack of candy or perhaps some nuts hidden under the plates on the breakfast table. She made a variety of candy and baked cookies by the dozens to sell at Christmastime.

In her later years, she loved to read her Bible which was precious to her, and she read the New Testament fifty times.She loved writing letters and keeping in touch with far away family, friends and missionaries. Although she lived for nearly ninety years she never grew old. She remained alert and interested in current events. Never did she look back and live in the past.

Grandma Carrie was active all her life. The last several years she spent in a wheel chair, living in a nursing home. Her many friends both young and old loved to visit her, and she enjoyed them all.

Even though she had many trials, struggles and heartaches, she was a wonderful Mother, Grandmother and friend. She kept the faith and now the torch has passed. The example Grandma Carrie set has encouraged succeeding generations. At the end she died quietly and with out fuss at almost ninety years of age. This book is a memorial to a good and great old lady.

"Let us, before we die, gather our heritage and offer it to our children."

For
My husband Willis, our son Mark, and our daughters Charmaine and Shana, who not only spent many hours helping with this book, but inspired me to keep at it until we turned the last page.

For
The dear family and friends who have shared their cherished family recipes with me or sent them from far away places and for the suggestions, and encouragements that helped make this family book possible.

For
The beautiful original art cover by Shirley Nichols and the illustrations by Gina Dedeaux

I am forever grateful and indebted to you and to a great many who have encouraged and stood by me through these months.

Arlene (Giesel) Koehn

Preface

We do not claim that any of these recipes are original, they have been collected from magazines, cookbooks and over the back yard fence and from friends and family far and near.

A recipe is like a poem, and a poem is not to be shut away in a drawer but read to anyone who will listen, for an unshared recipe is a poor thing.

Our heritage must not be tucked away and forgotten; but passed to our children and grandchildren, the cooks of tomorrow.

Contents

APPETIZERS

Avocado Dip

3 large avocados, mashed
1 tablespoon lemon juice
1 tablespoon mayonnaise

1 tablespoon chopped onion
3 tablespoons picante sauce
Salt and pepper to taste.

Mix together. Great to serve with chips as a snack or to give a taco or tostada added flavor, just top with a spoonful.

Valetta Koehn

Chip Dip

1 package cream cheese, softened

1 jar picante sauce

Mix in desired amount of picante sauce until it is as hot or mild as you like. Serve with Dorito chips.

Jolene Unruh

Curry Dip

1 cup miracle whip
¼ teaspoon garlic powder
3 tablespoons catsup
1 tablespoon Worcestershire sauce
pinch of salt

2 teaspoons curry powder
1 teaspoon Tabasco
1 teaspoon horseradish
1 to 2 tablespoons fresh lemon juice

Combine and let stand for several hours before using. (Keeps well in refrigerator up to a week.)

Arlene Giesel Koehn

Fruit Dip

1 (6 oz.) can frozen pink
  lemonade (undiluted)

1 can sweetened condensed milk
1 small carton cool whip

Mix lemonade and milk, gently fold into cool whip.

Mary, Mrs. Lee Giesel

Mexican Bean Dip

Make a white sauce with:
  4 tablespoons butter
  4 tablespoons flour
  ½ teaspoon salt

¼ teaspoon pepper
2 cups milk
1 can 15 ounce Mexican style beans

Mash 1 can 15 ounce Mexican style beans (I use a pint of pinto beans). Add to white sauce. Season with ½ teaspoon chili powder, 1½ tablespoons Worcestershire sauce, ¾ teaspoon Tabasco sauce, 1 cup shredded cheddar cheese. Serve with chips.

Sophie (Giesel) Koehn

Praline Dip

1 package (14 oz.) caramels
1 cup heavy cream
1 oz. square semisweet chocolate

6 ounces pecans, toasted and
  chopped
3 apples, sliced

Combine ingredients in order given and melt over medium heat. Serve with sliced apples that have been dipped in lemon juice to prevent browning.

Arlene Giesel Koehn

Vegetable Dip

1 cup sour cream
1 cup Hellmann's mayonnaise
  (Do not substitute)
1 tablespoon onion flakes
1 tablespoon parsley flakes

1 teaspoon Lawrey's season salt
1 teaspoon dill weed
½ teaspoon Worcestershire sauce
½ teaspoon accent
dash of garlic salt

Mix together and serve with assorted vegetables.

Kathy Wedel

Zesty Meatballs with Dip

2 eggs slightly beaten
⅓ cup milk
⅔ cup mashed potato flakes
2 tablespoons instant minced onion
1 teaspoon salt

⅛ teaspoon pepper
⅛ teaspoon garlic powder
1 teaspoon Worcestershire sauce
1 pound ground beef

Combine eggs, milk and potato flakes in bowl; let stand for about 1 minute. Add remaining ingredients; mix well. Shape into 1-inch meatballs. Cook until brown and well done; keep warm in oven until ready to serve. Serve with toothpicks. Dip; 1 cup chive or onion sour cream, 1 tablespoon brown gravy mix, 2 teaspoons milk. Combine all ingredients in saucepan. Heat through, stirring constantly; do not boil. Serve with meatballs.

Arlene (Giesel) Koehn

Appetizer Tortilla Pinwheels

1 (8 oz.) sour cream
1 package (8 oz.) cream cheese
  softened
1 can (4 oz.) diced green chilies,
  drained

1 cup grated cheddar cheese
½ cup chopped green onion
garlic powder to taste
seasoned salt to taste

Mix together spread over 5 10 inch tortillas, garnish with fresh parsley and salsa. Roll up cover tightly with plastic wrap. Refrigerate. When firm cut into 1" thick pinwheels.

Amy Giesel

Caramel Apples

54 caramels   1 cup oleo
1 can sweetened condensed milk

Melt together. This makes a yummy caramel that stays soft.

Donna, Mrs. Donovan Nikkel.

Christmas Cheese Ball

2 (8 ounces) cream cheese   2 tablespoons onion chopped
  room temperature   1 tablespoon seasoning salt
2-4 teaspoons green pepper   1 cup chopped nuts
  chopped

Form into 2 balls, chill until firm, roll in 1 cup additional chopped nuts.

Carolyn, Mrs. Wayne Holdeman

Cocktail Wieners

2 pounds cocktail wieners   1½ cups brown sugar
  (Little Smokies)   ½ (8 ounces) jar grape jelly
1½ pounds bacon

Cut bacon into thirds, wrap each wiener with a piece of bacon. (Use a toothpick to secure bacon around wiener) Place in crockpot and sprinkle brown sugar and jelly. Cook on high for 3 hours.

Jul Nightengale.

Date Nut Roll

½ cup butter   1 egg
1 (8 oz.) package chopped dates   1 teaspoon vanilla
1 cup sugar

Combine ingredients and cook on low heat for ten minutes, stirring constantly. Remove from heat and pour over 2 cups Rice Krispies, 2 cups chopped nuts, 1 cup coconut. Mix and shape into 2 rolls. May be frozen.

Cherylyn, Mrs. Mike Unruh

Ham and Cheese Ball

1 (8 ounce) package cream
  cheese softened
¼ cup salad dressing
2 cups shredded ham
¼ teaspoon dry mustard

½ cup chopped pecans
2 tablespoons parsley flakes
1 teaspoon minced onion
¼ teaspoon hot sauce

Mix well (except nuts) Form into a ball and roll in nuts. Chill. I got this recipe from a "Special Friend" of my Mother, Mrs. Susie Unruh, in Jan. 1981 when we stayed the last three weeks with Mother at Scott City.

Carol, Mrs. Gary Koehn.

Hidden Valley Ranch Pinwheels

2 (8 oz.) cream cheese
1 (1oz.) Hidden Valley Ranch
  Dressing mix
2 green onion, minced
4 12" flour tortillas

1 (4oz.) jar pimiento
1 (4 oz.) can chopped green
  chilies
1 (2.25 oz.) can black olives

Mix first 3 ingredients. Spread on tortillas. Drain vegetables and blot dry on paper towels. Sprinkle over cream cheese. Roll torts tightly. Chill 2 hours cut into 1" pieces.

LeAnne Nichols

Homemade Chicken Nuggets

Make nuggets from boneless chicken breasts, dip in melted margarine. Roll in seasoned flour and place in foil lined pan sprayed with cooking oil. Bake at 325 F. oven for 25 minutes. Dunk in your favorite sauce.

Carolyn, Mrs. Wayne Holdeman.

Indoors S'mores

2 graham crackers
marshmallow creme

peanut butter
chocolate chips

On one graham cracker spread some marshmallow creme. Sprinkle chocolate chips on top. Microwave for 30 seconds or until melted. Spread other cracker with peanut butter. Put one on top of the other and enjoy your snack!

Miss Eva Koehn.

Muddy Buddies

9 cups Double Chex
(or any kind Chex)
1 cup semi-sweet chocolate chips
½ cup peanut butter

¼ cup (½ stick) margarine
or butter
1 teaspoon vanilla extract
1½ cups powdered sugar

Pour cereal into large bowl; set aside. Combine chocolate chips, peanut butter and margarine. Microwave on HIGH 1 to 1½ minutes or until smooth, stirring after 1 minute. Stir in vanilla, pour chocolate mixture over cereals, stirring until all pieces are evenly coated. Put half of powdered sugar in large paper bag. Add cereal mixture, put rest of powdered sugar on top. Close bag and shake until all pieces are well coated.

Jolene Unruh

Party Mix

1 stick butter or oleo
1 tablespoon Worcestershire sauce
⅛ teaspoon Tabasco sauce
2 teaspoons seasoning salt

8 cups Crispix cereal
2 cups pretzels
2 cups cheese curls
½ can mixed nuts

Melt butter in microwave. Add sauces and seasoning salt. Mix remaining ingredients in large bowl. Pour butter mixture over cereal and stir until well coated. Microwave 7 minutes, stirring several times. May also be baked in oven at 250 degrees for 1 hour, stirring occasionally.

Jolene Unruh

Pimiento Spread (For Crackers)

2 (4oz.) jars diced pimiento
2 packages sharp Cracker Barrel cheese
¾ cup Kraft mayonnaise

⅛ teaspoon pepper
⅜ teaspoon garlic salt

Shred cheese and mix with other ingredients. Chill and serve.

Arlene Giesel Koehn

Puppy Chow

1 cup chocolate chips
1 cup smooth peanut butter

½ stick oleo

Melt together and pour over 8 cups Rice Chex, stir well. Sift 2½ cups powered sugar in a grocery sack, add mixture and shake. For "Meow Mix" use Cheerios in place of Chex!

Katie Nichols and Fonda, Mrs. Gareth Eicher.

Ranch Snack Mix

12 cups corn Chex
12 cups rice Chex
1 package oyster crackers
1 small package pretzels

2 packages dry Ranch dressing mix
2 tablespoons dill weed
1¼ cup oil

Place dressing and dill weed in bottom of a large bowl. Add cereal, crackers, and pretzels on top of dressing and dill weed. Mix well. Place in a paper sack and pour oil over all. Shake! Leave in bag for 2-3 hours, shaking every 30 minutes.

Jul Nightengale.

Salted Nut Roll

1 can sweetened condensed milk
1 stick margarine
1 (16 oz.) jar roasted peanuts

1 (12oz.) package Reese's peanut
butter chips
2 cups marshmallows

Sprinkle ½ jar peanuts on a greased 13 x 9 pan. Melt butter, chips and milk in a pan, add marshmallows, spread over nuts. Add remaining nuts on top. Chill. Cut into squares.

Ronda Giesel

Sausage Balls

1 pound sausage, pork mild or hot
1 pound sharp cheddar cheese, grated

3-4 cups Bisquick
¾ cup of water

Mix well. Roll in small ball (size of large marble) bake at 350 degrees 12-15 minutes.

Shana Koehn

Savory Chicken Bites

1 (8 oz.) cream cheese, softened
½ teaspoon lemon juice
½ teaspoon dried basil
¼ teaspoon onion salt
⅛ teaspoon oregano
⅛ teaspoon thyme

1 cup cooked chicken, finely chopped
⅓ cup finely chopped celery
1 (2 oz.) jar diced pimiento, drained
2 (8 oz.) cans crescent rolls
1 egg, lightly beaten
1½ teaspoons sesame seeds

Combine first 6 ingredients, add chicken, celery and pimiento. Set aside. Separate Crescents into 8 rectangles. Press perforations to seal. Spread about ¼ cup cream cheese mixture on each rectangle, leaving a ½" margin on one long side. Roll dough jelly roll fashion, starting with long side with filling spread to edge. Pinch seams to seal. Brush with egg. Sprinkle with sesame seeds. Cut each roll in 5 pieces; place seam down on lightly greased cookie sheet. Bake 375 degrees 12-15 minutes. Yield 40 appetizers. To reheat bake, uncovered, at 375 for 4-6 minutes.

LeAnne Nichols

Snack Crackers

1 cup Crisco oil
1 teaspoon dill weed
½ teaspoon garlic salt

1 package Ranch Salad Dressing
(original flavor)

Mix together and pour over 2 (12 oz.) packages oyster crackers. Mix well and let set for an hour or more. This is good at Christmas time when everything is so sweet.

Carol, Mrs. Gary Koehn

Spiced Pecans

½ cup sugar
1 tablespoon cinnamon
½ teaspoon salt

1 egg white
1 pound (6 cups) large pecan halves

Combine sugar, cinnamon and salt in small bowl, set aside. In a large mixing bowl, lightly beat egg white. Add pecans; stir until coated. Sprinkle sugar mixture over pecans; mix well. Spread in a single layer on a baking sheet. Bake at 300 degrees for 20 minutes. Remove nuts from baking sheet while warm to cool on waxed paper.

Jana, Mrs. Robert Nichols

Spinach Dip

2 (20 oz.) packages frozen
   chopped spinach
1 package 1⅜ ounce dry
   vegetable soup mix (Knorr)

½ cup water
1 (8 oz.) package cream cheese
1 (8 oz.) sour cream with chives

Thaw spinach and drain, place dry soup and water in a small bowl, cover with plastic wrap. Microwave on HIGH for 1 minute, let stand until vegetables are rehydrated. Place cream cheese in large bowl, microwave until soft, add the soup mix, sour cream, and drained spinach. Chill, serve with vegetables or bread sticks.

Mark Koehn

Texas Trail Mix

4 cups bite size pretzels
12 ounces Corn Chex
1 pound mixed nuts
½ teaspoon garlic powder
1 teaspoon chili powder

1 (1 oz.) package Ranch
   Dressing Mix
½ teaspoon cayenne pepper,
   if desired
½ cup vegetable or peanut oil

Mix dry ingredients in a large brown bag. Add oil and shake well. Bake in brown bag in a 200 degree oven for 1 hour.

LeAnne Nichols

BEVERAGES

Berry Punch

2 (10-oz.) packages frozen strawberries in syrup, thawed
1 (12 oz.) can frozen cranberry juice cocktail concentrate,
    thawed and undiluted
1 (12 oz.) can frozen lemonade concentrate, thawed and undiluted
2 (33.8-oz.) bottles club soda, chilled
1 (33.8-oz.) bottle gingerale, chilled

Place strawberries and syrup in blender; process until smooth, pour into punch bowl, add remaining ingredients.

Charmaine Wedel   Makes about 5 quarts

Citrus Slush

2-½ cups sugar
3 cups water
1 (12-oz.) can frozen orange juice
    concentrate
1 (12-oz.) can frozen lemonade
    concentrate

1 (46-oz.) can pineapple juice
3 cups cold water
4-quarts lemon-lime soda or
    gingerale, chilled

In 6-quart Dutch oven over high heat, bring sugar and 3 cups water to a boil, stirring until sugar dissolves; remove from heat. Stir in frozen orange juice and lemonade until melted. Stir in pineapple juice and 3 cups cold water until well blended. Pour into 2- 13"x 9"x 2" pans. Cover and freeze over night until firm. Cut each pan into 24 squares. Place squares in punch bowl. Slowly pour chilled soda over squares; stir until punch is slushy.

Kristin Giesel   Makes about 2 gallons or 32-1 cup servings

Crock Pot Punch

½ cup brown sugar
2 quarts apple cider
1 teaspoon whole Allspice

1-½ teaspoon whole cloves
2 cinnamon sticks
¼ fresh orange, cut in slices

Place brown sugar and cider into a crock pot, large enough to hold 2 quarts liquid. Place allspice, cloves, cinnamon and orange slices in a 12" square cloth and tie securely with string. Add to crock pot with the liquid. Cover and cook on HIGH for 1 hour, then on low for 2-8 hours. Remove spices before serving. I like to serve this on Christmas Day in the afternoon.

Betty, Mrs Gordon Unruh.

Hot Punch

Equal amounts of Apple juice, Cranberry juice, Pineapple juice. Add some raspberry Koolaide, ½ bag red hots, cinnamon stick. Heat all in crockpot. Serve hot.

Jul Nightengale

Hot Spiced Punch

Combine in a 30 cup automatic coffee maker:
- 9 cups unsweetened pineapple juice
- 9 cups cranberry juice cocktail
- 4½ cups water
- 1 cup brown sugar

Place the following in basket; 4½ teaspoons whole cloves, 4 cinnamon sticks broken, ¼ teaspoon salt. Plug in and perk. Serve hot.

Amy Giesel

Pina Colada Punch

Ice ring (see directions below)
20 oz. can crushed pineapple, undrained
15 oz. can cream of coconut

46 oz. can pineapple juice, chilled
2 cups ginger ale
32 oz. bottle club soda, chilled

Ice ring — Arrange pineapple chunks and maraschino cherries in 1-quart mold. Pour 1 cup cold water over fruit, Freeze. Pour 3 cups water over frozen mixture. Freeze. Prepare ice ring in advance. Place crushed pineapple and cream of coconut in blender, blend until smooth. In large punch bowl, combine pineapple juice, pineapple mixture and ginger ale, Add club soda and ice ring.

Arlene Giesel Koehn   Makes 4 quarts or 36 (5 oz.) servings

Punch

1 package red Koolaid
1 cup orange juice

1 cup sugar

Combine in a 2-quart pitcher and fill with cold water.

Fonda, Mrs Gareth Eicher

Wedding Punch

4 cups hot water
1 (6 oz.) box cherry Jell-O
3 cups sugar
1 (12 oz.) can frozen orange juice

1 (12oz.) can frozen lemonade
5 quarts water
2 quarts ginger ale

Dissolve Jell-O in hot water, add sugar and stir until dissolved, add orange juice, lemonade and water. Mix well. Just before serving add ginger ale. Serves 25. This is the punch we used at our wedding, although I've cut the recipe in fourths. I can still remember Mom and Barb Minninger opening all those juice cans the night before. I offered to help but they told me no, as they thought I needed my sleep!

Charmaine Wedel

Strawberry-lemonade Punch

1 (6 oz.) can frozen lemonade, thawed
1 (6 oz.) can frozen limeade, thawed
1 (6 oz.) can frozen orange juice, thawed

3 cups cold water
2 (10 oz.) packages frozen strawberries, thawed
1 (2 liter) bottle ginger ale, chilled

Blend strawberries add juices and ginger ale. Stir gently.

Charmaine Wedel   Makes 1 gallon

Sparkling Grape Refresher

1 cup water
1 cup sugar
1 quart Concord grape juice
2 cups apple juice

2 cups orange juice
⅔ cup lime juice
1 (28 oz.) bottle ginger ale
Ice Mold

Mix water and sugar in saucepan; bring to boiling point, stirring constantly until sugar is dissolved. Cool. Chill juices and ginger ale. Combine sugar syrup and fruit juices in punch bowl just before serving; add ginger ale. Float Ice Mold on surface of punch, fruit side up.

Arlene Giesel Koehn   Yield: About 3½ quarts

Wassail

¼ teaspoon nutmeg
¼ teaspoon cinnamon
¼ teaspoon allspice
3 tablespoons instant tea
2½ cups boiling water
1 (1 pound) can cranberry sauce

1½ cup water
¾ cup sugar
½ cup orange juice
¼ cup lemon juice
1 (1 quart) apple juice

Steep spices and tea in boiling water 5 minutes. Beat cranberry sauce into 1½ cups water with mixer. Heat on stove. Add sugar and juices. Combine mixtures and heat. Keep warm in crock pot. Serve hot. Really good at Christmas time!

Ronda, Mrs. Kenny Giesel

Hot Spiced Tea Mix

1 cup Tang
1 cup sugar
¼ to ½ cup lemon flavored instant tea

¼ teaspoon ground cloves
⅛ teaspoon ground nutmeg
⅛ teaspoon cinnamon

Store in covered container. Add 2 teaspoons mixture to 1 cup boiling water.

Kathy Wedel

Instant Tea

2 scant tablespoons Lipton's instant tea
⅛ cup water
¼ – ⅓ cup sugar

Place instant tea in microwave-safe coffee cup, add ⅛ cup water. Microwave on HIGH for approx. 1 minute. Measure sugar into 2 quart pitcher. Pour hot tea over sugar add water and ice to make 2 quarts, stir and serve.

Jolene Unruh

Tea Syrup

4 cups boiling water
½ cup loose tea
1 – 1½ cups sugar

Pour boiling water over loose tea. Let steep 5 minutes. Drain leaves and add sugar. Add enough water to fill a 1½ gallon container. Use 1⅓ cup brew to fill a 2 quart pitcher of ice water. Six batches serve approx. 85 people.

Jolene Unruh

Taste Boosts for Water

Add a splash of combined juices, such as cran-apple or pineapple-orange. Or freeze juice cubes and add a couple to chilled water.

A slice of fresh fruit adds a light hint of flavor to water. Try lime, pineapple, orange, kiwi, grapes, whatever's your favorite.

To make "juice" quickly, add cubes of low-cal frozen fruit-and-juice bars to a glass of water. There are lots of flavors to choose from.

For more intense flavor, freeze orange juice and use it in place of ice cubes. Add a splash of fruit nectar to a glass of water.

Arlene Giesel Koehn

Hot Chocolate Eggnog

Children detest eggs? They will never know Mr. Egg is hiding in this concoction.

3 cups whole milk
3 eggs
2 tablespoons cocoa
⅓ cup sugar
¼ teaspoon salt
1 teaspoon vanilla

In blender, whizz together all ingredients. Pour into saucepan and heat, stirring all the while, just until piping hot and steamy. DO NOT allow mixture to cook. as it will thicken and curdle. Serve in mugs and top with marshmallows.

Edna Giesel

Makes 1 quart of hot drink

SOUPS &
SANDWICHES

Beef and Onion Stew

1½ beef stew meat
flour
¼ cup butter or margarine
3 cups diced onion
1 garlic clove, minced
1½ cup beef broth
2 tablespoons cider vinegar

1 tablespoon tomato paste
1 bay leaf
1½ teaspoon salt
1 teaspoon lemon pepper
½ teaspoon dried thyme
Cooked rice or noodles

Dredge meat in flour. Brown in butter in Dutch oven. Add the onion and garlic; Cook, stirring occasionally, for 10 minutes. Add broth, vinegar, tomato paste and seasonings. Cover and simmer for 1½ to 2 hours or until meat is tender. Serve over rice or noodles.

Jana, Mrs. Robert Nichols   4 - 6 servings

Beef or Venison Stew

2 pounds round steak, cubed
2 tablespoons fat
3 tablespoons flour
3½ cups water
1 tablespoon salt
¼ teaspoon black pepper
2 tablespoons Worcestershire sauce

⅓ cup catsup
½ teaspoon paprika
1 medium onion, sliced
1 clove garlic, minced
1 bay leaf
¼ cup cooking wine

Brown beef in hot fat. Stir in flour and stir until flour is browned. Add water, salt, pepper, Worcestershire sauce, catsup, paprika, onion, garlic, bay leaf, and wine. Simmer 1½- 2 hours. Add 4-5 carrots, cubed, 4-5 medium potatoes, cubed. Simmer until vegetables are tender. This is especially good when made with venison.

Mary, Mrs. Lee Giesel.

Creamy Celery Soup

1 tablespoon oil
2 tablespoons flour
6-mushrooms
1 yellow onion
1 potato
1 bunch celery (trim off leaves)
5 or 6 green onions

2 cloves garlic
½ teaspoon basil
1 quart water
2 cups milk
3 thick slices Velveeta cheese
salt and pepper to taste

Dice all vegetables very fine or food process them. In large pan, saute onion, green onion, and garlic in oil. Add flour, potato, celery, mushrooms, and stir to coat with flour. Add spices, water and milk. if you did not process the vegetables, when they are tender, mash with a potato masher or wire whisk to a fine consistency. Add cheese and milk.

Julie, Mrs. Kieth Koehn

Creamed Soup Mix

2 cups nonfat dry milk
¾ cups cornstarch
¼ cup instant chicken
 bouillon (or other flavor)
2 tablespoons dried minced
 onion flakes

1 teaspoon dried basil, crushed
 (optimal)
½ teaspoon ground thyme
½ teaspoon pepper

Combine all ingredients, mixing well. Store in airtight container. To use soup mix; combine ⅓ cup milk with one cup water in a quart dish or glass measuring cup, microwave 2½-3 minutes or until thickened, stirring halfway through. Use in place of canned soups in a casserole.

Dawn Giesel Dyck   Yield: 3 cups mix (equivalent to about 9 cups soup)

Creamy Cheddar Cheese Soup

¼ cup (½ stick) butter
½ cup chopped onion
2 tablespoons all purpose flour
2 cups milk
2 cups canned chicken broth

2 large russet potatoes, peeled,
 diced
1 cup packed grated sharp
 cheddar cheese
chopped chives or green onions

Melt butter in heavy medium saucepan over medium heat. Add onion and saute until tender, about 5 minutes. Add flour and stir until just beginning to color, about 3 minutes. Gradually mix in milk and broth; add potatoes. Reduce heat to medium-low and simmer until potatoes are tender, stirring occasionally, about 20 minutes. Add cheese and stir until cheese melts and soup is smooth. Season to taste with salt and pepper. Garnish with chives and serve.

Arlene Giesel Koehn   Yield 4 servings

Cream of Potato Soup

6 cups sliced potatoes
¼ teaspoon pepper
½ cups sliced carrots
2 cups milk
6 slices bacon
2 cups light cream

1 cup chopped onion
1 cup sliced celery
1½ teaspoon salt
finely shredded cheddar cheese
parsley sprigs

Cook potatoes and carrots in water until tender, drain. Cook bacon until crisp; drain and crumble. Saute onion and celery in 2 tablespoons bacon fat. Combine cooked vegetables, bacon, salt, pepper, milk and cream. Simmer for 30 minutes. Do not boil. Garnish with cheese and parsley. Serve with Bran Muffins.

Elaine, Mrs. Bruce Unruh   Makes 2 quarts

Dad's Stew

Cut up pieces of beef, or chicken, place in Crock-pot. Add small pieces of potatoes, onion, carrots, turnips. If desired add some pre-soaked beans. Add 1½ cups water or beef broth. Stir and cover. Cook on LOW heat for 10-12 hours or on HIGH for 4-6 hours.

Nathan Giesel.

Hamburger Vegetable Soup

1 pound ground chuck	½ teaspoon pepper
½ cup chopped onion	1 bay leaf
5 cups water	¼ teaspoon basil, crushed
2 cans Tomato sauce	2 cups diced potatoes
4 instant beef bouillon cubes	2 cups sliced carrots
salt to taste	2 cups frozen corn

Brown hamburger with onion. Add water, tomato sauce, and seasonings and bring to a boil. Add vegetables, except corn, and simmer until vegetables are tender. Add corn and simmer.

Serena Amoth

"Hot Hamburger Soup"

1½ pounds ground beef, or venison	½ cup picante sauce, or to taste
1 large onion diced	1 tablespoon salt
½ bunch celery, diced	¼ teaspoon black pepper
1 large carrot, diced diagonally	⅛ teaspoon red pepper
1 large green bell pepper, finely chopped	1 tablespoon dried parsley flakes
1 cup green beans or asparagus cut	8 beef-flavor bouillon cubes
½ cup catsup	Ample water to cover
	3 large potatoes, cut in chunks
	⅓ cup rice

In skillet, brown meat (very brown) and chunky. Drain grease; Transfer meat to soup pot. Saute onion, celery, and green pepper in meat drippings until lightly browned. Drain drippings; add vegetables to meat along with remaining ingredients, excluding potatoes and rice. Bring mixture to boil, reduce heat and simmer 2 hours. Add potatoes and rice, simmer for 1 hour. Stir occasionally to prevent rice from adhering to bottom of pot.

Edna Giesel   Yield: 8-10 servings

Italian Vegetable Soup

1 pound ground beef
1 cup diced onion
1 cup sliced celery
1 cup sliced carrots
2 cloves garlic, minced
1 (16 oz.) can tomatoes
1 (15 oz.) can tomato sauce
1 (15 oz.) can red Kidney
   beans, undrained
2-3 cups water

5 teaspoons beef bouillon granules
1 tablespoon dried parsley flakes
1 teaspoon salt
½ teaspoon oregano
½ teaspoon sweet basil
¼ teaspoon black pepper
2 cups shredded cabbage
1 cup green beans
½ cup small elbow macaroni
Parmesan cheese

Brown beef in large heavy kettle; drain. Add all ingredients except cabbage, green beans and macaroni. Bring to boil. Lower heat. Cover and simmer 20 minutes. Add cabbage, green beans and macaroni, and simmer until vegetables are tender. If you prefer thinner soup, add additional water or broth, Sprinkle with Parmesan cheese before serving.

Jana, Mrs. Robert Nichols

Yield: 12 servings

Last Minute Chicken-noodle Soup

1 quart canned chicken or turkey
2 quarts water
4 or 5 teaspoons chicken bouillon

¼ cup chopped onion
Pepper
½ of 12 oz. package of noodles

Put all ingredients except noodles in a large pan and bring to a boil. Add dry noodles and stir. Simmer until noodles are done. This can be made at the last minute. Soup can be on the table in 15 minutes!

Jolene Unruh

Old Fashioned Vegetable Soup

2 pounds round steak
6 cups water
1 tablespoon salt
1 cup celery cut in ½ inch pieces
½ cup chopped onion
1 bay leaf

1 pound canned tomatoes
12 oz. can whole kernel corn
2 cups cubed potatoes
1 cup diced carrots
½ cup chopped green pepper

Combine round steak, water, salt, celery, onion and bay leaf in large sauce pan. Cover and simmer 3 hours until meat is tender. Tip: When soup is about done throw in a handful of noodles. Will make the soup thicker. Makes 6 servings.

Theresa, Mrs. Melvern Ratzlaff

Sarah's Hamburger Stew

1 pound ground beef	¼ cup diced onion
2 tablespoons butter	1 teaspoon salt
⅛ teaspoon pepper	½ cup water
½ Package frozen green beans	1 cup diced potatoes
1 cup diced carrots	1 cup diced celery

Brown meat and onions in butter(in heavy skillet) Add remaining ingredients. Cover and simmer 30-40 minutes, until vegetables are tender. (This recipe was given to me at my bridal shower by my Mother-in -law, Eva, Mrs. Alfred Koehn.)

Janice, Mrs. Jerry Ratzlaff   Makes 6 servings

Taco Soup

1½ pounds ground beef	1 (15 oz.) can Kidney beans
½ cup onion, chopped	1 (15 oz.) can whole kernel corn
2 cups water	1 (8 oz.) can tomato sauce
1 package taco seasoning mix	salt and pepper to taste
1 (28 oz.) can tomatoes	

Brown beef and onions in a large pot. Add water and taco mix. Stir over medium heat while adding all other ingredients. Let simmer for a few minutes to blend flavors.

LeAnne Nichols.

Taco Soup

2 pounds ground beef	1 package taco seasoning
1 small onion, chopped	1½ cups water
2 (4 oz.) cans chopped green chilies	1 package (1 oz.) ranch dressing mix
1 teaspoon salt	1 (14 oz.) can hominy, drained
1 teaspoon pepper	1 quart tomatoes
1 (16 oz.) can pinto beans	Shredded cheese
1 (16 oz.) can lima beans	Tortilla chips
1 (16 oz.) can kidney beans	

In large Dutch oven, brown beef and onions, drain. Rinse and drain all beans. Add all ingredients, (except cheese and chips) to hamburger, bring to a boil. Reduce heat and simmer 30 minutes. Serve over chips and top with cheese.

Charmaine Wedel

Vegetable Soup

Brown 2½ pounds hamburger, drain. Add 1½ onions chopped, while browning meat, Add 9 cups water and 1 can condensed tomato soup, Chop 1½ more onions, add to meat, soup mixture. Peel and slice 4 carrots, Add to soup mixture. Do the same with 2 stalks celery, Add the following: 2½ teaspoons salt, ⅓ teaspoon pepper, 1-2 tablespoons beef bouillon, 1 pint green beans, 3-4 cups frozen corn, 3 cups cabbage cut up. Simmer 1-3 hours. May add potatoes if desired.

Jolene, Mrs. Dennis Koehn.

Gumbo

⅔ cup oil (olive oil preferred
⅔ cup flour
1 cup chopped celery
1 onion chopped
2 pounds link sausage, cooked
   and browned (cut in ¼ slices)
4 cups chicken, turkey, shrimp, etc.

2 quarts broth
½ cup green onion tops
½ cup green onion bottoms
2 bouillon cubes
¼ teaspoon garlic powder
3-4 bay leaves

Make the roux by mixing oil and flour together and browning slowly over low heat, stirring all the while. Saute celery and onion in oil separately, Cool roux slightly before adding the broth, stir together as you would make gravy. Add remaining ingredients and simmer, the longer the better. Serve in soup bowls over rice.

Jolene Unruh.

Chicken Borscht

Cook 1 large chicken with salt and pepper; add enough water to end up with 2 quarts broth, Separate chicken from broth, debone and remove skin. Combine a handful of fresh parsley, 1½ bay leaf, 1 teaspoon peppercorns, ¼ teaspoon whole allspice, 2 teaspoons salt, tie in a cheese cloth or use a spice holder. Add 1 medium chopped onion, the spice bag, 1 teaspoon sugar, 1 large diced potato to the broth and cook. When potato is nearly done add 3-4 cups coarsely cut up cabbage, cook- (do not over cook). Add the chicken and 5 cups tomato juice. Bring to a boil, add ½ cup cream just before serving. Yield 1 gallon. Zion Church is required to make 23 gallons of this for Moundrige Manor gift day suppers.

Betty Giesel Martens.

Bacon and Potato Chowder

6 slices diced bacon
1 cup chopped onion
3 cups raw potatoes
3 cups water

3 chicken bouillon cubes
½ teaspoon salt
3 tablespoons flour
1 large can evaporated milk

Fry bacon in a large sauce pan until crisp, drain well, set aside. Reserve 2 tablespoons drippings, saute onions in drippings for 5 minutes. Add potatoes, water, bouillon cubes, and salt. Heat to boiling. Cover and simmer 15 minutes or until potatoes are tender. Mix flour with a little evaporated milk to make a paste. Gradually stir in remaining milk, add to potato mixture. Cook over medium heat, stirring constantly until mixture comes to a boil and thickens. Garnish with reserved bacon.

Marisa Giesel Wedel

Beef Chowder

2 pounds ground beef
1 cup chopped celery
½ cup chopped onion
⅓ cup chopped green pepper

1 quart corn
2½ cups tomatoes cut in pieces
2 cans celery soup, add 1½ cups
  water to soup

Cook beef, celery, green pepper, and onion until soft, add remaining ingredients (except the celery soup). Simmer 1 hour, add the soup and heat and serve.

Mornie Giesel Unruh

Cheesy Vegetable Chowder

½ cup chopped onion
1 clove garlic, minced
1 cup sliced celery
¾ cup carrots
1 cup cubed potatoes
3½ cups chicken broth
2 cups corn, canned or frozen
¼ cup butter or margarine

¼ cup flour
2 cups milk
1 tablespoon prepared mustard
¼ teaspoon white pepper
⅛ teaspoon paprika
2 tablespoons diced pimiento, optional
2 cups shredded cheddar cheese

Combine first 6 ingredients in a large Dutch oven; bring to a boil. cover, reduce heat, and simmer 15-20 minutes or until potatoes are tender. Stir in corn; remove from heat. Melt butter in heavy sauce pan over low heat; add flour, stirring until smooth. cook 1 minute, stirring constantly. Gradually add milk; cook over medium heat, stirring constantly, until thickened and bubbly. Stir in remaining ingredients. Cook just until cheese melts, stirring constantly. Gradually stir cheese mixture into vegetable mixture. Cook over medium heat, stirring until thoroughly heated. Serve immediately. Yield 2 quarts. This makes a good winter meal with ham or tuna sandwiches.

Michele, Mrs. Richard Ensz

Sausage-bean Chowder

2 pounds bulk pork sausage
2 (16 oz.) cans kidney beans
2 medium onions, chopped
2 medium potatoes, peeled
and chopped
½ teaspoon salt
¼ teaspoon garlic powder

4 cups water
2 (16 oz.) whole tomatoes,
undrained and chopped
½ cups chopped green pepper
1 large bay leaf
½ teaspoon dried whole thyme
¼ teaspoon pepper

Brown and drain sausage. Stir in all other ingredients and bring to a boil. Cover and reduce heat to simmer. Cook 1 hour. Good!

Janice, Mrs. Jerry Ratzlaff   Yields 3 quarts

Meat Ball Chowder

2 pounds ground lean beef
2 teaspoons seasoned salt
⅛ teaspoon pepper
2 eggs slightly beaten
¼ cup finely chopped parsley
⅓ cup fine cracker crumbs
2 tablespoons milk
3 tablespoons flour
1 tablespoon salad oil
6 cups water
6 cups tomato juice

6 beef bouillon cubes
6 carrots sliced
3 cups sliced celery
4-6 onions cut in eighths
2-3 cups diced potatoes
¼ cup long grain rice
2 teaspoons salt
½ to 1 teaspoon marjoram (optional)
1 tablespoon sugar
2 bay leaves
1 (12 oz.) can mexicorn

Combine meat, seasoned salt, pepper, eggs, parsley, cracker crumbs, and milk. Mix thoroughly, form into balls about the size of a walnut (makes 40) Dip in flour, heat oil in 8-10 quart kettle, lightly brown meat balls on all sides (or drop unbrowned into boiling vegetables). Add remaining ingredients (except add corn last 10 minutes of cooking). Bring to boil, cover, reduce heat, and cook slowly for 30 minutes or until vegetables are tender. If dinner must wait turn off heat at this point. Takes a few minutes to reheat.

Recipe from Mother Mornie Unruh,
sent in by Betty, Mrs Gordon Unruh   Yields 6-7 quarts

Potato-Bacon Chowder

Potatoes and bacon team up in this thick and nourishing cool-weather chowder.

8 slices bacon, cut up
1 cup chopped onion
2 cups cubed potatoes (2 medium)
1 cup water
1 can (10¾ oz.) cream of
  chicken soup

1 cup dairy sour cream
1¾ cups milk
½ teaspoon salt
dash pepper
2 tablespoons chopped parsley

Fry bacon until crisp in 3-quart saucepan; add onion and saute 2-3 minutes. Pour off fat; add potatoes and water. Bring to boil; cover and simmer 10-15 minutes or until potatoes are tender. Stir in soup and sour cream; gradually add milk. Add salt, pepper and parsley. Heat to serving temperature. Do not boil.

Mornie Giesel Unruh   Yield 4 servings

Chicken Chili

2 tablespoons vegetable oil
1 cup chopped onion
1 cup chopped green pepper
2 garlic cloves minced
4½ cups diced cooked chicken
2 (14½ oz.) cans stewed tomatoes

1 can (15 oz.) pinto beans drained
⅔ to ¾ cup picante sauce
1 teaspoon chili powder
1 teaspoon ground cumin
½ teaspoon salt

Optional toppings:
shredded cheddar cheese
diced avocado

sour cream

Saute onion, green pepper and garlic in oil, until tender. Add chicken, tomatoes, beans, picante sauce and seasonings; bring to a boil. Reduce heat; simmer for 20 minutes. Serve with cheese, avocado and sour cream if desired. (I double the beans and add a little water.) We like to eat it with cheese and saltines.

Jana, Mrs Robert Nichols   Yield: 6-8 servings

Chili

2 pounds ground beef
1 quart canned pinto beans
chili powder, to taste
sprinkle of garlic salt
2 cups tomato juice
water(add a little beef bouillon)

Drop or 2 of Tabasco sauce
picante sauce or salsa
sprinkle of red pepper
onion
salt
pepper

Fry ground beef, drain. Add all ingredients to taste. We like ours spicy. Bring to boil, reduce heat and simmer for a couple hours or all day. Amount of water depends on how soupy you like it.

Helen, Mrs. Emery Koehn

Chili

1½ pounds hamburger
1 package chili seasoning mix
1 large onion, chopped
3 (16 oz.) cans chili beans with gravy

1 (16 oz.) can tomatoes, mashed
1 (16 oz.) can red kidney beans, drained
½ cup green pepper chopped

Fill crock pot; cook on LOW 8-10 hours.

Theresa, Mrs. Melvern Ratzlaff

Large Recipe Chili

2 pounds hamburger
2 quarts canned tomato juice
OR
3-4 tablespoons flour or cornstarch
2 tablespoons chili powder
2 teaspoons salt
1 teaspoon seasoning salt
½ teaspoon minced garlic or garlic powder

1 quart canned pinto beans
2 packages chili seasoning

1 teaspoon sugar
1 teaspoon cumin
4 tablespoons minced onion
½ teaspoon crushed dried red pepper, (optional)

Mix all dry ingredients together, before adding to chili. Simmer, the longer the better.

Jolene Unruh

New River Chili

½ cup macaroni (uncooked)
1 pound ground beef
1 cup chopped onion
2 teaspoons seasoned salt (or less)
½ teaspoon pepper
1 tablespoon chili powder
1 tablespoon beef bouillon

1 (28 oz.) can tomatoes, and
1 (16 oz.) can tomatoes undrained and pureed
1 can kidney beans
1 can pinto beans
½ teaspoon Tabasco (optional)

Brown meat and onion in large Dutch oven. Combine all ingredients, simmer, covered for 1 hour. Garnish with shredded cheese if desired. Note add the macaroni the last 20 minutes, so they don't get mushy. We like to serve this with corn muffins.

LeAnne Nichols   Yield 3 quarts

Williams Chili

1 pound ground beef, browned
1 small can pork and beans
1 pint tomato juice, as needed
½ to 1 teaspoon salt

1 teaspoon sugar (if desired)
1 teaspoon Williams Chili Seasoning
  per pound of meat

Add chili powder, if desired. This is a mild chili.

Louise Wedel

Baked Cheese Burgers

2 pounds hamburger fried with 1 cup onion, drain, add 1 package spaghetti sauce mix, 1 tablespoon chili powder, 1 small can tomato sauce. Simmer. Using french bread dough, roll out. Cut into 3 inch squares. Roll again, Place ½ slice American cheese on dough with ⅓ to ¼ cup meat mixture on top. Bring corners together and seal, turn over and place on baking sheet. Let rise slightly. Bake at 350 degrees for 15 minutes. Very good to take to field and for lunches.

Jolene, Mrs. Dennis Koehn

Banana Sandwiches

Good for children and easy to make. Spread bread slices with peanut butter, place a layer of sliced bananas on peanut butter, sprinkle lightly with brown sugar. Top with another slice of peanut butter bread and you have a sandwich de luxe that will make any mouth water. Serve with a glass of ice cold milk. This is another recipe Grandma Mornie had written in the recipe book she made for me when I was 12 years old.

The above recipe brings to memory another sandwich, I remember to be delicious! When I was a small girl, Aunt Carolyn still lived at home. I loved to go to Grandpa's because Aunt Carolyn would make me one of her delicious sandwiches! I must of had enough, because I have no desire for them today! Aunt Carolyn's Sandwiches. 1 slice of bread, lots of thick mayonnaise.

Kathy Wedel

Barbecue

1½ pounds hamburger
1 cup chopped celery
½ cup chopped onion
2 tablespoons Worcestershire sauce

1 cup catsup
1 tablespoon mustard
2 tablespoons brown sugar
salt and pepper to taste

Cook together meat, celery and onion until done. Add the remaining ingredients. Simmer about 10 minutes. Spread on buns. I like mine a little thicker, so I add 1-2 tablespoons rice and cook a little longer.

Betty, Mrs. Gordon Unruh.

26

Egg Sandwich

1 egg
1 tablespoon butter-flavored
  shortening

salt and pepper to taste
2 slices buttered bread

In small dish, beat egg (with fork) add salt and pepper until blended. In hot skillet, melt shortening, add egg and fry. Turn once to brown both sides. Serve between slices of warm buttered bread.

Edna Giesel (From Mother-in-law Mary (Freeman) Giesel)

Ham Sandwiches

1 can Spam, ground
1 large onion finely chopped

½ pound Velveeta cheese, grated
½ cup mayonnaise

Mix together, spread on buns. Heat in oven until warm.

Arlene Giesel Koehn

Hearty Bologna Spread

1½ pounds bologna, ground
  (about 4½ cups)
¾ cup pickle relish
3 tablespoons minced onion

1 tablespoon Worcestershire sauce
1½ cup salad dressing
12 slices process American cheese
Lettuce leaves

Combine first 5 ingredients, mix well. Spread mixture on bun, using about ⅓ cup each. Top with cheese slice and then lettuce leaf.

Arlene Giesel Koehn   Makes 4-½ cups spread or fills 12 buns

Heinz Burgers

1 pound hamburger
¾-1 cup grated cheddar cheese
½ cup soft bread crumbs

¼ cup onion, chopped
3 tablespoons Heinz 57 sauce
¼ teaspoon salt

Mix and make into patties. Grill over medium coals. Place between hamburger buns. Serve.

Sharon Giesel

My Mamma Carrie Made, Old Time Hot Burger

5 pounds hamburger
1 can tomato soup
2-3 onions, chopped

4 tablespoons rice
salt
chili powder to taste

Brown hamburger and onion, add tomato soup and rice and seasonings. Cook until rice is done.

Mornie Giesel Unruh, Jul Nightengale   Yield 50 sandwiches

Peppy Burgers

1 pound ground beef
½ cup chopped onion
1 can Campbell's Pepper Pot Soup

2 tablespoons ketchup
2 tablespoons mustard

Brown meat and onion. Stir in one can soup (undiluted), ketchup and mustard. Simmer 5 minutes. Spoon on split, toasted buns.

Mary. Mrs. Lee Geisel

Pizza Burgers

1 pound browned hamburger
½ onion chopped or minced onion
1 (8 oz.) can pizza sauce

¼ teaspoon garlic salt
¼ oregano
salt and pepper to taste

Grate ½ pound American cheese. Add to cooled hamburger and mix. Spread on buns and put under broiler until cheese melts.

Louise Wedel

Sloppy Joes

1 pound bulk pork sausage
½ pound ground beef
1 cup barbecue sauce
¼ cup chopped green pepper

¼ cup chopped onion
10 hamburger split buns
pasteurized process cheese
   (sliced)

Brown meat, drain. Add barbecue sauce, peppers and onions. Cover, simmer 15 minutes. For each sandwich, cover bottom half of bun with meat mixture, top with process cheese spread slice. Serve with top half of bun. Yield: 10 sandwiches

Mornie Giesel Unruh

Sloppy Joes

1 pound hamburger, fried
   and drained
1 can tomato soup
1 teaspoon salt

1 tablespoon chili powder
Chopped onion or dried
   minced onion
8 hamburger buns

Mix first 5 ingredients together and simmer. Serve on buns.

Jolene Unruh

Sloppy Joes

2 pounds hamburger
¼ cup chopped onion
2 teaspoons chili powder
½ teaspoon salt
¼ cup ketchup
1 teaspoon mustard

½ (10½ oz.) can cream of
   chicken soup
½ (10½ oz.) can tomato soup
I add some sloppy joe seasoning,
   1-2 teaspoons or to taste

Brown meat with onion, add rest of ingredients and simmer. Yield: Serves 8 to 10.

Beulah, Mrs. Dennis Unruh

Tuna Buns

¼ cup chopped pickles
3 diced hard boiled eggs
2 tablespoons green pepper, chopped
2 tablespoons celery, chopped,
   (optional)

2 tablespoons stuffed olives
½ cup salad dressing
1 can tuna or (¾ cup chicken)
¼ pound grated American cheese

Combine, spread on buttered hamburger buns, Wrap in foil and bake 25-30 minutes at 250-300 degrees.

Arlene Giesel Koehn

CHEESE, EGGS, & PASTAS

Cackle-berries on a Shingle

How about breakfast you can fix the day before (boil eggs and cook bacon or sausage)?

1 slice buttered toast	1-2 strips bacon or sausage
1 square slice cheese	hard boiled eggs, sliced

Place cheese on toast, bacon or sausage on top of cheese, arrange egg slices on the bacon. Microwave or broil open face and serve hot.

Jennie, Mrs. Calvin Unruh

Scrambled Eggs

6 eggs	pepper
⅓ cup milk	oleo
1 teaspoon chopped onion, or to taste	cheese
¼ teaspoon salt	

Break eggs into bowl and add milk, stir until yolks are broken, add onion, salt and pepper. Melt oleo in skillet, pour in egg mixture and sprinkle shredded cheese across top. When eggs are half cooked turn and stir.

Jolene Unruh

Make Ahead Scrambled Eggs

3 tablespoons flour	1 dozen eggs
1½ cups milk	¼ teaspoon pepper
½ teaspoon salt	1 stick oleo

Options:

shredded cheese	chopped green chilies to taste
chopped ham	

In large bowl, beat together flour, salt pepper, and milk until smooth. Beat in eggs, mixing well. Melt oleo in large skillet over moderate heat, add eggs, cook over moderate heat until eggs are done, stirring gently. When eggs are almost done, add optional ingredients, if desired. Eggs may be kept hot 2 hours or longer in a chafing dish or in a 300 degree oven. Left over eggs that have been refrigerated, may be reheated. To reheat place in a greased dish, cover and place in a 325 degree oven until hot.

Janice, Mrs Jerry Ratzlaff

Deviled Eggs

6 hard boiled eggs	1 teaspoon mustard
¼ cup salad dressing	1 teaspoon salt
1 teaspoon vinegar	pepper to taste

Cut peeled eggs lengthwise into halves, slip out yolks, mash with fork, mix all ingredients together. Fill egg whites, sprinkle with paprika. Cover and refrigerate.

Coreen Holdeman, Carol, Mrs Gary Koehn

Oven-scrambled Eggs

4 tablespoons butter or margarine
13 eggs, well beaten
1 cup warm milk
¼ teaspoon salt

¼ teaspoon seasoning salt
1 tablespoon cheese, grated
½ can mushrooms, drained (optional)

Place butter in 13 x 9 inch baking dish, place in warm oven to melt. Combine eggs, milk, seasonings and cheese, stir well. Add mushrooms; pour into baking dish. Bake in preheated 350 degree oven for 10 minutes. Remove from oven; stir well. Return to oven for 20-25 minutes or until mixture is set. Cut into squares to serve.

Arlene Giesel Koehn

Egg Pizza

1 can mushrooms
¼ cup chopped green peppers
4 tablespoons butter
6 eggs
½ teaspoon salt

¼ teaspoon pepper
1 teaspoon crushed oregano
½ cup sliced pepperoni (2 oz.)
1 cup grated cheese

Saute mushrooms and green pepper in 2 tablespoons butter, remove from pan, melt remaining butter in pan. To make omelet, mix eggs, salt and pepper; pour in pan and cook slowly, tilt pan occasionally to lift cooked edge of omelet, to let uncooked part run underneath. When omelet is set, but surface is still moist, sprinkle with oregano and top with cheese, pepperoni, mushrooms and green pepper; cover and cook until cheese melts. Delicious!

Carolyn, Mrs. Wayne Holdeman

Fit for a King

This is a favorite dish of Bob's, that he ate at home and I still fix for him. I put three slices of toast on a plate, poach 3 eggs in milk, pour over the toast and serve.

Evelyn, Mrs. Bob Unruh

Breakfast Casserole

9 x 13 pan greased
8 slices french bread, broken in pieces, spread on bottom of pan
1 pound Velveeta cheese, cube and spread over bread
2 pounds sausage browned and drained, place over the cheese

Mix together:

½ stick margarine, melted	½ teaspoon salt
6 eggs beaten	1 teaspoon dry mustard
1 quart milk	

Pour over the top; refrigerate over night. Bake 1 hour at 350 degrees. May be reheated in microwave.

Arlene Giesel Koehn

Breakfast Casserole

8 slices bread	2¾ cup milk
1 pound ham, bacon or sausage	1 teaspoon mustard
¾ pound Velveeta cheese	4 tablespoons butter
8 eggs	salt and pepper to taste

Butter 9 x 13 pan place bread slices on bottom, next the meat layer, then the cheese. Mix eggs, milk, mustard, salt and pepper and pour over all; refrigerate over night; bake 1 hour 325 degrees.

Mary, Mrs. Lee Giesel

Baked Oatmeal

½ cup oleo melted	2 teaspoons baking powder
1 cup brown sugar	1 teaspoon salt
2 eggs beaten	1 cup milk
3 cups quick oatmeal	

Cream together first 3 ingredients, add all the other ingredients to creamed mixture. Bake in greased 10 x 10 pan and bake at 350 for 20-25 minutes or until golden. Note: May be mixed the night before. Variety: use ½ cup sugar and add raisins, coconut and nuts.

Carolyn, Mrs. Wayne Holdeman

Scrapple

½ pound chopped meat
(beef or pork head cheese)
1¼ teaspoon salt
⅛ teaspoon pepper

1 cup corn meal
1 medium onion chopped
1¼ quarts water

Brown onion in fat, add meat, seasonings and water. Cook at simmering point for 20 minutes; add corn meal, boil 1 hour; turn into a mold, cool and cut into slices; fry until brown; serve with gravy, tomato sauce and molasses.

Louise Wedel

Mac 'N' Cheese

A necessary recipe with children!
1 (7 oz.) package elbow macaroni
(2 cups uncooked)
2 tablespoons butter or margarine
2 tablespoons flour
1 teaspoon salt
2 cups milk

1 cup each shredded Colby, cheddar, and Monterey Jack cheese
¼ cup Parmesan cheese
2 teaspoons parsley flakes
2 tablespoons buttered bread crumbs

Prepare macaroni as package directs. Drain. In medium saucepan, melt butter. Stir in flour and salt, blend in milk; cook and stir till thickened; mix cheeses together, reserve ¼ cup. Add remaining cheese to sauce; stir until melted, mix in macaroni and parsley. Pour into 2 quart casserole, top with reserved cheese and bread crumbs. Bake at 350 for 25 minutes.

.Melissa, Mrs. Jason Koehn

Berrogge

Combine 5 eggs, slightly beaten, with 3 cups flour and enough milk to make a stiff dough. Roll out as noodles and cut in 3 inch squares. Fill squares with filling of 2 cups homemade cottage cheese (or dry curd), 1 egg, 1 tablespoon sugar (if desired), salt and pepper to taste. Fold dough in triangular shape and pinch edges together (real good). Cook slowly in salted water for 5 minutes, drain; brown in deep fat. Serve with sauce made by cooking equal amounts of cream and sugar. Squares made be filled with kraut in place of cheese.

Janice, Mrs. Jerry Ratzlaff

Kleetski

Grandma, (Evelyn) Unruh makes this for us and we love it! Heat 2 cups milk to boiling point, make a stiff dough with 2 eggs, a scant cup of flour and salt to taste, slice little bits of dough into the hot milk; cook 5-10 minutes.

Kendra and Melody Schmidt. Note: Freeman Giesel was fond of this dish also!

Homemade Noodles

Combine 1 beaten egg, 2 tablespoons milk, and ½ teaspoon salt. Add enough sifted all-purpose flour to make stiff dough- about 1 cup. Roll very thin on floured surface; let stand 20 minutes. Roll up loosely, slice ¼ inch wide, unroll, spread out and let dry 2 hours. (You may store in a container until needed.) Drop into boiling soup or boiling, salted water and cook uncovered about 10 minutes. Makes 3 cups cooked noodles.

Grandma Carrie must have multiplied this recipe many, many times the first time she had my husband John over for supper! He has a reputation for loving noodles and the story is that she had started making them the day before the meal she had invited us for. There may be some of you who were at that meal also- I don't recall who all were present. There was a huge bowl of noodles on the table as Grandma made it plain she expected John would eat a lot. He thought he could surely eat his share and more of those noodles. As soon as one bowl was emptied, another bowl of noodles would appear on the table as if by magic! John couldn't quite imagine how she could make so many as I, his wife, had trouble coming up with a few. As he proceeded to eat, depleting still another huge bowl of noodles - now beginning to feel "noodled out," still another bowl appeared. Now, let me explain that John was not the only one eating noodles, but he was the only one consuming huge amounts. Grandma was keeping her eye on him, enjoying the fact that her noodle making was not in vain. As it was apparent that there was a never ending supply of noodles coming at him, John decided to take a 'noodle' break to see what was happening in the kitchen and there he found two little ladies, still busily cooking up noodles! At this point, as he was the only one still eating noodles, he announced that he really could not eat one more! John recalls that he has never 'porked' down so many noodles, in one meal, in his entire life.

Barbara Jean, Mrs. John Jenkins

Never Fail Dumplings

Sift together 2¼ cup flour, 2 teaspoons baking powder and ¼ teaspoon salt. Blend well 2 beaten eggs and 1 cup milk. Add to above ingredients and mix well. Drop by tablespoon into boiling chicken, veal or beef broth or into vegetable stew. Cook for ten minutes or until done.

Sophie (Giesel) Koehn

Peroga or Cottage Cheese Dumplings

Dough:

4 cups flour

1 teaspoon salt

2 egg whites, beaten

1 tablespoon sugar

2 teaspoons baking powder

1 stick oleo

1 cup milk

1½ tablespoons cooking oil

Filling:

3½ to 4 cups dry cottage cheese
   (commercial may be used)

2 egg yolks

½ teaspoon salt

1 tablespoon sugar

¼ teaspoon pepper

Beat egg yolks, add cottage cheese, sugar, salt and pepper with enough cream to make it stick together. Mix the dry ingredients for dough. Mix milk and lightly beaten egg whites to make a stiff dough, roll out to ⅛ in thickness. Dampen the whole piece of dough. Start on one corner, put 1 tablespoon cottage cheese mixture and cover with dough and cut making a half circle. Pinch edges together well. Fry in oil until brown on both sides. Serve with homemade syrup.

Syrup for peroga:

1½ cups sugar

1½ cups water

Dash of salt

3 Tablespoons flour

1 stick butter

Bring to a boil and serve.

Here is my Mom, Grandma Carrie's, recipe. After frying peroga add some milk and sugar to drippings and heat. This is very good.

Sophie Giesel Koehn

SALADS & DRESSINGS

Ambrosia

½ pint sour cream
½ cup shredded coconut
1 cup drained mandarin oranges

1 cup drained pineapple
1 cup (miniature) marshmallows

Mix well and chill.

Mornie Giesel Unruh

Yield: 4 Servings

Angel Hash Salad

1 (1 pound) can crushed pineapple
1 can fruit cocktail, drained,
  save juice
2 tablespoons cornstarch
¼ cup sugar

2 egg yokes, well beaten
1 cup heavy cream, whipped
¼ cup chopped pecans
2 cups miniature marshmallows

Combine well beaten egg yolks with 1 cup juice, saved from fruit. Blend well. Add cornstarch and sugar. Mix well. Cook over medium heat, stirring constantly, until mixture thickens. Cool at room temperature. Fold in whipped cream, nuts, marshmallows and fruit. Chill overnight.

Serena Amoth

Black Cherry Jell-O (Mom's)

1 large box black cherry Jell-O
12 oz. Cool Whip

1 (8 oz.) package cream cheese

Soften cream cheese, whip together cream cheese and cool whip until smooth. Prepare Jell-O as directed on the box. Whip cream cheese mixture and Jell-O. Cool until set. Note: Cherry or mixed fruit may be substituted. This is a favorite in our family.

Serena Amoth

Butterfinger Salad

1 box vanilla instant pudding

1 box butterscotch instant pudding

Mix both boxes with 3 cups milk. Slice 3-4 Butterfinger candy bars. Add to pudding mixture. Then add 1 (12 oz.) carton frozen whipped cream. Mix all together. Cool.

Carol, Mrs. Gary Koehn

Cookie Salad

1 (11 oz.) package fudge stripe
  cookies, broken in pieces
1 (3 oz.) package instant vanilla
  pudding
1 (8 oz.) carton Cool Whip

1½ cups buttermilk
1 (15 oz.) can pineapple tidbits, drained
1 can mandarin oranges, drained
May add sliced bananas and
  miniature marshmallows

Mix pudding and buttermilk until smooth, adding remaining ingredients. Keeps well in the refrigerator.

Betty Giesel Martens

Cranberry Salad

2 cups cranberries
½ cup water
2 cups sugar

2 packages raspberry Jell-O
1 cup chopped pecans
Miniature marshmallows (optional)

Boil cranberries in ½ cup water, until skin pops, add sugar, set aside to cool. Prepare Jell-O, add cranberries, chopped nuts and 2-3 shredded apples.

Jul Nightengale

Cranberry Salad

1 large box red Jell-O
1 can jelled cranberry sauce
1¼ cups walnuts
½ cup celery

2 cups water
1 can cherry pie filling
1 cup apples

Dissolve Jell-O in boiling water. Add the rest of the ingredients and chill.

Janice, Mrs. Jerry Ratzlaff

Cranberry Holiday Salad

2 cups fresh cranberries
1 orange, peeled
1 cup red apples, diced
½ cup green seedless grapes,
  halved
⅓ cup crushed pineapple

½ cup nuts, chopped
1¾ cup sugar
⅛ teaspoon salt
1 package cranberry/raspberry
  Jell-O

Combine cranberries, and orange in food processor and chop. Add sugar and let set at least 2 hours or over night. Prepare Jell-O according to package directions. Chill until Jell-O begins to congeal. Add all other ingredients, mix well, and refrigerate.

Arlene Giesel Koehn

Makes 8-10 servings

Creamy Mandarin Orange Salad

This is a very quick and simple recipe. If all ingredients have been refrigerated, it can be stirred together right before serving.

1 small box orange Jell-O
1 small box instant vanilla pudding
8 oz. Cool Whip, thawed

11 oz. can mandarin oranges
8 oz. can crushed pineapple

Drain juices from canned fruits. (Should be about 1 cup liquid) Add instant pudding to juices and stir well. Add box of dry Jell-O, stir. Add cool whip and stir well. Stir in fruits and refrigerate. A 15 oz. can of oranges can be used instead of oranges and pineapple. Drain juice and add water to make one cup and proceed with recipe.

Jolene Unruh

Choice Salad

1 cup pineapple juice
2 tablespoons cornstarch
¼ cup sugar
1 beaten egg

1 cup diced pineapple
½ cup diced cheese
½ cup chopped nuts
1 cup miniature marshmallows

In a saucepan, combine pineapple juice, cornstarch and sugar. Cook until thick, stirring constantly. Cool slightly, then slowly add beaten egg, stirring well. Return to heat and cook two minutes longer, continuing to stir. Pour mixture over diced pineapple, cheese, nuts and marshmallows.

Carolyn, Mrs. Wayne Holdeman

Cool Summer Salad

1 small Cool Whip
1 large can crushed pineapple
1 small package miniature
   marshmallows

½ cup English walnuts, broken
1 small carton large curd cottage
   cheese

Mix and Chill.

Mornie Giesel Unruh

Yield: 4 Servings

Easter Salad

2 (3 oz.) packages lemon Jell-O
2 cups boiling water
2 cups chilled lemon-lime soda
3 large bananas, diced

Frosting
1½ cups sugar
3 tablespoons flour
1 egg, well beaten

2 (8¼ oz.) cans crushed pineapple,
    drained, reserve juice
1 cup miniature colored
    marshmallows

1 cup pineapple juice
1 cup whipped topping
Grated cheese

Mix gelatin in boiling water until dissolved. Add soda. Refrigerate until consistency of egg whites. Add pineapple (save juice for frosting). Add bananas and marshmallows. Spread on frosting. To make frosting: Combine sugar, flour, egg and pineapple juice. Cook until thick. Let stand until cold, then fold in whipped topping. Sprinkle grated cheese on top. Note: This is a pretty, spring-looking salad and yummy, too!

Donna, Mrs. Donovan Nikkel, Charmaine Wedel

Delicious Fruit Salad

1 (15½ oz.) can pineapple
    chunks, drained
1 can mandarin oranges, drained

⅓ bag of frozen whole strawberries
3 sliced bananas
1 can peach pie filling

Drain canned fruit and add strawberries and bananas. Stir in peach pie filling. Refrigerate. Will keep 2-3 days. In season, fresh strawberries and a few fresh, sliced peaches are good in this recipe. 1 cup fresh blueberries, apples, seedless grapes may be added.

Charmaine Wedel, Jolene Unruh.

Juiced-up Jell-O

1 (3 oz.) package raspberry Jell-O
1 cup boiling water

1 cup cold grape juice

Dissolve Jell-O in boiling water. Add juice. Pour into individual bowls. Chill. Other combinations to try: orange Jell-O and apple juice, lime Jell-O and canned pineapple juice or strawberry Jell-O and orange juice.

Charmaine Wedel

Fruit Salad

1 can mandarin oranges
1 small can pineapple tidbits
2 apples, sliced

1 small bunch seedless grapes
1 (3 oz.) package instant
    vanilla pudding

Drain oranges and pineapple, reserving the juice. Mix juice with pudding mix and pour over fruit.

Charmaine Wedel

Frozen Fruit Cup

May use for breakfast, brunch, salad or dessert. Heat and dissolve 2 cups hot water and 1¾ cup sugar.

Add:

1 (6 oz.) can crushed pineapple (sweetened)

6 sliced bananas

1 quart fresh or frozen strawberries

1 quart fresh or frozen peaches

4-6 kiwi, sliced

grapes, optional

1 (12-16 oz.) can apricot nectar

Put all ingredients into fix-n-mix bowl and stir well. Freeze. Take out of freezer before serving and put into little fruit bowls. Return leftover to freezer.

Gayla, Mrs. Duane Martens

Frozen Fruit Salad

Mix together:

1 pint sour cream

1 cup sugar

2 large cartons Cool Whip (tint pink)

Add:

1 cup milk

1 cup marshmallows and ½ cup maraschino cherries (cut in half)

1 (16 oz.) fruit cocktail, drained well

Mash 5 bananas with 2 tablespoons lemon juice, add to mixture. Freeze in 9" x 13" pan.

Jul Nightengale

Fruity Chicken Salad

1 (15¼ oz.) can pineapple tidbits, undrained

4 cups chopped, cooked chicken

1 (11 oz.) can mandarin oranges, drained

1 (8 oz.) can sliced water chestnuts, drained

1 (2½ oz.) package slice almonds, toasted

1 cup chopped celery

1 cup seedless green grapes, cut in half

1½ cup mayonnaise

1 tablespoon soy sauce

1 teaspoon curry powder

1 (3 oz.) can chow mein noodles

Lettuce leaves, (optional)

Drain pineapple, reserving 2 tablespoons juice. (Reserve remaining juice for use in other recipes.) Combine pineapple tidbits and next 6 ingredients: mix well. Combine 2 tablespoons pineapple juice, mayonnaise, soy sauce, and curry powder; stir well, and add to chicken mixture. Chill. Stir in noodles just before serving. Serve on lettuce leaves, if desired.

Arlene Giesel Koehn

Yield: 8 servings

Frozen Fruit Salad

1 (8 oz.) package cream cheese
¾ cup granulated sugar
3 large ripe bananas, not over ripe
1 large can pineapple tidbits

1 pint frozen strawberries
½ cup chopped nutmeats
1 large container Cool Whip

Cream together the cream cheese, sugar and Cool Whip. Fold in fruits and nuts. The original recipe says to pour mixture into a jelly roll pan and freeze. It is very hard to cut into nice squares this way, so I usually spoon into cupcake liners. Just before serving, remove liners and arrange in bowl. Keeps well in freezer for 4-6 weeks. This recipe comes from Grandma Mary Giesel. Make it ahead of time when you are planning on Sunday dinner company or expecting a new baby in the family.

Finette Giesel Koehn

Fruit Salad (Sophie's)

2 bananas
1 can pineapple

1 can mandarin oranges, reserve juice
1 box instant vanilla pudding

Mix with 1 ½ cups reserved juice. (Made for German Sing, October 14, 1976)

Mornie Giesel Unruh

Fruit Salad

2 cups sliced strawberries
1½ cup cubed cantaloupe
1½ cup cubed watermelon
1½ cup cubed honeydew melon
2 cups sliced peaches

2 cups seedless whole grapes
2 cups fresh whole blueberries
2 cups cubed apples
¼ cup water
1½ tablespoons sugar or sweetener

Mix all ingredients in a large bowl and chill for 1½ to 2 hours and serve. Use ½ watermelon as a serving bowl.

Arlene Giesel Koehn

Fruit Salad

1 (20 oz.) can pineapple, chunks
    or tidbits
1 (16 oz.) can mandarin oranges
2 cups blueberries
2 cups grapes

2 eggs
¼ cup sugar
3½ tablespoons flour
½ teaspoon salt
2 cups Cool Whip

Drain pineapple and oranges. Reserve juice. Beat eggs; add sugar, flour and salt. Add fruit juice. Cook over low heat, stirring constantly, until thick. Cool. Fold in Cool Whip and fruit. This was the salad we served at our wedding. It's especially good in summer when grapes and blueberries are in season.

Michele, Mrs. Richard Ensz

Fruit Salad (24 Hour)

1 large can fruit cocktail, drained
1 large can crushed pineapple
1 (16 oz.) Cool Whip
⅓ cup lemon juice

1 cup eagle brand condensed milk
1 cup chopped and toasted pecans
1 cup miniature marshmallows

Next 3 items are optional:
½ cup raisins
½ cup coconut

½ cup maraschino cherries

Mix condensed milk with lemon juice. Add Cool Whip by hand. Fold in all other ingredients. Decorate with pecans and cherries. Chill.

Kathy Wedel

Glazed Fruit Salad

1 can pineapple chunks
1 can fruit cocktail
2 cans mandarin oranges

7 or 8 bananas, peeled and sliced
2 tablespoons lemon juice
1 can apricot pie filling

Drain the canned fruits thoroughly. Mix all the ingredients together and chill several hours, or overnight. It's apricot pie filling that makes salad glisten-also adds fine flavor.

Arlene Giesel Koehn   Makes 12 servings

1 box strawberry or raspberry Jell-O, 1 cup hot water dissolved in Jell-O, chill then whip. Chill and whip 1 can carnation milk, beat 1 cup sugar and 8 oz. of cream cheese and 1 teaspoon vanilla together. When Jell-O is set, whip milk and Jell-O and cream cheese mixture together. Add 1 stick of butter or oleo to 30 crushed graham crackers. Add 1 tablespoon powdered sugar. Line bowl with graham cracker mixture and fill with Jell-O mixture. This is one of my favorites. I can plainly remember Grandma Giesel fixing this when she would come to visit. Charmaine has carried on the tradition. I always ask her to make this for family dinners.

Shana Lea Koehn

Microwave Fruit Salad

1 package Cook'n' Serve vanilla
    pudding
1 (15 oz.) can pineapple tidbits

1 (10 oz.) can mandarin oranges
2 medium bananas
Maraschino cherries

Pour pudding into 1½ to 2 quart glass measuring dish. Stir in juice from pineapple and oranges (should be around 1 cup liquid). Microwave on high for four minutes, stirring after 2 minutes. Remove and add pineapple and oranges. Stir. Chill several hours, then add sliced pineapple and desired amount of cherries, halved or whole. Instant pudding can be used. Simply add the juice from canned pineapple and oranges to the pudding, stir, then add all the rest of the fruits. (Do not cook).

Jolene Unruh

Million Dollar Rice Salad

1 (8 oz.) package cream cheese,
    softened
1½ tablespoons sugar
1 tablespoon mayonnaise
2 cups cooked rice, cooled
12 maraschino cherries, halved

1 (20 oz.) can crushed pineapple,
    drained
1 (10 oz.) package miniature
    marshmallows
½ pint whipping cream, whipped
1 cup chopped pecans

Combine cream cheese, sugar and mayonnaise until smooth. Add rice, cherries, pineapple, and marshmallows and mix well. Fold in whipped cream and pecans.

Arlene Giesel Koehn

Mornie's Fruit Salad

Dressing:
5 tablespoons tapioca (minute)
¾ cup sugar

dash salt
2½ cups water or fruit juice

Soak 5 minutes, bring to a boil. Add 2 teaspoons lemon juice after dressing is boiled. Add any fruit you like. Grapes, bananas, strawberries, pineapple, fruit cocktail, sweetened, fresh oranges. Take pineapple and fruit juices and use for the dressing instead of water.

From Elma Giesel Koehn's recipe collection

Orange Jell-O Cranberry Salad

2½ cups fresh cranberries
1⅔ cup water
1 cup sugar
dash salt

1 (3 oz.) package orange Jell-O
1 (11 oz.) can mandarin oranges
   or 2 cups peeled, chopped oranges

Mix together cranberries, water, sugar and salt. Cook slowly, stirring occasionally until berry skins pop and become soft. Drain liquid from berries and measure juice; adding enough more boiling water to make 2 cups. Dissolve orange Jell-O in hot liquid, stir berries back into mixture, and chill until Jell-O begins to congeal. Fold in chopped oranges and continue to chill until set. Serve plain or with sweetened whipped cream.

Mary, Mrs. Lee Giesel

Orange Slice Salad

1 (20 oz.) can crushed pineapple
2 tablespoons flour
½ cup sugar
1 pound orange slice candy

1 pound quartered marshmallows
1 cup chopped walnuts
1 cup heavy cream

Cook pineapple with flour and sugar until thick. Pour over orange slices, marshmallows and nuts. Fold in whipped cream and chill. I got this recipe on one of our visits to Greensburg, Kansas at a very young age from Aimee, Mrs. Willard Dirks. No doubt, I must have been impressed!

Shana Lea Koehn

Overnight Salad

2 eggs
¼ cup sugar

¼ cup white vinegar
2 tablespoons butter

Beat eggs, add vinegar, sugar and butter. Cook until thick. Cool.

1 cup heavy cream, whipped
1 (14 oz.) can pineapple tidbits,
   drained

2 cups seedless grapes, halved
2 oranges peeled and diced
2 cups miniature marshmallows

Fold in whipped cream, fruits and marshmallow. Chill 24 hours. (substitute for grapes 1 can royal cherries, drained, pitted and halved.

Louise Wedel.

Peach Jell-O Salad

2 small boxes peach Jell-O
1½ cups boiling water

1½ cups cold water
1 can peach pie filling

Dissolve Jell-O in boiling water. Add cold water and pie filling. Chill till set. Other flavor Jell-O and pie filling may be substituted for peach, such as cherry.

Jolene Unruh

Peaches in a Cloud

This is a speedy salad recipe!

1 large package vanilla instant
    pudding
1½ cup juice (from peaches)
12 oz. Cool Whip

2 small packages peach Jell-O
    (or one large)
2 (16 oz.) cans sliced peaches in
    unsweetened pineapple juice

Drain juice from peach cans, adding water to make 1½ cups. Mix with pudding in large bowl. Add dry Jell-O and stir well. Stir in Cool Whip. Stir in peaches, reserving six slices for garnish. Spoon into large serving bowl. Arrange peach slices on top of salad in starburst design. Refrigerate. Try with other flavors; such as lime Jell-O and pears. Try with sugar-free pudding and/or sugar free Jell-O for a sweet salad with less sugar.

Jolene Unruh

Pineapple Cheese Salad

1 #2 can pineapple chunks
½ pound Velveeta cheese
20 large marshmallows
1 egg

2 tablespoons sugar
1 tablespoon oleo
juice from one can of pineapple

Drain the pineapple and place juice in top of double boiler. Combine flour, sugar and salt. Add to beaten egg. When blended, stir into heated pineapple juice; add oleo and cook until thickened. Cut cheese in ¼ inch cubes, cut marshmallows in quarters, add pineapple and pour cooked mixture over this and mix well. Chill for 2-3 hours. I usually refrigerate overnight. This recipe was given to me at my wedding shower in 1962. I'm not sure who gave it to me, but I've used it many times. It's a little more trouble to make, but well worth it.

Kathy Wedel

Pineapple Marshmallow Salad

1 can pineapple tidbits
¼ pound American cheese cut in cubes or shredded, (optional)
20 large marshmallows cut in small pieces or you may use small marshmallows, as many as you like

Drain pineapple, heat juice and add:

1 beaten egg
2 tablespoons flour
2 tablespoons sugar

⅛ teaspoon salt
1 tablespoon butter

(I add some more marshmallows to the sauce while it is hot.) Cook until thick. When cool, add pineapple, cheese and marshmallows. This can be made a day ahead. It is very good to take to picnics.

Sophie Giesel Koehn

Pineapple Salad

1 box instant vanilla pudding
1 large can crushed pineapple

1 cup shredded cheese
1 (9 oz.) Cool Whip

Mix pudding with pineapple (undrained). Add remaining ingredients. Fast and easy salad!

Coreen Holdeman

Raspberry Delight

The following recipe can be used for a salad or dessert

1 (3 oz.) package raspberry Jell-O
1 cup hot water
1 can (8 oz.) crushed pineapple
and juice

1 (10 oz.) package frozen raspberries
and juice
1 cup whipped topping

Dissolve Jell-O in hot water and chill until syrupy. Fold in pineapple, raspberries and their juices. Refrigerate until thickened. Fold in whipped topping, making a marbled effect.

Mornie Giesel Unruh

"Red Hot" Jell-O

½ cup red hots
2 cup boiling water

2 (3 oz.) packages raspberry Jell-O
3 cups applesauce

Dissolve candy and Jell-O in boiling water. Add applesauce. Chill until firm. This is easy to make and children LOVE IT!

William Nichols, Mornie's Great-Grandson

Rosie Pink Salad

1 (17 oz.) can pears in heavy syrup
1 (20 oz.) can pineapple chunks in
heavy syrup, reserve half the juice
1 (16 oz.) or 2 (10 oz.) packages
frozen strawberries in heavy syrup

1 (20 oz.) can peach pie filling
3 or more bananas, sliced
1 cup chopped pecans

Drain and cut up pears. Mix all ingredients and add reserved juice. Let sit in refrigerator for at least 2 hours before serving. Delicious!

Arlene Giesel Koehn

Simple Salad Suggestions

1 can pie filling
8 oz. cool whip

8 oz. yogurt or 1 small box Jell-O or
1 can sweetened condensed milk

Stir cool whip and pie filling together, add yogurt or condensed milk or dry Jell-O, mix; chill. Try blueberry pie filling with berry blue Jell-O or grape; cherry pie filling with cherry Jell-O or black cherry yogurt; peach pie filling with peach Jell-O, or orange or orange-pineapple Jell-O; lemon pie filling with orange-pineapple Jell-O or lemon.

Jolene Unruh

Striped Knox Blox

3 envelopes Knox unflavored
    gelatine
4 cups boiling water

3 packages 3 oz. flavored gelatine,
    any flavor

Mix 1 package Knox gelatine and 1 package of flavored gelatine together, add 1⅓ cup boiling water. Pour into 9 x 13 pan. Chill; repeat this with the other 2 gelatine flavors. Make sure each layer is set before you add the next layer. Cut in squares.

Ronda, Mrs. Kenny Giesel

Summer Fruit Salad

Ascorbic-citric powder
2 large apples, unpeeled and sliced
2 fresh nectarines, unpeeled and
    cut into wedges
2 fresh peaches, peeled and
    cut into wedges
1 (11 oz.) can mandarin oranges

1 (16 oz.) can pear halves sliced
1 (6 oz.) jar maraschino cherries
¼ cup sugar
1½ teaspoons cornstarch
½ cantaloup
1 cup seedless green grapes

Prepare ascorbic-citric solution according to directions. Toss apples, nectarines, and peaches separately in solution; drain and set aside. Drain the canned fruit and combine juices; stir well and set aside 1 cup of the juice mixture. Combine sugar and cornstarch in a saucepan; stir in reserved juice mixture. Cook over medium heat, stirring constantly, until mixture is thickened and bubbly. Scoop out cantaloupe balls. Layer apples, mandarin oranges, grapes, cantaloupe, pears, nectarines and peaches in a 3-quart bowl; garnish with a few maraschino cherries; serve with fruit juice dressing.

Arlene Giesel Koehn

Yield: 10-12 servings

Super Fruit Salad

2 (11 oz.) cans mandarin oranges, drained
2 (13½ oz.) cans pineapple tidbits, undrained
2 cups miniature marshmallows
2 cups cantaloupe balls
2 cups watermelon balls
½ cup slivered almonds
Fluffy Dressing *(Recipe follows)*

Combine drained mandarin oranges, pineapple tidbits with their juice and marshmallows. Let stand in refrigerator at least 1 hour so marshmallows absorb some of the juice. Drain off excess juice; add melon balls and almonds. Serve in large bowl. Let guests help themselves to salad and dressing. Yield 8 cups.

Fluffy Dressing:
2 eggs, beaten
2 tablespoons sugar
¼ cup light cream
4 tablespoons lemon juice
1 cup heavy cream, whipped

Combine eggs, sugar and cream. Cook over hot water, stirring constantly, until slightly thickened. Beat in lemon juice with rotary beater (this makes mixture smooth). Remove from heat and chill. When ready to serve, fold in whipped cream.

Arlene Giesel Koehn

Tapioca Salad

4 cups boiling water
½ cup plus 1 tablespoon baby pearl tapioca

Cook above mixture for 10-15 minutes; remove from heat, cover until tapioca is clear.

Add:
1 package orange or strawberry Jell-O
½ teaspoon salt
⅔ cup sugar

Let cool ; add fruit, oranges with orange Jell-O, strawberries with strawberry Jell-O; refrigerate. If desired add 1 package dream whip.

Betty, Mrs. Gordon Unruh

Quick Graham Cracker Fluff

2 packages instant vanilla pudding
3 cups milk

Whip with mixer until thick. Stir in:
9 oz. cool whip

Crush 15 graham crackers, mix in 3 tablespoons sugar and 3 tablespoons oleo, softened. Pat in bowl, reserving enough to sprinkle on top. Fill bowl top with remaining crumbs.

Arlene, Mrs. Randy Giesel   Yield: 12 servings

Avocado Salad

1 ripe avocado
1 stalk celery
½ large tomato

½ small onion
1 teaspoon chopped black olives
salt and pepper to taste

Cut all vegetables in small pieces. Mix together the following: mayonnaise, cream Parmesan, Tabasco, salt and pepper, and garlic powder to taste, stir in vegetables. Serve. This may be served in a burrito shell or pita sandwich.

Julie, Mrs. Kieth Koehn

Broccoli Salad

1 bunch broccoli
1 cup shredded cheese

1 diced onion

Mix the following and pour over ingredients: ½ cup salad dressing, ¼ cup sugar, 2 tablespoons vinegar, ½ pound bacon, fried crisp and crumbled, salt and pepper to taste. Serve.

Mary, Mrs. Lee Giesel

Broccoli Salad

4 cups chopped broccoli
1 cup raisins
1 cup shelled sunflower seeds

½ cup chopped sweet onion
6-8 slices bacon cooked crisp
and crumbled

Combine ingredients. Dressing: 1 cup mayonnaise, ¼ cup sugar, 1 tablespoon vinegar; mix together and pour over broccoli mixture.

Carolyn, Mrs. Wayne Holdeman

Nutty Broccoli Salad

4 cups chopped tender broccoli
½ pound bacon
1 cup white raisins
1 medium red onion, chopped

1 (4 oz.) package salted sunflower
seeds, or 1 cup unsalted roasted
peanuts
1 (2 oz.) package almonds sliced

Fry bacon and crumble. Combine all ingredients and refrigerate. One hour before serving add dressing.

Dressing:
2 tablespoons red wine vinegar
2 tablespoons sugar

1 cup mayonnaise

Mix and pour over salad.

Arlene Giesel Koehn

Broccoli Delight Salad

5 cups fresh broccoli
½ cup raisins
¼ cup chopped red onion
2 tablespoons sugar

3 tablespoons vinegar
1 cup mayonnaise
10 bacon slices, fried and crumbled
1 cup sunflower seeds

In large bowl, combine broccoli, raisins and onion. In small bowl combine sugar, vinegar and mayonnaise. Pour over broccoli; toss to coat. Refrigerate. Just before serving, sprinkle with bacon and sunflower seeds; toss.

Jana, Mrs. Robert Nichols   Yield 6-8 servings

Crunchy Cabbage Salad

2 tablespoons sesame seeds, or
    sunflower seeds
½ cup slivered almonds
½ large head cabbage shredded,
    about 5 cups

4 green onions chopped
1 package (3 oz.) oriental ramen
    style noodles (chicken flavor)

Dressing:
flavor package from noodle mix
2 tablespoons sugar
⅓-½ cup oil

3 tablespoons vinegar
½ teaspoon pepper

Make dressing early in the day, combine all ingredients, mix well and refrigerate. Toast sesame seeds and almonds in 350 degrees oven for 15 minutes or until golden; set aside. Combine cabbage, onions, and uncooked noodles (which have been broken in pieces by hand) mix lightly. Just before serving add dressing, seeds and nuts. Toss, and serve immediately.

Betty, Mrs. Gordon Unruh, Jolene Unruh

Cabbage Salad

Dressing:
Flavor package from Ramen Noodles
2 tablespoons sugar

¼ teaspoon pepper
½ cup cole slaw dressing

Mix together and set aside:
½ head cabbage shredded
2 tablespoons sunflower seeds
¼ cup slivered almonds

4 green onions chopped
1 (3 oz.) package ramen noodles
    (chicken flavor)

Mix altogether just before serving.

Connie, Mrs. Kevin Koehn

Cabbage Salad

1 small head cabbage, shredded
1 small onion chopped
1 green pepper chopped

½ cup salad oil
½ cup vinegar
1 cup sugar

Arrange cabbage, onion, and green pepper in bowl in layers, seasoning each layer with celery seed, salt and pepper. Combine oil, vinegar and sugar and bring to a boil. Pour hot syrup over cabbage mixture. Refrigerate over night, do not stir until the next morning. This salad keeps well in refrigerator for several days, also freezes well.

Arlene Giesel Koehn

Cabbage Salad and Crunchy Noodles

4½ cups shredded red or green
    cabbage
5 green onions thinly sliced,
    including tops

11 oz. niblets corn, drained
9 oz. package frozen peas, thawed
2 oz. sliced mushrooms (undrained)

Dressing:
¼ cup tarragon vinegar
¼ cup oil
3 oz. package oriental noodles with
    chicken flavor seasoning

½ cup slivered almonds (toasted)
3 tablespoons sugar
2 tablespoons sunflower seeds
½ teaspoon pepper

In large bowl combine all salad ingredients; In small bowl combine seasoning packet, vinegar, oil, sugar and pepper, salt to taste, blend well; pour dressing over salad, toss to coat; refrigerate at least 2 hours; Break noodles into ¾ inch pieces; just before serving add noodles, seeds, and nuts into salad mix.

Carolyn, Mrs. Wayne Holdeman

Cauliflower and Broccoli Salad

Mix following ingredients:
cauliflower
broccoli
cheese, grated
onion, chopped

raisins
sunflower seeds
bacon, crumbled

Dressing:
1 cup miracle whip
½ cup sugar

2 tablespoons vinegar

Elaine, Mrs. Bruce Unruh

Cauliflower - Broccoli Salad

1 head cauliflower
1 bunch broccoli

1-2 onions
⅓ cup cooked diced bacon

Dressing:
⅓ cup vinegar
⅓ cup salad oil
¼ cup sugar

½ cup mayonnaise
½ teaspoon salt

Mix together and pour over salad.

Marisa Giesel Wedel

Cauliflower - Broccoli Salad

½-1 head cauliflower
1 bunch broccoli
8-10 slices bacon, cooked and
    crumbled

2 small onions, chopped
grated cheese
sunflower seeds

Mix together, add dressing just before serving.

Dressing:
1 cup miracle whip
½ cup sugar

2 tablespoons vinegar

Karen, Mrs. Rick Penner

Crisp Cucumbers in Cream

1 large cucumber, sliced thin
½ cup vinegar
⅓ cup ice water
1 teaspoon salt

4 whole black peppers
1 medium onion, sliced thin
1 cup sour cream
tomato wedges

Slice cucumber into bowl. Combine vinegar, water, salt, and peppers and pour over. Cover and chill in refrigerator at least 2 hours. Drain well and remove peppers. Mix cucumber and onion slices and toss with sour cream. Serve in small bowls with tomato wedges.

Arlene Giesel Koehn

Chow Mein Salad

1 cup diced celery
1 cup shredded carrot
⅓ cup diced onion

1 large can tuna
mayonnaise to moisten

Chill; add 1 small can chow mein noodles just before serving. Sprinkle with soy sauce to taste.

Jennie, Mrs. Calvin Unruh

Chef's Garden Salad

1 large head lettuce, torn into
   bite-size pieces
1 tomato, cut into wedges
1 small cucumber, sliced
½ cup sliced celery
½ cup chopped green pepper

½ cup thousand island dressing
1 cup julienne strips cooked ham
1 cup julienne strips cooked chicken
1 cup julienne strips cheddar cheese
2 hard boiled eggs, sliced

Combine vegetables in a large bowl. Add ½ cup dressing, tossing well. Arrange ham, chicken, cheese, and eggs on salad. Serve with additional dressing if desired.

Arlene Giesel Koehn

Garden Salad

Marinade:
1 cup sugar
½ cup oil
¾ cup vinegar

½ teaspoon pepper
1 teaspoon salt
1 teaspoon bean juice

Vegetables:
1 can (16 oz.) tiny peas, drained
1 can (16 oz.) white whole
   kernel corn
1 can (16 oz.) french style green
   beans, drained

1 small jar chopped pimiento
   chopped
1 cup celery, chopped
½ cup onion, chopped
1 cup green pepper, finely chopped

In saucepan, combine sugar, oil, vinegar, pepper, salt and bean juice and bring to a boil. Cool. Combine vegetables and pour cooled marinade over them. Refrigerate overnight. Salad will keep for 1 week.

Mornie Giesel Unruh

Gazpacho Salad

4 tomatoes, seeded and diced
2 cucumbers, peeled and diced
2 green peppers, seeded and diced
1 medium onion, diced

1 can sliced ripe olives
1 teaspoon salt
½ teaspoon pepper

Dressing:
½ cup olive oil
¼ cup vinegar
¼ cup lemon juice
1 tablespoon parsley

2 garlic cloves, minced
2 teaspoons chopped green onions
½ teaspoon salt
¼ teaspoon cumin

In a 1½ quart glass jar or bowl, layer one third or one half of the tomatoes, cucumbers, green peppers, onion, olives, salt and pepper. Repeat layers 2-3 times. In a small bowl combine all dressing ingredients. Pour over vegetables. Cover and chill several hours or over night.

LeAnne Nichols

Yield: 10-12 servings

Lima Bean Salad

Green onions and basil make this special.

¾ cup salad oil
½ cup vinegar
3 tablespoons finely chopped
    basil leaves, or 1 teaspoon
    dried basil leaves

1 teaspoon salt
1 tablespoon sugar
½ cup chopped green onions
6 cups cooked lima beans
lettuce

Mix oil, vinegar, basil, salt sugar and onion. Pour over beans; mix lightly. Cover and chill at least 4 hours. Serve on crisp lettuce or other greens.

Arlene Giesel Koehn   Yield: 8 servings

Macaroni Salad

1 (8 oz.) box small macaroni
1 cup cubed cheddar cheese
¼ cup chopped onion
1 (16 oz.) can English peas, drained
½ cup grated carrots
salt to taste

1 bell pepper, chopped
3 boiled eggs, chopped
½ cup chopped pimiento
1 cup chopped celery
½ cup mayonnaise

Cook macaroni according to package directions; drain. Add remaining ingredients; mix well. Chill before serving.

Janice, Mrs. Jerry Ratzlaff   Yield: 8-10 servings

Microwave Potato Salad

5 cups diced raw potatoes
⅓ cup cold water
1 cup mayonnaise
½ cup each: chopped onion, celery
    slices, chopped dill pickle

1 tablespoon mustard
½ teaspoon celery seed
½ teaspoon salt

Combine potatoes and water in a 2 quart glass dish, cover. Microwave on HIGH 10 to 12 minutes or till tender, stirring after 6 minutes. Drain; In large bowl, stir together remaining ingredients. Add potatoes, mix lightly. Chill. Diced cucumber may be substituted for sliced celery, and diced cooked eggs are a good addition.

Jolene Unruh

Oriental Salad

1 package cole slaw (or 8 cups
    cabbage and carrots shredded)
1 cup slivered almonds

2 packages Ramen Noodles,
    oriental flavor
1 cup sunflower seeds

Dressing:
½-1 cup oil
½ cup sugar

⅓ cup vinegar
2 seasoning packages from noodles

Mix the dressing ingredients and pour over the other ingredients; serve immediately.

Jana, Mrs. Robert Nichols

Pasta Salad

1 (10 oz.) package pasta, spirals,
    bowties, or mostaccioli
1 large cucumber
2-3 tomatoes
1 large onion
1 green pepper
¾ cup oil
1½ cup sugar

1½ cup vinegar
2 teaspoons prepared mustard
1 teaspoon salt
1 teaspoon pepper
1 teaspoon parsley
1 teaspoon garlic salt
1 teaspoon Accent

Cook pasta according to directions; drain and rinse in cold water. Slice all vegetables and mix well. Combine oil, vinegar, sugar and other spices in bowl. Mix thoroughly. Pour over pasta and vegetables. Toss lightly and chill over night in covered bowl. Keeps for several days in refrigerator. A good salad to take to basket dinners.

Pat, Mrs. Mitchell Unruh

Pea Salad

2 (10 oz.) packages frozen tiny
    green peas, thawed
2 cups chopped celery
1 cup cashews
½ cup chopped green onions

12 slices bacon, cooked and crumbled
1 cup sour cream
¼ teaspoon salt
¼ teaspoon pepper

Combine peas, celery, cashews, green onions, and bacon in a large bowl. Add sour cream, salt, and pepper; toss lightly to coat. Cover and chill thoroughly.

Arlene Giesel Koehn

Yield: 8-10 servings

Pizza Salad

1 pound spiral macaroni, cooked
  and drained
3 medium tomatoes, seeded
  and diced
1 pound cheddar cheese, cubed
1-2 bunches green onions, sliced
3 oz. sliced pepperoni
¾ cup vegetable oil

⅔ cup grated Parmesan cheese
½ cup red wine vinegar
2 teaspoons oregano
1 teaspoon garlic powder
1 teaspoon salt
¼ teaspoon pepper
croutons, optional

Combine macaroni, tomatoes, cheese, onions, and pepperoni. In a small bowl combine oil, Parmesan cheese, vinegar and spices. Pour over macaroni mixture. Cover and refrigerate several hours. Top with croutons just before serving.

LeAnne Nichols.   Yield: 16 servings

Sauerkraut Salad

Drain 1 2 ½- pound can sauerkraut. Chop 1 medium pepper, and 1 medium onion in small pieces. Combine sauerkraut, pepper, onion, ¼ cup chopped pimiento and 1 teaspoon dill seed. Combine 1-½ cups sugar with ½ cup vinegar. Heat until sugar dissolves; add ½ cup salad oil; mix well. Pour over sauerkraut mixture and toss to mix. Cover and refrigerate overnight to blend flavors.

Janice, Mrs. Jerry Ratzlaff   Makes 1 quart

Tossed Taco Salad

My family loves this salad. It's a complete meal
1 head lettuce
1 bunch green onions, chopped
4 tomatoes, chopped
1 package (5½ oz.) taco chips
12 oz. grated cheese

1 (15 oz.) can red kidney beans,
  drained
1 pound ground beef
1 bottle (8 oz.) thousand island
  dressing

Mix the first 6 ingredients together. Brown ground beef and drain. Add to salad while still hot. Toss with salad dressing.

Arlene Giesel Koehn   Makes a large salad

Taco Salad

1 head lettuce
1 cup shredded cheddar cheese

½ can chili beans, do not drain
taco flavored tortilla chips, crushed

Toss together well. Add creamy Italian dressing to taste.

Finette Giesel Koehn

Vegetable Refrigerator Salad

1 can french-styled green beans
1 can yellow niblets corn, drained
1 green pepper, diced
1 pimiento, chopped
3 small carrots, shredded
1 can water chestnuts, sliced and drained

1 can bean sprouts, drained
1 (4 oz.) can mushrooms, drained and sliced
1 medium onion, sliced
1 cup diced celery
1 head cauliflower, cut in florets

Heat the following until sugar dissolves; 2 cups sugar, 1 cup salad oil, cracked pepper, 2½ cups vinegar, half white, half red or cider; pour over vegetables that have been drained. Toss. Cover lightly then refrigerate overnight.

Arlene Giesel Koehn

Hot Chicken Salad

2 cups diced chicken or turkey
2 cups diced celery
1 cup sliced almonds
2 teaspoons grated onion
2 tablespoons lemon juice

1 cup mayonnaise
½ teaspoon salt
½ cup grated Parmesan cheese
1 cup crushed potato chips

Combine chicken, celery and almonds. Blend onion, lemon juice, mayonnaise, and salt (pepper if desired) and mix lightly with chicken mixture. Put into greased casserole and top with cheese and crushed chips. Bake in 400 degree oven 15 minutes.

Momie Giesel Unruh

Hot Chicken Salad

4 chicken breasts cooked and cut up
2 cans cream of chicken soup
2 cans water chestnuts, drained and cut up

2 cups chopped celery
4 cups corn flakes
4 tablespoons chopped onions

Mix all ingredients except corn flakes, put in buttered pan. Top with buttered corn flakes. Bake at 350 degrees for 30 minutes.

Barbara, Mrs. Ervin Koehn

Roast Beef Salad

3 cups cubed cooked beef
½ cup chopped dill pickles
½ cup chopped celery
⅓ cup finely chopped onion

⅓ cup mayonnaise or salad dressing
1 teaspoon prepared mustard
1 teaspoon Worcestershire sauce
1 teaspoon salt

Combine first four ingredients. Blend mayonnaise with remaining ingredients. Mix lightly with meat mixture; chill.

Arlene Giesel Koehn

Yield: 4-6 servings

Salmon Salad

(Mary, Mom Giesel's recipe)

1 (14¾ oz.) can pink salmon, drained and deboned

3 hard boiled eggs, peeled and diced

3 tablespoons chopped pickles (sweet or dills)

¼ cup diced celery

2 tablespoons minced onions

mayonnaise for dressing to taste

Mix lightly and chill. Aunt Mornie suggested I include this recipe. I didn't have Mom's written recipe, only memories... I think Mom used cream for the dressing, as we did not buy mayonnaise many years ago. I am not sure she added the celery, but I like it that way.

Betty Giesel Martens   Serves 4

Turkey Salad

8 cups cooked turkey, cut into bite-size pieces

1 large can water chestnuts, diced

1½ cups celery, chopped fine

⅔ cup seedless grapes

1¼ cup slivered almonds

2 cups mayonnaise (may need more)

1½ tablespoons lemon juice

1 tablespoon curry powder

2 tablespoons soy sauce

lettuce leaves

1 can pineapple chunks

Combine turkey, water chestnuts, celery, grapes, and almonds. Blend mayonnaise with lemon juice, curry powder, and soy sauce. Stir gently into turkey mixture. Chill in large glass bowl for several hours. Serve on crisp lettuce and garnish with pineapple chunks.

Arlene Giesel Koehn

Banana Poppy Seed Dressing

Light sweet refreshing dressing, good over fresh fruit or crisp greens.

1 ripe banana

1 cup (8 oz.) sour cream

¼ cup sugar

1 tablespoon poppy seed

1 tablespoon lemon juice

1 teaspoon dry mustard

¾ teaspoon salt

In a small bowl mash banana, add sour cream, sugar, poppy seeds, lemon juice, mustard and salt. Chill for at least 30 minutes. Arrange salad greens and fruit on platter, serve with dressing.

Connie Martens Koehn   Yield: 1¾ cup

Best Ever Cole Slaw Dressing

1 cup sugar
½ cup vinegar
1 cup salad oil
1 teaspoon celery seed

1 teaspoon salt
1 teaspoon dry mustard
1 small onion, diced

Beat ingredients together until very creamy. Store in a covered pint jar in refrigerator. Keeps very well.

Charmaine Wedel

Birmingham Slaw Dressing

1 cup sugar
2 cups mayonnaise
½ cup catsup
¼-½ cup white vinegar

1 tablespoon mustard
1 teaspoon Worcestershire sauce
½ teaspoon salt

Mix well and serve over finely shredded cabbage.

Arlene Giesel Koehn

Dressing for Mixed Fruit

5 tablespoons minute tapioca
¾ cup sugar

¼ teaspoon salt
2½ cup fruit juice or water

Soak the above ingredients together for 5 minutes. Bring to a boil over medium heat, stirring constantly, remove from heat and add juice of 2 lemons. Cool; add desired fruit, peaches, strawberries, grapes, pineapple and bananas.

Carolyn, Mrs. Wayne Holdeman

French Dressing

1 cup catsup (thick)
1 cup sugar
1 cup salad oil
½ cup vinegar

1 teaspoon salt
2 teaspoons paprika
1 small onion grated (to taste)

Mix well. Vary with celery seed or blue cheese

Arlene Giesel Koehn

Mexican Dressing

½ cup onion
1 cup sugar
1 teaspoon salt
½ teaspoon pepper
1 teaspoon celery seed

3 teaspoons prepared mustard
⅓ cup vinegar
1 cup oil
4 tablespoons mayonnaise or
    salad dressing

Blend in blender. This recipe was given to me by Gloria Dirks.

Jackie Koehn

Thousand Island Dressing

1 quart mayonnaise
1 can tomato soup

½ cup sweet relish
¼ cup white vinegar

Mix well and store in refrigerator in tightly covered container. Keeps indefinitely.

Jul Nightengale.

ENTREES

Baked Steak

Round steak- sprinkle with Lipton onion soup mix, salt and pepper. Slice green pepper over top and pour beef broth to cover the bottom. Bake at 220 degrees all night.

Jackie Koehn.

Brisket, Oven Barbecue

6-7 pounds boneless brisket

Sprinkle liberally with onion salt, garlic salt, and celery salt. Sprinkle with ⅔ small bottle liquid smoke. Rub in. Cover and marinate overnight in refrigerator.

In the morning salt and pepper both sides. Sprinkle with ¼ cup Worcestershire sauce. Rub in. Bake covered (fat side up) at 275 degrees for 4 to 5 hours. Turn to lean side and cover with barbecue sauce. Bake covered 1 hour longer at 275 degrees.

Barbecue Sauce:

1 cup catsup	3 tablespoons sugar
2 tablespoons Worcestershire sauce	1 tablespoon dry mustard

If desired, make more sauce to pour over meat when serving.

Bev, Mrs. Lonnie Unruh

Beef Brisket

1 3-6 pound beef brisket	1 envelope Lipton's onion soup mix
1 can Campbell's mushroom soup	(I use golden onion)
(I use golden mushroom)	

Preheat oven to 275 degrees. Lay brisket in roasting pan, fat side up. Mix the can of mushroom soup with the packet of dry soup mix. Spread the mixture on top of the brisket. Cover the pan tightly with foil, put on the lid, and bake for 45 minutes to 1 hour per pound—2½ to 6 hours, depending on the size of brisket. When meat is tender, trim fat from top. Make gravy from pan drippings. Slice against the grain of the beef.

My mother-in-law gave me this recipe.

Lelain Lorenzen Epstein

Beef Stroganoff

1 pound round steak
2 tablespoons fat
2 onions, sliced
8 oz. can tomato sauce
½ cup water

1 teaspoon salt
1 teaspoon Worcestershire sauce
4 oz. wide noodles
½ cup sour cream

Cut meat into one half inch cubes; heat fat in heavy skillet and brown meat and onions. Stir in tomato sauce, water, salt, and Worcestershire sauce; cover and simmer about 45 minutes or until meat is tender. Prepare noodles; cook noodles in 3 quarts boiling water and 2 teaspoons salt. Boil rapidly 2 minutes; cover, remove from heat, and let stand 10 minutes. Rinse with hot water and drain. Fold noodles and sour cream into meat mixture and reheat, or can be served separately.

Mary, Mrs. Lee Giesel

Chicken Fried Steak and Cream Gravy

2 pounds boneless round steak
1 cup all-purpose flour
1 teaspoon salt
1 teaspoon pepper
½ teaspoon garlic salt

2 eggs
¼ cup milk
Vegetable oil
Cream Gravy (see below)

Trim excess fat from steak; pound steak to ¼ inch thickness, using a meat mallet. Cut into serving size pieces. Combine flour, salt, pepper, and garlic salt. Combine eggs and milk; beat well. Dredge steak in flour mixture; dip in egg mixture, and dredge in flour mixture. Lightly pound steak. Heat 1 inch of oil in a skillet to 375 degrees. Fry steak in hot oil until browned, turning steak once. Drain steak on paper towels. Reserve ¼ cup pan drippings for gravy. Serve steak with Cream Gravy

Yield: 6 to 8 servings

Cream Gravy:
¼ cup all-purpose flour
¼ cup pan drippings
2 to 3 cups milk

½ teaspoon salt
¼ teaspoon pepper

Add flour to pan drippings; cook over medium heat until bubbly, stirring constantly. Gradually add milk; cook until thickened and bubbly, stirring constantly. Stir in salt and pepper.

Arlene Giesel Koehn

Yield: 2¾ cups

Hobo Dinners

Round steak, as much as you like.

Marinate in the following:

1 tablespoon meat tenderizer
3 tablespoons liquid smoke
1 teaspoon salt
¼ teaspoon pepper
½ teaspoon celery salt

½ teaspoon onion salt
½ teaspoon paprika
¼ teaspoon nutmeg
½ cup brown sugar

Marinate at least 12 hours. Cut up carrots, onions, green peppers, and the meat and place some of each on a square of foil. Fold and seal tightly. Place in a pit of hot coals and charcoal till done. Serve out of a wheelbarrow.

Jackie Koehn

Poor Man's Fillet Mignon

2 pounds extra lean ground beef
4 slices bread, crumbed
2 eggs, beaten
½ cup milk
2 teaspoons salt
1 tablespoon minced onion

2 teaspoons dried celery flakes
½ teaspoon chili powder
1 bottle (18 oz.) smoke flavored
  barbecue sauce, divided
12 slices uncooked bacon

Combine the first eight ingredients and 2 tablespoons barbecue sauce. Form into 12 thick patties. Wrap a bacon slice around the sides of each patty and secure with a toothpick. Bake on a rack at 350 degrees for 50-60 minutes or until desired doneness is reached. Baste frequently with remaining barbecue sauce the last 30 minutes. These are especially good grilled.

Arlene, Mrs. Randy Giesel   Yield: 12 servings

Rdk's Hamburger Steak

2 pounds hamburger
4 eggs mixed with milk or cream

1 package crushed saltine crackers

Shape meat into patties. Dip into milk and roll in cracker crumbs. Fry. May be served with gravy, mashed potatoes, and corn. Sure to please a growing boy's appetite.

Ridgel Koehn

Salisbury Steak

1 and ½ pounds ground beef
¼ cup chopped onions
dash of pepper
½ cup bread crumbs
1 egg slightly beaten

salt to taste
1 can mushroom soup or cream
of chicken soup
⅓ cup water

Combine ¼ cup soup with all of the remaining ingredients except the ⅓ cup water. Mix and shape into six patties. Brown patties. Place in a shallow baking dish. (9 x 13) Bake at 350 degrees for 30 minutes. Spoon off fat. Mix remaining soup and ⅓ cup water, pour over meat. Bake for 10 minutes.

Sophie Giesel Koehn

Slow Cooked Pepper Steak

1½ - 2 pounds beef round steak
2 tablespoons cooking oil
¼ cup soy sauce
1 cup chopped onion
1 garlic clove, minced
1 teaspoon sugar
½ teaspoon salt
¼ teaspoon pepper

¼ teaspoon ground ginger
4 tomatoes, cut into eighths or
1 can (16 oz.) tomatoes with
liquid, cut up
2 large green peppers cut into strips
½ cup cold water
1 tablespoon cornstarch
cooked noodles or rice

Cut beef into 3 inch by 1 inch strips. Brown in oil in a skillet. Transfer to a slow cooker and combine the next 7 ingredients. Pour over beef. Cover and cook on low for 5-6 hours, or until meat is tender. Add tomatoes and green peppers. Cook on low 1 hour longer. Combine the cold water and cornstarch to make a paste. Stir into liquid in slow cooker and cook on high until thickened. Serve over noodles or rice.

Connie, Mrs. Kevin Koehn   Yield: 6-8 servings

Steak Kabobs

Round steak
onion
green pepper

mushroom
chunk pineapple

Any amount you wish. Cut the steak into 2 inch cubes and marinate at least 12 hours in the following marinade sauce.

Soy Marinade:
⅓ cup vegetable oil
5 tablespoons soy sauce
2 tablespoons catsup
1 teaspoon garlic powder

1 tablespoon vinegar
1 tablespoon Worcestershire sauce
dash of pepper

Combine all ingredients and mix well.

Awhile before serving time, cut up onion, green peppers and mushrooms(if large). Skewer starting and ending with meat. It is best to place everything fairly close together as it tends to dry out. Place on medium coals and turn often as they burn easily. These are delicious!

Jackie Koehn

Makes ½ cup

Sukiyaki

1½ pounds round or sirloin steak
3 tablespoons cooking oil
1 large onion, thinly sliced
1 cup sliced celery
1 medium green pepper, cut in strips
½ cup (or less) canned mushroom
  pieces (4 oz. can)

½ cup green onions, cut into 1 inch
  lengths
2 (10 oz.) cans beef broth
2 tablespoons soy sauce
¼ cup cold water
2 tablespoons cornstarch

Cut partially frozen steak into ½ inch pieces. Stir-fry meat in skillet or wok over high heat until brown, about 10 minutes. Combine soy sauce and beef broth and add to meat. Bring to a boil, reduce heat to simmer. Simmer for about 40 minutes or until meat is tender. Add the vegetables and cook over low heat about 10 minutes, stirring often. Combine cornstarch and water. Mix into sukiyaki to thicken. Serve over hot rice. It may need more thickening. If you like more sauce, you can double the beef broth, soy sauce, water and cornstarch.

Michele, Mrs. Richard Ensz

Serves 4-6

Teriyaki Steak

½ cup packed brown sugar	1 teaspoon ground ginger
½ cup soy sauce	¼ teaspoon garlic powder
½ cup sherry	T-bone or sirloin steak

Mix all ingredients except steak. Microwave at HIGH 1-1½ minutes until sugar is dissolved. Place steak in plastic bag. Pour marinade over steak and seal bag. Refrigerate 6-8 hours. Drain steak, grill over hot coals. Chicken, turkey or pork chops may be used in place of steak.

Jane Giesel

Veal or Round Steak Birds

6 pounds round steak

Cut steak into 4 inch squares, pound to flatten and sprinkle with salt. Spread dressing on each square, roll and fasten with a toothpick.

Dressing:

1½ large onion, chopped	2 beef bouillon cubes dissolved in
1½ teaspoons ground sage	2 cups hot water
salt and pepper to taste	¼ cup margarine
1 loaf toasted bread crumbs	

Saute onion in margarine, add to ingredients. Mix lightly.

Gravy:

2-3 tablespoons flour or cornstarch	3 bouillon cubes, dissolved in
seasonings to taste	6 cups hot water

Cook until thickened. Pour over meat before baking. Meat rolls absorbs a good amount of gravy, and you want some for potatoes. Bake at 300 degrees for 2 to 3 hours. This recipe was Aunt Mary Giesel's. I remember eating it at their house for Sunday dinner. It was always special!

Carolyn, Mrs. Wayne Holdeman

Hearty Fiesta Burgers

1 pound ground beef	1 can mushroom soup or tomato soup
¾ cup oatmeal or cracker crumbs	1 can kidney or chili beans,
2 eggs	drained (15 oz.)
¼ cup ketchup	⅓ cup fresh or frozen green pepper,
2 teaspoons instant minced onion	chopped
2 teaspoons Worcestershire sauce	½ cup shredded cheese (2 oz.)

Combine first 6 ingredients, a dash of pepper and ⅛-¼ teaspoon salt, Shape into 6-8 patties, brown in large skillet. Spread soup over meat, top with green peppers and beans. Cook covered, over low heat 10-15 minutes. Sprinkle with cheese, cover and cook till cheese melts.

Jolene Unruh

Stuffed Hamburgers

2 pounds hamburger
2-3 fresh sliced mushrooms
1 green pepper diced

1 onion chopped
Velveeta cheese, cubed or sliced

Divide hamburger into 8 portions. Flatten each portion as for hamburger. Top 4 patties with mushrooms, peppers and onion and cheese. Place a second plain pattie on top of each and seal the edges well, so ingredients will not spill out. charcoal until done, may be broiled.

Nancy, Mrs Kenneth Unruh

Corn Dogs

½ cup cornmeal
1 cup flour
1 tablespoon baking powder
1 teaspoon salt
1 tablespoon sugar
1 cup evaporated milk

1 egg, beaten
¼ teaspoon paprika
½ teaspoon dry mustard
dash pepper
10-16 hot dogs
vegetable oil for deep frying

In bowl mix cornmeal, flour, baking powder, salt, sugar, milk, egg, paprika, mustard, and pepper. Pour mixture into tall glass; skewer hot dogs with wooden skewers; dip in mixture, deep-fry at 375 degrees, until golden brown. (about 2 minutes) drain on paper towels.

Coreen Holdeman

Barbecue Wieners

Fry ¼ cup chopped onions in hot fat until tender, add 1 cup ketchup, ½ cup water, 2 tablespoons brown sugar, ½ teaspoon salt, dash of pepper, 2 tablespoons vinegar, 3 tablespoons Worcestershire sauce and ½ teaspoon mustard, simmer 20 minutes. Pour over wieners, bake in oven for 1 hour, or simmer on stove top.

Jul Nightengale

Amish Casserole

2 pounds hamburger
1 (10 oz.) bag krinkly noodles
½ pound Velveeta cheese, grated
1 quart green beans

1 (10½ oz.) can mushroom soup
1 (10½ oz.) can chicken soup
1 (10½ oz.) celery soup
1 (10½ oz.) can tomato soup

Fry hamburger with salt, pepper, onion, and 1 teaspoon chili powder. Drain. Cook noodles with 1 tablespoon salt. Follow directions on bag. Layer in order given, noodles, hamburger, green beans, cheese, and soups. baked covered 350 degrees for 20 minutes, stir gently and bake 10-15 minutes.

Bev, Mrs. Lonnie Unruh

Beef Pot Pie

Crust:

1¾ cups all-purpose flour
¼ cup fine whole wheat flour
1 teaspoon salt

⅛ teaspoon baking powder
⅔ cup butter flavor Crisco
5-6 tablespoons cold water

Roll and press into 9" pie plate.

Filling:

¼ cup chopped celery
¼ cup chopped potatoes
¼ cup chopped carrots
¼ cup frozen corn
¼ cup frozen peas
3 tablespoons minced onion
1 teaspoon minced fresh parsley
3 tablespoons salted sunflower seeds
1 ½ cups water divided
¾ cup beef broth
1½ tablespoons cornstarch

½ teaspoon instant chicken flavor
   bouillon granules
½ teaspoon instant beef flavor
   bouillon granules
¼ teaspoon pepper
⅛ teaspoon salt
1½ tablespoons ketchup
1 cup cubed cooked roast beef
¾ cup condensed cheddar cheese soup
1 tablespoon butter or margarine
¼ cup grated American cheese

Combine celery, potatoes, carrots, corn, peas, onion, parsley, sunflower seeds, and 1¼ cups water in medium saucepan. Bring to boil, reduce heat, simmer for 10 minutes. Heat beef broth in separate medium pan. Combine cornstarch, beef bouillon granules, chicken bouillon granules, pepper, salt, ketchup, and remaining ¼ cup water in small bowl. Stir into beef broth. Cook and stir until thickened. Add beef, cooked vegetables and liquid and soup. Spoon into unbaked pie shell, dot with butter. Sprinkle with cheese. Top with crust, cut slits or design, and bake at 400 degrees for 15 minutes. Reduce temperature to 350 degrees, bake for 20-30 minutes. Serve while hot.

Arlene Giesel Koehn

Bierocks

I remember going to Grandpa's house in town (Ike and Mornie) and finding Grandma in the kitchen baking Bierocks, they were delicious!

1 pound hamburger, browned
   and drained
1 small head cabbage, shredded

1 medium onion, chopped
salt and pepper to taste
yeast dough

Add cabbage, onion and seasonings to cooked hamburger. Cover and saute slowly till vegetables are soft. Drain and cool. Roll out dough and cut 6- 8 inch squares. Place filling in center and bring corners up and seal. Bake 15-20 minutes at 400 degrees. (You may let them rise 30 minutes before baking).

Jolene Unruh

Biscuit and Beef Casserole

1 pound ground beef
1 teaspoon salt
1 (16 oz.) can pork and beans
¾ cup barbecue sauce

2 tablespoons brown sugar
1 tablespoon instant minced onion
1 can refrigerated biscuits
1 cup shredded cheese

Preheat oven to 375 degrees. Brown beef, drain. Stir in the next 5 ingredients. Heat till bubbly. Pour into a 2 quart casserole. Cut biscuits in half to form 20 half circles. Place cut side down around edge of casserole. Sprinkle with cheese. Bake 375 degrees for 25-30 minutes. Refrigerate left overs.

Reva, Mrs Steve Yoder

Cheeseburger Bake

1½ pounds ground beef
2 tablespoons flour
¼ cup chopped onion
8 oz. can tomato sauce
½ cup ketchup

½ teaspoon salt
½ teaspoon pepper
¼ pound sliced or 1 cup
   shredded cheese

Combine beef and flour, brown with onion in skillet. Stir in tomato sauce, ketchup, salt and pepper. Heat. Turn into 8" square baking dish. Top with cheese and 1 can refrigerator biscuits. Tip: may also use baking powder biscuits. Bake at 425 degrees.

Theresa, Mrs. Melvern Ratzlaff

Cheese Topped Family Casserole

1 pound ground beef
½ cup chopped onion
4 slices bacon chopped
½ cup firmly packed brown sugar
½ cup catsup
1 tablespoon vinegar
1 tablespoon prepared mustard
1 teaspoon salt

16 oz. can baked beans, undrained
16 oz. can wax beans, drained
8 oz. can blue lake green beans,
   drained
1 cup crushed corn chips
1 cup shredded process American
   cheese

In 10" skillet combine ground beef, onion, and bacon. Cook over medium heat, stirring occasionally, until beef is browned; drain. In ungreased 3 quart casserole combine beef mixture and remaining ingredients except corn chips and cheese; mix well. Bake at 375 degrees for 50-60 minutes or until bubbly around edges. Remove from oven and sprinkle with corn chips and cheese. Return to oven; continue baking 4-5 minutes or until cheese is melted.

Arlene Giesel Koehn

Chili Skillet

1 pound ground beef	1 teaspoon dried oregano
1 cup chopped onions	1 teaspoon salt
½ cup green pepper	½ cup uncooked rice
1 garlic clove, minced	1 cup canned or frozen corn
1 cup tomato juice	½ cup sliced black olives
1 (8 oz.) can kidney beans	1 cup shredded or Monterey
4 teaspoons chili powder	Jack cheese

In a large skillet over medium heat, cook beef, onion, pepper and garlic until meat is brown and vegetables are tender. Drain fat. Add tomato juice, kidney beans, chili powder, oregano, salt and rice; cover and simmer about 25 minutes or until rice is tender. Sir in corn and olives; cover and cook 5 minutes more. Sprinkle with cheese, cover and cook only until cheese melts, about 5 minutes.

Jana, Mrs. Robert Nichols   Yield: 4-6 Servings

Covatini

½ pound Curlyroni	½ pound mozzarella cheese
½ pound hamburger	2 cups tomato juice
½ pound Jimmy Dean sausage	1 quart Ragu spaghetti sauce
½ pound pepperoni	with mushrooms

Cook spaghetti and drain. Brown hamburger and sausage. Drain. Add to meat the following: spaghetti sauce, pepperoni (cut in pieces), tomato juice and ¼ cup of cheese. Mix well and then add the noodles. Stir well. Put in two large casseroles. Sprinkle remaining cheese on top. Cover with foil. Bake at 350 degrees for 30-45 minutes.

Jolene, Mrs. Dennis Koehn

Dad's Casserole

2 cups uncooked noodles	1 cup milk
1 pound hamburger	1 egg
1 tablespoon salt	1 cup cottage cheese
1 tablespoon diced onion	1 cup grated cheese
1 can cream of mushroom soup	

Fry hamburger and onion until color of meat changes. Add cottage cheese and set aside. Cook noodles until half tender. Layer noodles and hamburger in casserole, starting and ending with noodles. Mix soup and milk together and pour over casserole. Beat egg and pour over top. Sprinkle with cheese. Bake at 350 degrees for 1 hour.

Charmaine Wedel

Green Bean Casserole

1 pound ground beef
1 small onion, chopped
salt and pepper to taste
1 quart green beans, drained

1 (8 oz.) can tomato sauce
mashed potatoes
grated cheese

Cook meat and onion; add tomato sauce and green beans. Place in 9 x 9 casserole dish and top with mashed potatoes. Sprinkle with grated cheese. Bake for 30 minutes at 350 degrees.

Ronda, Mrs. Kenny Giesel

Goulash, Blender Style

1 pound hamburger
2 cups macaroni
1 quart tomato juice
1 carrot
1 celery stalk
1 onion (small or medium)

2 or 3 teaspoons chili powder
2 teaspoons salt
¼ - ½ teaspoon pepper
⅛ - ¼ teaspoon garlic powder
1 or 2 inches Velveeta cheese
    (from a 2 pound block)

Cook macaroni and drain. Brown hamburger and drain. Blend carrot, celery and onion with tomato juice in blender, completely. (Cut the vegetables into one inch pieces before blending.) Combine all ingredients in skillet and simmer an hour or so, stirring several times.

Jolene Unruh

Hamburger Casserole

2 pounds ground beef
1 medium onion, chopped
¼ teaspoon salt
Dash of pepper
1 (6 oz.) box long grain wild rice mix
1 (10¼ oz.) can chicken with rice
    soup

2 (10¾ oz.) cans cream of
    mushroom soup
1 (8 oz.) can chopped mushrooms,
    drained
¼ cup water
½ cup blanched almonds

In skillet, brown beef and onion. Add salt and pepper as browning begins. Drain off excess juice. Add seasoning packet with wild rice, chicken and rice soup, 1½ cans of the cream of mushroom soup, and mushrooms; stir and simmer for 5 minutes. Place in a 9 x 13 inch casserole dish and bake at 350 degrees for approximately 40 minutes. For the last ten minutes, spread the top of the casserole with the remaining ½ can cream of mushroom soup diluted with ¼ cup water. Sprinkle with almonds.

Arlene Giesel Koehn   Yield: 6-8 Servings

Hamburger Casserole

Two pounds hamburger, fix like sloppy Joe meat. Layer in bottom of pan, top with cooked potatoes, and cooked carrots. Cover with Velveeta cheese and bake in oven till cheese is melted.

Jul Nightengale

Hamburger Main Dish

8 oz. noodles	1 medium onion, chopped
2 pounds ground beef	1 teaspoon oregano
1½ teaspoons salt	2 (8 oz.) cans tomato sauce
¼ teaspoon pepper	8 oz. cream cheese
2 tablespoon green pepper	½ cup dairy sour cream
½ teaspoon garlic salt	1½ cups cottage cheese

Cook and drain noodles. Brown meat with salt, pepper, onion, garlic salt and green pepper. Stir in tomato sauce and oregano. Set aside. Soften cream cheese, blend with sour cream, add cottage cheese and mix well. Put half the noodles in 9X13 pan, cover with cheese mixture. Put remaining noodles on top. Pour the beef mixture over. Bake at 350 degrees for 20 minutes.

Mary, Mrs. Lee Giesel   Yield: 12 servings (Recipe can be halved for 6 servings.)

Main Dish Casserole

1 pound hamburger	1 small onion, chopped

Brown hamburger and onion.

1 pkg. Lipton Beefy onion soup mix	1 tablespoon liquid smoke
1 can cream of chicken soup	1 tablespoon Worcestershire sauce
¾ cup minute rice or ½ cup	2 medium potatoes, cubed
regular rice	2 carrots, sliced
1½ cups water	salt and pepper to taste

Mix all together and add to hamburger and onion. Bake at 350 degrees for 1½ hours.

Finette Giesel Koehn

Mexican Casserole, Revised

(Quick, mild and delicious)

2 pounds ground beef	1 cup minute rice (instant)
1 can tomato soup	½ teaspoon salt
1 can mushroom or celery soup	Dorito chips
12 oz. picante sauce	Velveeta cheese

Brown meat, drain. Add remaining ingredients except chips and cheese. Simmer till rice is done. Crush chips and line bottom of large pan (lightly greased) or 2 smaller pans. Put meat mixture on top of chips and cover with slices of cheese. Bake in oven till cheese melts.

Jolene Unruh

Mexican Casserole

2 pounds ground beef
1 small can tomato paste
1 can cream of chicken soup
1 can cream of mushroom soup
2 small cans taco sauce
1 small can green chilies, diced

1½ cups cooked rice
1 medium onion
¾ tablespoon Accent
Dorito chips (large)
small box Velveeta cheese

Brown meat and onions, add rest of ingredients(except chips and cheese), and simmer. Break chips and place in bottom of casserole. Add meat mixture. Slice cheese and lay on top of meat mixture. Put in moderate oven until cheese is melted and casserole is thoroughly heated.

Carolyn, Mrs. Wayne Holdeman

Mexican Mix

1 pound hamburger
1 can cheddar cheese soup
8 to 12 oz. picante sauce

1 pint jar pinto beans (or 16 oz. can)
  undrained

Mix altogether, heat and serve on crushed Dorito chips or rice. Top with lettuce and diced tomato.

Jolene Unruh

Mix 'N' Go Skillet Supper

1 pound hamburger, fried and
  drained
1 can tomato soup (or mushroom
  or celery)

1 soup can water
1 package onion soup
2 or 3 cups frozen mixed vegetables

Mix together all ingredients and bring to a boil. Stir, then let simmer uncovered till thickened and vegetables are done.

Jolene Unruh

Nachos Casserole

1 cup chunky taco sauce
1 can green chilies
1 pound ground beef
½ cup chopped onion
¼ teaspoon cumin

1 cup mashed pinto beans
2 cups grated cheese
½ cup water
4 cups corn flakes

Combine taco sauce and chiles, set aside. Brown meat and onions. Add cumin and beans, 1 cup cheese, ½ of taco sauce mixture and water. Pour 2 cups of corn flakes in lightly greased 2 quarts casserole. Cover with meat mixture. Top with remaining sauce and remaining cereal. Bake at 350 degrees about 25 minutes. Sprinkle with remaining cheese. Bake until cheese melts. Garnish with sour cream, chopped tomatoes, green onions, sliced olives, if desired. (We garnish with lettuce and Ranch dressing!)

LeAnne Nichols

Pizza Casserole

1 pound hamburger, browned
   and seasoned
14 oz. jar pizza sauce

2 cups mozzarella cheese

Layer in 8 x 8 pan. Combine ¾ cup Bisquik mix, 1½ cups milk and 2 eggs. Beat till smooth (Batter will be runny). Pour over rest of ingredients. Bake at 400 degrees 30-35 minutes.

Reva, Mrs. Steve Yoder

Pizza Potato Casserole

1 pound hamburger
1 pint home-canned pizza or
   spaghetti sauce (or 2 cups
   ready-made sauce)

4 or 5 medium potatoes, thinly sliced
Shredded mozzarella cheese

Brown hamburger, drain. Place half of the sliced potatoes in a greased casserole. (Potatoes can be peeled or left unpeeled.) Spread ¼ of the pizza sauce over the potatoes. Next spread on half of the ground beef. Drizzle with ¼ cup of the pizza sauce. Repeat with remaining potatoes and hamburger. Bake one hour at 350 degrees. Top with mozzarella cheese and bake till cheese is lightly browned.

Jolene Unruh

Quick Mexican Casserole

12 corn tortillas (soft)
1 pound hamburger
1 can mushroom soup
12 oz. picante sauce

Shredded cheese or sandwich
cheese slices
diced tomato

Fry hamburger, drain. Add soup and sauce. Make layers of torn tortillas and the hamburger mixture. Bake at 350 degrees for 15 minutes. Top with cheese, then diced tomato. Bake 15 minutes more.

Jolene Unruh

Shepherd's Pie

Brown 1½ pounds hamburger with salt and pepper. Drain grease. Add ½ teaspoon garlic powder, ½ cup diced onion and 1 cup cooked vegetables-peas, carrots, green beans, etc., your choice. Place in 8 x 8 pan and smother with seasoned mashed potatoes. Bake at 350 degrees for 45 minutes. Garnish with grated cheese and paprika for last few minutes of baking time.

Jana, Mrs. Robert Nichols

Smothered Beef Cubes

2 pounds boneless beef, (chuck, round) cut in 1 inch cubes
1 clove garlic, minced
1 (8 oz) can tomato sauce
1 cup water
1 teaspoon salt

1 teaspoon sugar
¼ teaspoon dry mustard
⅛ teaspoon pepper
1 pound small white onions, peeled
4 cups seasoned cooked rice

Trim fat from beef cubes; brown in Dutch oven. Add garlic, tomato sauce, water and seasonings. Cover, simmer 1 hour. Add onions and simmer about 45 minutes, or until meat and onions are tender. Skin off any fat. Serve in ring of hot seasoned and buttered rice.

Mary, Mrs. Lee Giesel   Yield: 6 servings

Spicy Meat Stuffed Tomatoes

6 large tomatoes
2½ cups garlic-onion flavored
    croutons
¾ cup water
2 tablespoons chopped parsley
1 teaspoon basil, crushed
½ teaspoon oregano, crushed

½ teaspoon thyme
2 tablespoons butter
1½ teaspoons salt
dash of pepper
1 pound ground beef
1½ pounds fresh mushrooms,
    chopped (optional)

Slice off tops of tomatoes. Carefully scoop out pulp to form shell, invert to drain. Crush croutons; reserve ⅓ cup, combine remaining crumbs, water and herbs. Saute ground beef until browned; drain off fat. Add meat to crouton mixture. In same skillet, melt 1 tablespoon butter; add mushrooms. Saute until brown and liquid evaporates. Add to meat mixture. Season with salt and pepper to taste. Spoon mixture into tomatoes; do not pack tightly, but mound slightly. Melt remaining tablespoon butter, stir in ⅓ cup crouton crumbs; sprinkle over tomatoes. Place in shallow baking dish and bake at 375 degrees for 20 minutes.

Betty Giesel Martens

Souper Hamburger Helper

1 quart home-canned tomato soup
1 pound hamburger, fried and
    drained
1 cup macaroni, uncooked
¼ teaspoon oregano

¼ teaspoon basil
⅛ teaspoon garlic salt
Velveeta cheese (approximately
    1 inch from a 2 pound block)
Salt and pepper

Combine all ingredients except macaroni and cheese. Bring to boil. Add uncooked macaroni. Stir a bit to keep macaroni from sticking, then cover skillet and simmer awhile. Add Velveeta cheese and stir until melted.

Jolene Unruh

Spuds-n-meat Casserole

(Very simple, very good)
1 pound ground beef
½ of a medium onion, chopped
1 can cream of mushroom or
    chicken soup

1 tablespoon Worcestershire sauce
1½ teaspoons salt
¼ teaspoon black pepper
4 or 5 small potatoes, thinly sliced

Brown beef and onion together. Drain drippings; mix in remaining ingredients with meat. Bake in a 2 quart casserole dish, covered for 45 minutes to an hour or until potatoes are fork tender. Serve hot and bubbly.

Edna Giesel

Sweet and Sour Beef

2 pounds round steak, cut in
   ½" x 2" strips
¼ cup flour
cooking oil
1 cup water
½ cup ketchup

¼ cup brown sugar
¼ cup vinegar
1 tablespoon Worcestershire
   sauce
1 cup chopped onion
1 teaspoon salt

Roll steak strips in flour; brown in large skillet in small amount of oil. Combine water, ketchup, brown sugar, vinegar, Worcestershire sauce, salt and onion. Add mixture to steak. Bring to a boil, reduce heat and simmer, covered, about 45 minutes until steak is tender and sauce is thickened. Stir occasionally to prevent scorching. Serve over rice or noodles.

Pat, Mrs. Mitchell Unruh

Spanish Rice Casserole

1 cup instant rice
1 pound hamburger, fried
   and drained
1 pint tomato juice

½ package taco seasoning
   (more if you wish)
shredded cheese
lettuce salad with tomato

Sprinkle dry rice in bottom of casserole dish. Cover with fried hamburger. Sprinkle taco seasoning over hamburger. Pour tomato juice evenly over hamburger. Cover with shredded cheese (or slices of sandwich cheese), Cover dish and bake 30 minutes at 350 degrees or microwave 5 minutes on full power, then 5 minutes on medium power. Top with lettuce salad and serve.

Jolene Unruh

Quick Spanish Rice

1 pound hamburger
1 pint tomato juice
¾ cup water
chopped onion
chopped green pepper

1¼ teaspoons salt
1 tablespoon chili powder
1 cup minute rice, instant
4 sandwich cheese slices

Fry hamburger, drain. In skillet, mix hamburger and the rest of the ingredients except rice and cheese. Bring to a boil, then stir in rice. Place cheese on top, cover skillet and reduce heat to simmer. In a few minutes the melted cheese can be stirred in and the Spanish Rice should be done.

Jolene Unruh

Barbeque Meatballs

3 pounds hamburger
1 can evaporated milk
3 cups quick oatmeal (scant)
2 eggs

1 cup onion, chopped
2 teaspoons salt
½ teaspoon chili powder

Mix all ingredients together and shape into balls. Place in flat pan, only one layer at a time. Do not fry brown. Pour sauce over meatballs and bake at 350 degrees for 1 hour. Sauce: 2 cups ketchup, ¾ cup brown sugar, 1 tablespoon liquid smoke, ½ teaspoon garlic powder.

Marisa Giesel Wedel

Barbecued Meatballs

3 pounds ground beef
1 (12 oz.) can evaporated milk
1 cup cracker crumbs
1 cup quick oatmeal
2 eggs

½ cup chopped onion
½ teaspoon garlic powder
2 teaspoons salt
½ teaspoon pepper
2 teaspoons chili powder

Sauce:
2 cups ketchup
½ teaspoon liquid smoke
    (or to taste)

1 cup brown sugar
½ teaspoon garlic powder
¼ cup chopped onion

To make meatballs, combine all ingredients(mixture will be soft) and shape into walnut size balls. Place meatballs in a single layer on wax paper-lined cookie sheets; freeze until solid. Store frozen meatballs in freezer bags until ready to cook. To make sauce, combine all ingredients and stir until sugar is dissolved. Place frozen meatballs in a 13x9x2 baking pan; pour sauce over. Bake at 350 degrees for 1 hour.

Marisa Giesel Wedel   Yield: 80 meatballs

Barbecue Meatballs

An easy delicious dish to take to a basket dinner

3 pounds hamburger	2 cups saltine crackers, crushed
1 (13 oz.) can evaporated milk	1 medium onion, diced
2 eggs, beaten	½ teaspoon garlic powder
½ teaspoon pepper	2 teaspoons chili powder
1 teaspoon salt	

Mix all ingredients together and form into balls. Place in two 9x13 baking dishes; cover with sauce (recipe) below and bake 1 hour at 350 degrees.

Sauce:

2 cups ketchup	2 tablespoons liquid smoke
½ cup diced onion	2 cups brown sugar, firmly packed
½ teaspoon garlic powder	

In sauce pan, mix all together and bring to a boil. Pour over meat balls and bake. These are great for parties, too. Just make balls smaller and serve with a tooth pick, right out of the crock pot.

Valetta, Mrs. John Koehn   Serves 16-18 people

Barbeque Meatballs

1 pound hamburger	2 tablespoon chopped onion
1 teaspoon salt	½ cup oatmeal
½ teaspoon pepper	⅔ cup evaporated milk

Combine the above ingredients and form into small meatballs. Place in covered casserole.

Sauce:

1½ cups ketchup	1½ tablespoons water
¾ cup brown sugar, packed	1 teaspoon mustard

Combine and pour over meatballs. Bake at 350 degrees for 1 hour. This is one of Randy's favorites.

Arlene, Mrs. Randy Giesel

Meatballs

1½ pounds hamburger
¼ cup minute rice
2 tablespoons chopped onion
¾ teaspoon salt

½ teaspoon pepper
1 teaspoon chili powder
¼ cup ketchup

Mix all ingredients together. Roll into medium sized balls and roll in flour. Fry in skillet with little shortening until brown on both sides. Drain; pour sauce over balls. Simmer or bake 45 minutes.

Sauce:
¼ cup ketchup
2 cups tomato soup

½ cup brown sugar
2 teaspoons chili powder

Blend together.

Fonda, Mrs. Gareth Eicher

Blender Meatloaf

1½ pounds ground beef
¾ cup oatmeal
1 egg
½ cup ketchup and ½ cup milk
   (or 1 cup tomato juice)

1 small onion
1 carrot
1 celery stalk
1½ teaspoons salt
¼ teaspoon pepper

Place all ingredients except hamburger and oatmeal in blender and blend thoroughly. Mix with hamburger and oatmeal, pack into pan and bake one hour at 350 degrees.

Jolene Unruh

Individual/Italian Meat Loaves

1 egg, beaten
1 cup soft bread cubes
¼ cup milk
1 ½ teaspoons onion salt
1 teaspoon parsley flakes

dash pepper
1½ pounds lean ground beef
7 sticks (2½" x ½" each) cheddar
   or mozzarella cheese

Sauce:
2 (15 oz.) cans tomato sauce
½ cup chopped onion
1 tablespoon parsley flakes

½ teaspoon oregano
¼ teaspoon garlic salt
¼ teaspoon salt

In a mixing bowl, combine first 6 ingredients. Mix in beef. Divide into 7 portions. Shape each portion around a cheese stick and form into a loaf. Set aside. In a large skillet combine all sauce ingredients. Add loaves and spoon sauce over each. Cover and bring to a boil. Reduce heat to simmer; cook until done, about 20 minutes. Serve over noodles.

Charmaine Wedel, Melissa, Mrs. Jason Koehn   Yield: 6 servings

Meaty Meat Loaf(microwave)

1 pound ground beef
⅔ cup evaporated milk
2 tablespoons onion soup mix
1 slice of bread, crumbled

¼ teaspoon salt
2 tablespoons brown sugar
½ teaspoon dry mustard
2 Tablespoons ketchup

In 1½ quart loaf dish; combine beef, milk, soup mix, and bread crumbs. Mix well. (Mixture will be very moist.) Press evenly in pan or form into a ring in a 9" glass cake pan with a custard cup inverted in the center. Combine brown sugar, mustard and ketchup; spread over top of meat mixture. Cover with a plastic wrap with a slit cut to allow steam to escape. Cook on high for 7 minutes or until done. Let stand 5 minutes before serving.

Betty Giesel Martens   Yield: 4-5 servings

Meatloaf

1½ pounds ground round steak
  or ground beef
½ pound ground pork
2 teaspoons salt
pepper
2 eggs, slightly beaten
1 onion, minced

1 cup minced celery
1 carrot, grated
½ cup corn flakes
1 teaspoon Worcestershire sauce
1 tablespoon shortening
½ cup water

Have meat ground twice. Combine the beef and pork and season with salt and pepper. Add eggs, onion, celery, carrot, corn flakes and sauce. Combine all ingredients well and form into two small loaves. Wrap in wax paper and chill several hours in refrigerator. Heat cooker and add shortening. Brown each loaf well on all sides, turning with a pancake turner. Place meat on rack and add water. Close cover securely. Place pressure regulator on vent pipe and cook 15 minutes with pressure regulator rocking slowly. Let pressure drop of its own accord. Later add potatoes, carrots, cabbage. A good one dish meal. I like to add a few canned tomatoes.

Jennie, Mrs. Calvin Unruh

Meatloaf

1½ to 2 pounds hamburger
salt and pepper to taste
¼ cup milk
small onion

1 (8 oz.) can tomato sauce
16 crackers
green pepper

Mix all ingredients, shape into loaf, top with sauce.

Sauce:
⅓ cup ketchup
1 tablespoon brown sugar

1 tablespoon mustard
1 tablespoon honey

Mix together. Bake 1 hour at 350 degrees.

Coreen Holdeman

Meatloaf

Soak ⅔ cup bread crumbs in 1 cup milk. Add 1 pound ground beef, 1 pound sausage, 2 beaten eggs, ¼ cup grated onion, 1 teaspoon salt, ⅛ teaspoon pepper, ½ teaspoon sage, ¼ teaspoon dry mustard, ¼ teaspoon poultry seasoning, 1 tablespoon Worcestershire sauce, and 2 tablespoons chopped celery. Mix lightly, form into loaf. Cover with sauce. Sauce: mix ¼ cup ketchup, 3 tablespoons brown sugar, and 1 teaspoon mustard. Bake 1 hour at 350 degrees.

Betty Giesel Martens

Sweet and Sour Meatloaf

1 pound ground beef
¼ cup chopped onion
¼ teaspoon pepper
⅛ teaspoon thyme leaves
2 eggs, slightly beaten

4 shredded wheat biscuits (crushed)
½ teaspoon salt
¼ teaspoon crushed marjoram leaves
⅓ cup chili sauce

Bake at 375 degrees for 30 minutes. Then 15 minutes longer with sauce.

Sweet and Sour Sauce: Drain 1 (20 oz) can pineapple chunks, reserving syrup. Add water to make 1 cup liquid. Combine ¼ cup light brown sugar, 2 tablespoons corn starch and ½ teaspoon salt in a saucepan. Add pineapple syrup, ⅓ cup cider vinegar and 1 tablespoon soy sauce. Cook, stirring constantly, until mixture thickens and comes to a boil. Remove from heat. Add 1 large green pepper, thinly sliced, ¼ cup thinly sliced onion, 1 (2 oz.) jar sliced pimiento, drained and pineapple chunks.

Janice, Mrs. Jerry Ratzlaff

Chow Mein

¼ cup butter
2 cups (1 pound) pork, cut thin
¼ cup onion
1 teaspoon salt

1/16 teaspoon pepper
1½ cup hot water
1 cup celery
1 can chow mein vegetables

Thickening:
2 tablespoons cold water
2 tablespoons corn starch

2 teaspoons soy sauce
1 teaspoon sugar

Mix thickening ingredients. Melt butter in hot skillet. Add meat, stir quickly without browning, add onions and fry for 5 minutes. Add salt, pepper, celery and hot water. Cover and cook for 5 min. Add drained vegetables, Stir, heat to boiling. Add thickening. Stir and cook 1 minute. Serve over Chow Mein noodles.

Jane Giesel

Baked Pork Chops

8 pork chops
2 tablespoons flour
2 tablespoons mustard
¼ cup chopped onion
¼ teaspoon cloves

½ teaspoon pepper
1 cup juice from canned peaches
1 teaspoon salt
1 cup catsup
2 tablespoons Worcestershire sauce

Brown pork chops. Make a paste with flour and mustard. Add onions, cloves, salt, pepper, Worcestershire sauce, juice and catsup. Place chops in casserole and pour liquid mixture over them. Bake at 300 for 90 minutes.

Janice, Mrs. Jerry Ratzlaff

Barbequed Ham Balls

1 pound ground ham
1½ pounds ground pork
1 cup cracker crumbs rolled fine

2 eggs beaten
1 cup milk

Mix well then form into balls

Sauce:
1½ cups brown sugar
½ cup water

½ cup vinegar
1 tablespoon dry mustard

Heat sauce on stove top. Pour over balls in baking dish. Bake at 325 for 2 hours. Turn and baste balls frequently.

Dawn Giesel Dyck

Ham from Pork Roast

Rub 1½ tablespoons Morton's Tenderquick and 1 tablespoon liquid smoke on top of 3-4 pounds pork roast. Pierce with fork and rub again. repeat on other side. Put in Tupperware and let marinate in refrigerator for a day. Turn over and marinate another half day. Rinse the roast well, and let soak in water one half hour. Place in heavy pan, add some water, and bake all night and all morning at 250 degrees.

Jolene Unruh.

Ham Loaf

1½ pounds ground ham
½ pound ground pork (lean)
¾ cup cracker or bread crumbs

3 tablespoons catsup
1 teaspoon mustard
¼ cup evaporated milk

Mix and form into loaf. Place in foil lined pan, cover; Place pan in a pan of water and steam for 2 hours at 325 degrees. Uncover and bake for 30 minutes to brown.

Arlene Giesel Koehn.

Ham, Mushroom and Noodle Casserole

8 ounces egg noodles
¼ cup margarine
1 cup celery, chopped
½ cup canned mushroom pieces
and stems, drained
¼ cup chopped onion
¼ cup flour
2½ cups milk

1 cup shredded cheddar cheese
2 cups diced cooked ham
¼ cup sliced stuffed green olives
2 tablespoons chopped pimiento
1 teaspoon salt
⅛ teaspoon pepper
¼ cup bread crumbs

Cook noodles as directed on package until tender. Melt ¼ cup margarine in sauce pan. Add celery, mushrooms, and onion; saute until tender. Stir in flour, gradually add milk. Cook over medium heat, stirring constantly, until mixture thickens. Add cheese, stir until cheese melts. combine with noodles, ham, olives, pimiento, salt and pepper. Place in 2 quart casserole. Melt 1 tablespoon margarine, stir in bread crumbs, sprinkle over casserole. Bake at 375 degrees for 30-35 minutes, until golden brown.

Theresa, Mrs Melvern Ratzlaff   Yield: 6 servings

Pork Chops with Baked Beans

1 (16 oz.) can pork and beans
½ cup chopped onion
¼ cup firmly packed brown sugar
¼ cup catsup
1 teaspoon prepared mustard

4 (½ inch thick) boneless pork chops
¼ cup catsup
1 tablespoon brown sugar
1 teaspoon Worcestershire sauce

Combine first 5 ingredients in a lightly greased 2-quart baking dish. Place pork chops on beans. Combine ¼ cup catsup and remaining ingredients; spread on pork chops. Cover and bake at 350 degrees for 25 minutes. Uncover and bake an additional 10 minutes.

Arlene Giesel Koehn   Yield: 4 servings

Pork Chops and Rice

Flour, salt and pepper 10 pork chops. Brown in skillet with 2 tablespoons Crisco. Prepare 3 cups minute rice, 2 packages (1 box) dry Lipton onion soup, 2 cans cream of celery soup and 2 cans of water; mix and pour in baking pan. Arrange pork chops on top of rice mixture, cover. Bake at 250 degrees for 2 hours.

Delores, Mrs. Isaac Unruh, Jr.

Pork Chop Suey

4 tablespoons soy sauce
1½ pounds pork steak
4 cups celery, sliced thin
4 onions, sliced thin
3 tablespoons cornstarch

3 teaspoons sugar
1 cup water
1 can beansprouts
Cooked rice and chow mein noodles

Cut up pork and brown in a little hot oil. Chop onion and fry with meat until tender, add celery and enough water to cover; cook until celery is tender, add beansprouts and bring to boil; mix cornstarch, water, sugar, and soy sauce. Stir into meat mixture and simmer 15 minutes. Serve on rice. Sprinkle noodles on top.

Connie, Mrs. Marlon Giesel

Rice and Pork Chops

4 pork chops
1 medium onion, diced
1 cup raw rice

1 can cream chicken soup
1½ cans milk
soy sauce

Brown pork chops and put in casserole dish, sprinkle diced onion over chops, then the rice; combine soup, milk, salt and pepper to taste and pour over chops; cover and bake 325 degrees for 1½ hours. Serve with soy sauce.

Ronda, Mrs. Ryan Wedel

Stuffed Pork Loin

3-4 pound pork loin (cut in
    half lengthwise)
1 apple, chopped
¼ cup raisins

brown sugar and cinnamon to taste
1 clove garlic, chopped
½ onion, chopped

Saute garlic and onion in small amount of olive oil. Add apple, raisins, brown sugar and cinnamon. Spread mixture on half loin. Top with other half and tie at one inch intervals with string. Season outside of loin with pepper and Nature's Seasons. Bake at 350 degrees for 1½ hours.

Arlene Giesel Koehn

Serves 6-8

Sweet and Sour Pork

Pork loin roast, 4 pounds
¼ teaspoon Accent
⅓ cup soy sauce

4 cloves garlic, crushed
2-3 tablespoons sugar
3-4 tablespoons vinegar

Cut loin off bone, into small pieces. Mix Accent, soy sauce, garlic, sugar, vinegar, salt and pepper to taste, pour over meat and marinate several hours. Add 4-5 tablespoons flour to meat and fry in fat until done. Set aside; cover with sauce just before serving.

Sauce:

¾ cup water
2-3 tablespoons oil
4-5 tablespoons soy sauce
dash Accent
2 tablespoons red wine vinegar
2 tablespoons sugar

2 tablespoons corn starch to thicken
salt to taste
1 bunch green onions, cut into
    1 inch pieces
3-4 tomatoes cut into wedges

Mix all ingredients except onions and tomatoes; bring to boil, reduce heat and cook a few minutes. Add onions and tomatoes just before pouring sauce over meat. Serve.

Arlene Giesel Koehn

Winter Sausage Supper

1 quart green beans
1 quart canned potatoes
1 quart canned sausage

cheese, thinly sliced
salt and pepper

Place drained beans in a 3 quart casserole; cover with cheese; shred canned potatoes and place on top of cheese. Top potatoes with cheese. Cut sausage into ½ inch pieces and place on cheese layer. Bake uncovered 350 degrees for 30 minutes or until sausage is browned.

Jolene Unruh

Aunt Virginia's Bar-b-que Chicken

Mix:

1 cup catsup
2 tablespoons B.B.Q. sauce
¼ cup vinegar
1 teaspoon chili powder

1 teaspoon celery seed
½ cup water
1 cup brown sugar
salt and pepper to taste

Brown chicken and pour mixture over chicken. Bake at 350 degrees for 2½ hours. Delicious if grilled in place of fried, then bake.

Melissa, Mrs. Jason Koehn

Cheese Baked Chicken Breasts

2 cups Cheese-It cracker crumbs
  (6¼ oz. package)
1 teaspoon salt
1 teaspoon garlic salt
½ teaspoon marjoram

1 egg
1 tablespoon water
6 whole chicken breasts split,
  deboned and skinned
1 cup butter

Crush crackers (very coarse); mix well with salt, garlic salt, and marjoram. Beat eggs and water together. Dip chicken pieces in egg mixture and then in the crumbs; Place in a buttered shallow pan, 1 inch apart. Drizzle with melted butter. Bake 350 degrees for 35-40 minutes.

Reva, Mrs. Steve Yoder

Chinese Chicken

1 chicken cooked and cut into
  bite-sized pieces
1 (16 oz.) package wild rice with
  seasoning, cooked as directed
1 (10 oz.) can cream of celery
  soup, undiluted
1 onion, chopped
½ cup mayonnaise

1 cup chicken broth
1 (14 oz.) can mixed Chinese
  vegetables
1 (2 oz.) jar pimiento
1 (16 oz.) can french style green
  beans, drained
salt and pepper to taste
dash of soy sauce and red pepper

Mix above ingredients. Bake at 350 degrees until hot and bubbly. Freezes well.

Arlene Giesel Koehn   Yield: 8 servings

Chicken Squares

2 cups uncooked macaroni
2-3 cups cooked chicken pieces
2 cans mushroom soup
2 cups milk

½ green pepper, chopped (optional)
½ onion, chopped
4 hard boiled eggs
1 cup shredded cheese

Mix all ingredients together and refrigerate over night. Bake in greased 9 x 11 pan at 350 degrees for 1 hour or until done. Cut in squares. This recipe can be made with hamburger and peas in place of the chicken and eggs.

Jolene Unruh

Country Chicken

¼ cup all-purpose flour
½ teaspoon pepper
⅛ teaspoon salt
1 (2½ to 3 pound) broiler fryer,
    cut up
3 tablespoons butter or margarine
3 tablespoons vegetable oil
1 large onion, chopped

½ cup chopped green pepper
3 cloves garlic, minced
2 (14½ oz.) cans stewed tomatoes,
    undrained
1 tablespoon curry powder
1 cup chopped dry roasted peanuts
½ cup golden raisins
Hot cooked rice

Combine flour, pepper, and salt. Skin chicken if desired. Dredge chicken in flour mixture. Heat butter or oil in a large skillet over medium heat; add chicken and cook until golden brown. Remove chicken from skillet; set aside. Reduce heat to low, and saute onion, green pepper, and garlic in pan drippings until tender. Add tomatoes and curry powder; stir well. Return chicken to mixture; cover and cook 25-30 minutes or until chicken is tender. Remove from skillet; set aside. Cook sauce over medium heat, stirring constantly, until liquid is reduced and sauce is thickened. Stir in peanuts and raisins. Spoon rice around chicken on platter; pour sauce over chicken and rice.

Arlene Giesel Koehn

Yield: 4 servings

Chicken Rellenos

6 boneless chicken breasts (halves)
1½ cups shredded Monterey
    Jack cheese
3 tablespoons diced green chilies
3 tablespoons sliced pimiento
30 Ritz crackers, coarsely crushed
    (1½ cups)

½ teaspoon chili powder
¼ teaspoon cumin
2 tablespoons flour
1 egg beaten
3 tablespoons margarine, melted
salsa

Pound each chicken breast to ¼" thickness, top each with ¼ cup shredded cheese. Combine chilies and pimiento. Sprinkle 1 tablespoon mixture over cheese. Roll up chicken from short edge. Secure with toothpicks. Mix cracker crumbs, cumin and chili powder. Coat chicken rolls with flour, dip in beaten egg, then roll in crumb mixture. Place chicken rolls in 12 x 8 baking dish. Drizzle margarine over chicken. Bake at 350 for 35 to 40 min. Remove toothpicks, serve with salsa.

LeAnne Nichols

Chicken with Sweet and Spicy Barbecue Sauce

1⅓ cups firmly packed brown sugar
1 (15 ounce) can tomato sauce
1 cup cider vinegar
1 large onion, chopped
6 tablespoons Dijon mustard

1 tablespoon plus 1 teaspoon dried
  thyme, crumbled
1 teaspoon salt
1 teaspoon cayenne pepper
2 chickens, each cut into 6 pieces

Combine first 8 ingredients in heavy sauce pan. Simmer 15 minutes to blend flavors. Season with pepper. (Can be made 2 days ahead. Cover, chill.) Arrange chicken in single layer in large baking pan. Brush with some sauce. Roast until cooked through, basting occasionally with sauce, about 1 hour at 375 degrees. Serve hot.

Arlene Giesel Koehn

Gourmet Chicken

This is good and can be prepared a day ahead.

6 chicken breasts, skinned
6 chicken thighs, skinned
bacon
1 can cream of mushroom soup

8 ounces sour cream
1 package (4 oz.) dried beef,
  cut in strips

Place chicken pieces in shallow casserole dish and top each with a half strip bacon. Combine remaining ingredients and pour over chicken. Bake in 325 degree oven for 2 hours.

Mornie Giesel Unruh

Chicken, Dominican Meal

Beans:

1 cup dry pinto beans	1 slice onion
1 clove garlic, crushed	1 tablespoon oil

Add water to cover beans and bring to a rapid boil, cook hard for about 2 hours, adding water as necessary. Heat ¼ cup oil, 2 slices onion, chopped, and 5 cloves garlic, crushed. Cook together until it smells good. Add 2 tablespoons tomato paste, 1 cube chicken bouillon, ½ teaspoon pepper, ⅛ teaspoon oregano. Add beans to this mixture and cook slowly for 1 hour. Serve over rice.

Rice:

2 cups rice	2 teaspoons salt
3 cups boiling water	3 teaspoons oil

Heat oil, add rice and stir fry for 2 minutes, add boiling water, cook and stir until water has boiled away. Reduce heat to very low and cover tightly. After 10 minutes stir rice , cover and set aside for 5 minutes.

Chicken:

1 chicken, cut up	1 teaspoon oregano
1 teaspoon salt	3-4 cloves garlic
1 teaspoon pepper	1 small green pepper, chopped
½ onion, chopped	¼ cup vinegar

Mix together and marinate. Later, heat a little oil and add ¼ cup brown sugar, let brown. Add to chicken and stir well. (sugar will turn to hard crystals) Cook until done or put in oven.

Cabbage salad:

1 tablespoon oil	shredded cabbage
1 tablespoon vinegar	sliced cucumbers, optional
1 teaspoon salt	

To serve this meal Dominican style, set table with large bowls. Pass rice first, then put soupy bean mixture on top of rice, top with cabbage.

LeAnne Nichols

Easy Baked Chicken

1 (2 oz.) package chipped beef	1 (10¾ oz.) can cream of
4 deboned chicken breasts	mushroom soup
4 slices of bacon	1 (8 oz.) carton sour cream

Grease a 7½ x 11 inch casserole dish. Line casserole with chipped beef. Wrap chicken breasts with bacon and place on chipped beef. Make a sauce of soup and sour cream and pour over chicken. Bake at 275 degrees for 3 hours.

Arlene Giesel Koehn

Huntington Chicken

½ cup cream
4 cups chicken broth
8 tablespoons flour
½ pound diced Velveeta cheese

2 cups uncooked macaroni
4 tablespoons butter or oleo
1 chicken, cooked and diced

Save broth from chicken, add cream to broth and thicken with flour. Add chicken, cheese and macaroni, pour into baking dish. Sprinkle buttered bread crumbs over top. Bake at 350 degrees for 35 minutes. This is a favorite dish at our house.

Elaine, Mrs. Bruce Unruh

Lemon Chicken

1 pound skinned, deboned chicken
    breasts cut into strips
1 medium onion, chopped
2 garlic cloves, crushed
2 tablespoons butter
1 tablespoon corn starch
13¼ ounces chicken broth

1 large carrot, sliced diagonally
2 tablespoons fresh lemon juice
½ teaspoon grated lemon rind
½ teaspoon salt
1 cup snow pea pods
3 tablespoons chopped parsley
1½ cups minute rice

Saute chicken, onion, and garlic in butter till chicken is slightly browned, about 5 minutes. Stir in cornstarch and cook 1 minute. Add broth, carrot, lemon juice, lemon rind, and salt. Bring to a full boil. Stir in pea pods, parsley, and rice. Cover ; remove from heat, let stand 5 minutes. Fluff with fork.

Jackie Koehn   Serves 4

Nutty Oven Fried Chicken

1 cup biscuit mix
2 teaspoons paprika
½ teaspoon salt
½ teaspoon poultry seasoning
½ teaspoon rubbed sage

⅓ cup finely chopped pecans
1 (3 pound) broiler-fryer, cut up
½ cup evaporated milk
⅓ cup butter or margarine, melted

Combine first 6 ingredients; mix well. Dip chicken in milk; coat generously with pecan mixture. Place in a lightly greased 13 x 9 inch baking pan. Drizzle butter over chicken; bake, uncovered, at 350 degrees for 1 hour or until done.

Arlene Giesel Koehn   Yield: 4 servings

Oven Fried Chicken

1 (3 pound) fryer
½ cup butter or oleo
1 egg
½ cup evaporated milk
1 cup flour

1 teaspoon baking powder
2 teaspoons paprika
1 teaspoon garlic powder
1 teaspoon salt

Cut fryer into serving pieces. Line cookie sheet with foil and melt oleo in cookie sheet. Dip chicken in egg and milk, coat chicken with flour and seasonings. Place chicken, skin side down on cookie sheet, bake 30 minutes, uncovered at 400 degrees; turn chicken pieces and bake an additional 30 minutes.

Ronda, Mrs. Kenny Giesel

Plantation Style Chicken

½ cup butter or margarine, melted
⅓ cup flour
1 teaspoon seasoned salt
⅛ teaspoon pepper

1 (3 pound) chicken, cut up
5 cups Corn Chex cereal,
  crushed to make 1⅔ cups

Combine butter, flour, seasoned salt, and pepper. Dip chicken in butter mixture. Roll in Chex crumbs. Place chicken in shallow baking dish. Let stand 10 minutes. bake uncovered 50-55 minutes or until brown and crisp at 400 degrees.

Bev, Mrs. Lonnie Unruh

Ramen Chicken

2-3 cups cooked chicken
1 package ramen noodles,
  chicken flavor, crushed
½ cup celery, chopped
½ cup onion, chopped

½ cup green pepper, chopped
½-1 cup sour cream
1 can mushroom soup
butter or margarine

Saute vegetables in butter or margarine; add all other ingredients, including seasoning packet from noodles. Bake at 350 degrees 20-30 minutes.

Jana, Mrs. Robert Nichols

Stir-fry Chicken and Broccoli

1 pound chicken breast strips
2 tablespoons oil
4 cups vegetables (broccoli, pepper
   strips, onion, cauliflower, carrots,
   water chestnuts, etc.)
1½ cups chicken broth

3 tablespoons soy sauce
2 tablespoons cornstarch
2 teaspoons brown sugar
1 teaspoon garlic powder
¾ teaspoon ground ginger
baked rice

Stir fry chicken in hot oil in large skillet until browned. Add vegetables; stir fry until crisp tender. Mix broth, soy sauce, cornstarch, sugar, garlic powder and ginger; add to skillet. Bring to boil; boil 1 minute. Serve chicken and vegetables over rice.

Helen, Mrs. Emery Koehn   Makes 4 servings

Hush Puppy Chicken Casserole

8½ ounce box corn muffin mix
1 tablespoon chili powder
4 boneless, skinless, chicken breast
   halves, cut into ½ inch chunks
1-2 tablespoons olive oil
16 ounce can oven baked beans

14½ ounce can Mexican-style
   stewed tomatoes, undrained
1 tablespoon smoky barbecue sauce
14½ ounce can dilled green beans,
   drained
1 tablespoon maple syrup

Prepare corn muffin mix to batter stage, according to package directions. Set aside. Sprinkle chili powder on chicken chunks; toss with fork to coat well. Heat oil in large skillet. Saute chicken chunks over medium heat, stirring frequently until opaque; drain fat. Reduce heat. Stir in baked beans, stewed tomatoes, barbecue sauce and dilled green beans. Simmer mixture 5-10 minutes, stirring occasionally until heated through. Spoon mixture into greased 9 x 13 baking dish. Spoon corn muffin batter on top of bean mixture around outside edge of baking pan. Bake in a 400 degree oven for 20-25 minutes or until topping is golden. Remove from oven and brush lightly with maple syrup.

Arlene Giesel Koehn   Makes 6-8 servings

Chicken and Rice

1 cup long grain rice
1 can cream of mushroom soup
1 can cream of chicken soup
2 soup cans milk (a little more if
   this has to be in the oven longer)

1 fryer, cutup or approximately 8-10
   pieces of chicken. (We like the
   breasts and thigh pieces used
   this way.)
1 package onion soup mix

Grease bottom of 13 x 9 pan. Put rice in pan. Combine soups and milk. Pour over rice. Lay chicken pieces on top. Sprinkle onion soup mix on top. Cover with foil and bake at 325 degrees for 2 hours.

Mary, Mrs. Lee Giesel

Club Chicken Casserole

4 tablespoons butter or margarine
5 tablespoon flour
1 cup chicken stock
1½ cup evaporated milk
1 teaspoon salt
3 cups cooked rice

1½ cups cooked, diced chicken
1 (3 oz.) can broiled mushrooms, sliced
¼ cup chopped pimiento
⅓ cup chopped green pepper
½ cup slivered blanched almonds

Melt butter; add flour and blend. Add stock and milk and cook over low heat until thick. Stirring constantly. Add salt. Alternate layers of rice, chicken and vegetables in greased 6 x10 inch baking dish. Pour the sauce over top with slivered almonds. Bake at 350 degrees for 30 minutes.

Deanna Giesel   Yield: 8-10 Servings

Chicken Hashbrown Potato Casserole

1 package frozen hashbrowns
1 cooked chicken, (deboned)
½ cup oleo
12 ounces shredded American or Velveeta cheese

1 can cream of chicken soup
chopped onion, (to taste)
½ teaspoon salt
8 ounces sour cream

Layer potatoes and chicken in a 9x13 pan. Mix remaining ingredients together. (I add a little chicken broth to the soup mixture) Pour mixture over chicken and potatoes. Mix 2 cups crushed cornflakes and ½ cup melted oleo. Sprinkle over casserole. Bake at 350 degrees for 45 minutes.

Serena Amoth

Chicken Noodle Casserole

Boil 5 pounds chicken. Debone and cut into small pieces. Saute in oleo: 1 chopped onion, 1 stalk celery, chopped, 1 small green pepper, chopped. Cook 10-12 ounces noodles in chicken broth, add chicken, 1 can cream of mushroom soup, 1 can cream of chicken soup, ½ pound Velveeta cheese, cubed, sauteed vegetables. Pour into 9x13 pack or large casserole. Heat in oven, until hot and bubbly.

Reva, Mrs. Steve Yoder

Chicken with Rice

4 pieces chicken
½ can mushroom soup
½ can chicken soup

1½ cans water
¾ cup rice
½ teaspoon minced onion

Arrange pieces of chicken in covered casserole. Mix remaining ingredients and pour over chicken. Bake at 250 degrees for 2 hours.

Arlene, Mrs. Randy Giesel

Chicken with Wild Rice Casserole

3 to 4 chicken breasts
1 (5 oz.) box wild rice
1 medium onion, chopped
1 (8 oz.) can sliced mushrooms, drained
½ cup margarine
1 (10¾ oz.) can cream of mushroom soup

1 (10¾ oz.) can cream of chicken soup
3 tablespoons flour
1½ cups milk
1 cup grated cheddar cheese

Cook chicken breasts and debone. Cook rice according to package directions. Set aside. Saute onion and mushrooms in margarine. Add soups and mix well. Combine flour and milk and add to mixture. Layer in casserole rice, chicken and cheese. Bake at 350 degrees until heated through and cheese is melted.

Arlene Giesel Koehn   Yield: 4 servings

Souper Rice and Chicken Casserole

Basic Recipe:
1 can mushroom, chicken or celery soup
1 can instant rice, (measure with soup can)

1 can milk or broth
Chunks of cooked chicken (desired amount)
1 tablespoon chicken bouillon

Optional extras (desired amounts): frozen peas, chopped onion, diced hard-boiled eggs, shredded cheese or sandwich cheese slices.

First, make the "souper rice" by mixing together the can of soup, can of milk, and can of rice. Then add the bouillon and cooked chicken meat. If the extras are desired, mix it together any way you like; casserole-style. Bake 30 minutes at 350 degrees or microwave 10-15 minutes, turning once or twice.

Jolene Unruh

Quick and Easy Chicken Casserole

5 boneless chicken breasts
1 (15½ oz.) can French style green beans, drained
1 (10¾ oz.) can cream of celery soup

1 (8oz.) can water chestnuts, drained
3 tablespoons minced onion
1 cup mayonnaise
1 cup chicken broth

Boil chicken breasts in salted water; cool and cut into bite size pieces. Combine all ingredients in a 2 quart casserole. Bake at 400 degrees for 25 to 30 minutes. Serve over rice.

Arlene Giesel Koehn   Yield: 4 servings

Chicken and Dumplings

Cook one hen or chicken
  (hen is tastier)
1 large onion chopped

1 stalk of celery, whole
salt and pepper to taste

Cover with plenty of water so you have lots of broth when done. Cook slowly until tender. Remove from heat and remove hen, and celery from broth. Let cool and debone, set aside while you make the dumplings.

Dumplings:
2½ cups flour
1 teaspoon salt
¼ teaspoon baking powder

¼ cup shortening
1 egg beaten

Mix all dry ingredients together, cut in shortening, then add egg and cold water until it looks like pie crust. Flour surface and roll real thin. Cut in approx. one inch strips. Dissolve 6 or 8 chicken bouillon cubes in the broth and simmer while you drop pieces of dumplings into broth. Stir often as you are putting dumplings into broth so they don't stick together. Cook slowly until dumplings are done. Add hen and heat through and enjoy! If you need more broth, add water and more bouillon. It should be rather thick.

When we moved to the South, dumplings were new to us, but we really liked them. I was working for a southern lady who had a black lady to do all the cooking. She made delicious dumplings. One day she taught me how and I've been hooked ever since! Some people use canned biscuits for their dumplings but they're not the same. This dish is now one of my specialties that I love to cook. Try 'em they'll grow on you, in more ways than one.

Kathy Wedel

Stewed Chicken, Homemade Noodles

Put a 5-pound hen or two 3-pound fryers in a big pot with 2 quarts cold water. Add an onion cut in half, 2 stalks of celery, some parsley and ¼ teaspoon each of thyme and marjoram. Cover and cook gently. Simmer until tender - from 1 to 2 hours. When almost done, add 1 tablespoon salt. Noodles: Break 2 eggs into mixing bowl. Add a pinch of salt and beat. Work in 1¼-1½ cup flour to make a very stiff dough. Form into a ball and invert the mixing bowl over it. Let rest 30 minutes or more. Divide the dough into two pieces. On a floured surface, roll each piece out as thin as possible, then roll into a log. Cut with a sharp knife into ¼ inch slices. Unroll each pinwheel and let them stand until ready to cook. When chicken is tender, remove it from broth. Take out the limp vegetables and skim off some of the fat. Bring the chicken broth back to a slow boil and slide in the noodles, a handful at a time, so that the broth keeps bubbling. Simmer until done. It should take 10-20 minutes. Debone chicken and cut into serving pieces. When noodles are tender; put the chicken back in and reheat. Salt to taste. Add a little white pepper and just a whisper of nutmeg. Serve! This is the recipe my mom, Carolyn, uses for chicken noodle soup. The homemade noodles are what makes it special!

Jana, Mrs. Robert Nichols

Chicken Normandy

Crust:

1 package (8 oz) seasoned bread
    stuffing mix
½ cup melted butter

1 cup water

Filling:

2½ cups cooked diced chicken
½ cup chopped onion
½ cup chopped celery
½ cup mayonnaise or salad dressing

1 teaspoon salt
2 eggs
1½ cups milk

Topping:

1 can condensed cream of
    mushroom soup, undiluted

1 cup grated cheddar cheese

The day before serving; combine crust ingredients. Mix lightly. Spread ½ of crust mixture in buttered 13 x 9 baking pan. In a bowl, combine chicken, onion, celery, mayonnaise and salt. Spread chicken mixture over bottom crust. Top with reserved crust mixture. Beat together eggs and milk, pour over top. Cover with foil and refrigerate overnight. (May freeze for future use.) One hour before cooking, remove casserole from refrigerator. (Let thaw if frozen.) Spread mushroom soup over the top. Bake at 325 for 40 min. Sprinkle with cheese and bake 10 minutes more. P.S. I have used left over turkey and it's just as good.

Betty, Mrs. Gordon Unruh

Makes 12 servings

Chicken Pot Pie

Pastry for 2 2-crust pies

Gravy:

½ cup margarine or chicken fat
2 cups chicken broth
1 can cream of chicken soup

1 cooked chicken, cubed
1 cup sliced carrots, cooked
1 cup frozen peas

Melt margarine and blend in flour. Add broth and boil 1 minute. Add soup. Add chicken, carrots, and peas. Pour mixture into pastry lined pans. Put top pastry on. Bake at 425 for 30 - 40 minutes. These pies freeze very well unbaked. One pie serves about 4 people. This was a favorite with my family. It was a special treat when Mom made chicken pot pie on a cold winter evening!

Michele, Mrs. Richard Ensz

Chicken

(For freezer or table use.)

Soak chicken in salt water, 1 tablespoon salt to 1 pint water. Set in refrigerator for twelve hours or more. Pack in containers and fill with fresh water. Freeze. For table use you may leave it in refrigerator for 3 or 4 days. I use this recipe for thawing my turkey. Put turkey in big granite cooker and soak at least 24 hours. The meat is salted through. I put some ice with it if it sets too long, and put it in the garage where it is cold. Chicken, I put in the refrigerator.

Sophie (Giesel) Koehn

Chicken Spaghetti

1 chicken	¼ cup butter or oleo
12 ounce package spaghetti	1 cup chopped celery
1 can cream of mushroom soup	1 small chopped onion
1 can cream of chicken soup	½ to 1 cup chopped green pepper
1 small jar pimiento	½ to ¾ pound Velveeta cheese
salt and pepper, to taste	chili powder, to taste

Cook chicken and debone. Save broth and cook spaghetti noodles in it. Saute' onions, celery and pepper in butter. Add the remaining ingredients. If too dry, add chicken broth. Heat thoroughly. This is also good frozen, thawed and reheated.

Ronda, Mrs. Ryan Wedel   Yield: 12 servings

Party Spaghetti

3 cups chicken or turkey, cooked and cubed	1 can cream of mushroom soup
2 green peppers, chopped	1 can tomato soup
2 celery stalks, chopped	1 small jar pimiento, drained and chopped, optional
2 medium onions, chopped	½ pound American cheese, grated
2 garlic cloves, minced or crushed	4 ounces spaghetti, cooked,
½ stick margarine	salt to taste
dash of Worcestershire sauce	½ pound cheddar cheese, grated

Preheat oven to 325 degrees. Saute peppers, celery, onions, and garlic in margarine. Add Worcestershire sauce. Stir in remaining ingredients, except for cheddar cheese. Season to taste and pour into buttered casserole. Sprinkle with grated cheese on top and bake 30 minutes.

Finette Giesel Koehn   Yield: 8 servings

Spaghetti Pie

5 ounces cooked Italian spaghetti, broken into short pieces
2 tablespoons oleo

2 eggs, well beaten
⅓ cup Parmesan cheese

Mix well; form into crust in buttered large pie pan. Spread 1 cup cottage cheese over crust. Lightly brown 1 pound hamburger or sausage, ½ cup chopped onion, ¼ cup chopped green pepper; drain fat. Add 8 oz tomatoes with juice; 1 (6 oz.) can tomato sauce, 1 teaspoon sugar, ½ teaspoon oregano, ½ teaspoon garlic salt, simmer for 20-30 minutes. Pour into crust; top with ½ cup shredded mozzarella cheese. Bake at 350 degrees for 20 minutes. May make early, store in refrigerator and bake later.

Betty Giesel Martens

Easy Cheesy Lasagna Squares

½ cup cottage cheese
¼ cup Parmesan cheese
1 pound ground beef, fried and drained
1 teaspoon oregano
½ teaspoon dried basil leaves
6 ounces tomato paste

1 cup shredded mozzarella cheese
1 cup milk
2 eggs
⅔ cup Bisquick
1 teaspoon salt
¼ teaspoon pepper

In a square 8 x 8 pan, layer cottage cheese and then Parmesan cheese. Mix fried beef, herbs, tomato paste and ½ cup mozzarella cheese; spoon evenly across top. Beat eggs, milk, Bisquick, salt and pepper one minute until smooth and pour on top. Bake at 350 degrees about 30-35 minutes, or until knife inserted comes out clean. Halfway through baking, add the other ½ cup of mozzarella cheese on top.

Jolene Unruh

Golden Lasagna

½ cup chopped onion
½ cup chopped green pepper
3 tablespoons butter
1 can cream of chicken soup
⅓ cup milk
½ teaspoon basil leaves
8 ounces lasagna noodles, cooked and drained

1½ cups cottage cheese
3 cups hamburger, browned and seasoned
2 cups shredded cheddar cheese
½ cup Parmesan cheese

Saute onion and green pepper in melted butter (do not brown). Stir in soup, milk and basil. Heat well. Arrange ½ noodles in greased 13 x 9 x 2 baking dish. Then layer in ½ of sauce, cottage cheese, hamburger, cheddar cheese and Parmesan cheese. Repeat layers. Bake at 350 degrees for 45 minutes or until hot.

Barbara, Mrs. Ervin Koehn

Lasagna Roll-ups

⅔ (16 oz.) package lasagna noodles
  (12 noodles)
1 tablespoon salad oil
1 (10 oz.) package frozen chopped
  broccoli, thawed and squeezed dry
2 tablespoons minced green onions
¼ cup grated Parmesan cheese

1 (15 oz.) container ricotta cheese
  (2 cups)
½ teaspoon salt
1 egg
1 (14 oz.) jar spaghetti sauce
1 (4oz.) package shredded mozzarella
  cheese (1 cup)

About 1¼ hours before serving, cook lasagna noodles as label directs. Meanwhile, in 2 quart saucepan over medium heat, in hot salad oil, cook broccoli and green onions until tender, about 5 minutes, stirring frequently. Remove saucepan from heat. Stir in ricotta cheese, Parmesan cheese, salt and egg. Preheat oven to 375 degrees. Drain noodles; place in single layer on wax paper. Evenly spread some cheese mixture on each lasagna noodle. Roll up each noodle jellyroll fashion. In bowl, mix spaghetti sauce with ½ cup water. Into 11" x 7" glass baking dish, spoon about ¾ of spaghetti sauce. Arrange rolled noodles, seam side down, in sauce. Top with mozzarella cheese and remaining sauce. Cover dish loosely with foil; bake 30 minutes or until hot and bubbly and the cheese is melted.

Arlene Giesel Koehn   Yield: 6 main dish servings

Mexican Lasagna

1½ pounds ground beef
1½ teaspoons cumin
1 tablespoon chili powder
⅛ teaspoon garlic powder
¼ teaspoon red pepper
1 teaspoon salt
1 teaspoon pepper (to taste)
1 (16 oz.) can tomatoes, chopped
10-12 corn tortillas

2 cups small curd cottage cheese,
  drained
1 cup grated Monterey Jack cheese
1 egg
½ cup grated cheddar cheese
2 cups shredded lettuce
½ cup chopped tomatoes
3 green onions, chopped
¼ cup sliced black olives (optional)

Brown beef; drain thoroughly. Add cumin, chili powder, garlic powder, red pepper, salt, pepper and tomatoes; heat through. Cover bottom of a 13x9x2 baking dish with tortillas. Pour beef mixture over tortillas;place a layer of tortillas over meat mixture and set aside. Combine cottage cheese, Monterey Jack cheese and egg; pour over tortillas. Bake at 350 degrees for 30 minutes. Remove from oven. Sprinkle on cheddar cheese, lettuce tomatoes, green onion and olives.

Sharon Giesel

Mexican Lasagna

2 pounds ground beef
½ cup chopped onion
1 (16 oz.) jar picante sauce
1 can refried beans
1 teaspoon salt

¼ teaspoon pepper
1 (24 oz.) carton cottage cheese
flour tortillas
shredded mozzarella cheese

Brown beef, drain. Stir in onion, picante sauce, beans, salt and pepper; set aside. Spread ⅓ of meat mixture in bottom of 9 x 13 pan. Sprinkle with shredded cheese, then half the cottage cheese. Next put on a layer of tortillas, overlapping slightly. Repeat layers, ending with meat. Sprinkle or cover with mozzarella cheese. Bake at 350 degrees for 30-45 minutes or till cheese is browned.

Jolene Unruh

Burritos

24 flour tortillas
3 pounds hamburger
1 onion
1 can cream of celery
1 quart jar pinto beans, drained
    and mashed
2 can green chilies, chopped

salt and pepper
½ jar Pace picante sauce
    (mild or to taste)
chili powder, to taste
shredded mozzarella and cheddar
    cheese

Fry hamburger, drain. Add all ingredients except cheese and tortillas. Spread meat mixture on tortillas. Sprinkle amount of cheeses desired and roll. Wrap in foil and heat for 20 minutes at 350 degrees or freeze. These are really handy to have in your freezer.

Joyce, Mrs. Leland Koehn

Easy Burritos

1 pound hamburger
1 can refried beans
7-10 flour tortillas

shredded cheese or sliced sandwich
    cheese

Fry hamburger, drain. Mix with refried beans. Place meat mixture and cheese on tortillas, fold up and wrap in foil. Bake till heated through. Or place in pan, cover and microwave.

Jolene Unruh

Fajitas

I got this recipe from mom. I add a little Claude's fajita seasoning while simmering. 2 pounds round steak (tenderized) cut into ½" strips, 1 large onion, cut in strips, 1 large bell pepper, cut into rings, the following ingredients, to taste: minced garlic, salt, pepper, seasoning salt and chili powder. In large skillet, saute strips of steak while adding onions and peppers, stirring lightly. Add garlic and seasonings. Stir till steak is brown and tender. Warm flour tortillas and layer with 3 ounces meat mixture, chopped tomatoes, grated cheese, guacamole, salsa or vary to your own taste.

Donna, Mrs. Quinn Schmidt   Yield: 8 servings

Taco Casserole

1 package Dorita chips, crushed
2 pounds hamburger, brown with
   1 chopped onion
1 can tomato soup

1 can mushroom soup
1 package taco seasoning
1 cup water
1½ cups cheese

Mix all together and bake at 350 degrees for 1 hour.

Louise Wedel

Tortilla Pie

2 tablespoons salad oil
1 medium onion, diced
1 medium green pepper, diced
2 whole large chicken breasts,
   skinned and boned
½ teaspoon chili powder
1 (8oz.) bottle mild or hot taco sauce

2 tablespoons drained, chopped
   canned green chilies
3 (7-8 inch) flour tortillas
¼ pound Monterey Jack cheese,
   shredded (1 cup)
½ small head iceberg lettuce,
   thinly sliced

About 40 minutes before serving, in 12-inch skillet over medium heat, in hot salad oil, cook onion and green pepper 5 minutes, stirring occasionally. Meanwhile, cut chicken breasts into ½ in. pieces. Increase heat to medium high; add chicken and chili powder; cook 5 minutes, stirring frequently. Add taco sauce and green chilies; heat to boiling. Reduce heat to low; simmer for 10 minutes, stirring mixture occasionally. Add salt to taste. Meanwhile, preheat oven to 350 degrees. Place tortillas in cookie sheet; bake 5 minutes or until crisp. To assemble, on same cookie sheet, on 1 tortilla, place ⅓ chicken mixture and ⅓ cheese. Repeat layering 2 times. Bake 10 minutes or until cheese melts and filling is hot. Place stack on platter with lettuce. Cut into wedges to serve.

Carolyn, Mrs. Wayne Holdeman   Yield: 4 servings

Cheesy Chicken Enchilada

½ cup chopped onion
1 garlic clove, minced
1 tablespoon oil
2 cups chopped cooked chicken
1 can (4 oz.) chopped green chilies
¼ cup chicken broth
2 teaspoons chili powder

1 teaspoon ground cumin
4 ounces cream cheese, cubed
6 flour tortillas (6 inch)
¼ pound Velveeta process cheese
  spread, cubed
2 tablespoons milk
½ cup chopped tomato, divided

Microwave onion, garlic, and oil in a 2-quart casserole on HIGH 2-3 minutes or until tender, stirring after 2 minutes. Stir in chicken, chilies, broth and seasonings. Microwave on HIGH 4 minutes or until thoroughly heated. Add cream cheese, stir until cheese is melted. Spoon ⅓ cup chicken mixture onto each tortilla; roll up. Place, seam side down, in 8-inch square microwave dish. Microwave Velveeta cheese, milk and ¼ cup tomato in medium bowl on HIGH 2-3 minutes or until cheese is melted, stirring after each minutes. Pour sauce over tortillas, top with remaining tomatoes. Microwave on HIGH 6-8 minutes or until thoroughly heated, turning dish after 3 minutes.

LeAnne Nichols

Chicken Enchiladas

1 cooked chicken or 4 chicken
  breasts, cut up
¼ cup onion
1 can cream of chicken soup
1 can cream of mushroom soup

1 can beans
salt and pepper
taco sauce to taste
grated cheese
flour tortillas

Add all ingredients together, except cheese and tortillas; heat through. Break up 3-4 tortillas in bottom of buttered pan. Place ½ of meat mixture over tortillas, Sprinkle with grated cheese; repeat layers, ending with cheese. Bake 350 degrees for 30-45 minutes.

Barbara, Mrs. Ervin Koehn

Chicken or Pork Enchiladas

Brown 1 onion in ¼ cup oleo, add 1 can cream of mushroom soup or 1 can of cream of chicken soup. Add 1 quart pinto beans, ¼ cup broth from meat, 1 (8 oz.) can tomato sauce, 1 small can diced chilies, and 1 cooked chicken, diced, or 1 quart canned pork. Add chili powder, salt and pepper to taste. Layer all with tortillas and cheese. Bake until hot and bubbly, 350 degrees.

Jul Nightengale

Chicken Enchiladas

24 small flour tortillas
1 stick margarine, melted
4 cups cooked white chicken pieces
2 cans (1 quart) pinto beans
1 can cream of chicken soup

16 ounces sour cream
1 (4 oz.) can green chilies
1 package Williams taco seasoning
1 chopped onion
grated cheese

Dip tortillas in melted butter; mix all other ingredients, except cheese; divide mixture among tortillas. Add grated cheese. Roll up tortillas and place in two 9 x 13 pans. Bake uncovered at 350 degrees for 30 minutes. Top with grated cheese and return to oven until cheese is melted.

Charlene, Mrs. Glen Unruh

Creamy Green Enchiladas

1 pound ground beef
8 ounces cheddar cheese, grated
1 can cream of celery soup
¾ cup milk
8 ounces Velveeta cheese, cut in
  chunks

1 envelope green onion dip mix,
  or french onion soup mix
1 (4 oz.) can chopped green chilies
8-12 tortillas

Brown beef, drain; add cheddar cheese, set aside; combine soup, milk, Velveeta, dip mix, and chilies in a saucepan. Place over low heat, stirring occasionally, till melted. Spread on tortillas, with meat mixture, roll tightly and place in a 13 x 9 inch baking pan. Pour cheese sauce over the top. Bake at 350 degrees for 30 minutes.

Joyce, Mrs. Leland Koehn

Enchilada Casserole

1 pound hamburger
1 can cream of celery soup
1 can cream of mushroom soup
1 can enchilada sauce

1 cup shredded cheese
onion to taste
12 corn tortillas

Brown hamburger and onion, add salt and pepper to taste. Add remaining ingredients, mix well. Bake at 350 degrees for 30 minutes.

Julie Nightengale

Enchilada Casserole

2 pounds ground chuck
1 cup chopped onions
2 cloves garlic, minced
1 (10¾ oz.) can condensed cream
  of chicken soup
1 (10¾ oz.) can condensed cream
  of mushroom soup
1 (10 oz.) can enchilada sauce
1 cup milk

1 cup sliced, pitted, ripe olives
  (optional)
1 (4 oz.) can green chilies, chopped
½ teaspoon ground cumin
12 flour tortillas, each cut into
  4 strips
2 cups shredded Monterey
  Jack cheese

Brown meat, onions and garlic in large Dutch oven; drain fat, stir in soups, milk, enchilada sauce, olives, chilies and cumin; Bring to boil, remove from heat. Spread ¼ of the sauce in a 13 x 9 baking dish, then layer ⅓ of the tortilla strips, ¼ of the sauce, ⅓ shredded cheese. Repeat these 3 layers, ending with cheese. Cover with foil. Bake at 350 degrees for 30 minutes; remove foil, and bake for 20 minutes, or until hot and bubbly.

Mary, Mrs. Lee Giesel   Yield: 8-10 servings

Martha's Enchilada Casserole

Brown 2 pounds hamburger with onion and green pepper. Heat 1 can cream of chicken soup and 1 can enchilada sauce, add shredded cheese, stir until cheese is melted, add 1 small can diced green chilies. Combine with meat mixture; spread a layer of Dorito chips in bottom of a baking dish; place meat mixture over chips. Bake 25-30 minutes at 350 degrees.

Jul Nightengale

Skillet Enchiladas

1 pound beef
1 onion, chopped
1 can (10½ oz.) mild enchilada sauce
1 can (10½ oz.) cream of mushroom
  soup

½ cup milk
1 can (4 oz.) chopped green chilies
6 flour tortillas
shredded Cheddar cheese

Brown ground beef and onion; drain. Add enchilada sauce, milk, and chilies. Simmer 20 minutes. Warm tortillas in microwave and put ¼ cup cheese in each tortilla. Roll up and place on meat mixture in skillet and warm until cheese melts. Serve by spooning some meat mixture over each enchilada.

Pat, Mrs. Mitchell Unruh

Smothered Enchiladas

8 flour tortillas (or corn tortillas)
1 pound hamburger
1 can mushroom soup
½ cup chopped onion
Enchilada sauce (⅓ of recipe below)

⅓ cup milk
2 tablespoons green chilies
½ teaspoon salt
pepper
2½ cups shredded cheese

Heat hamburger (fried and drained), mushroom soup, onion, enchilada sauce, milk, and chilies together. Spread a little of this mixture across bottom of 7 x 11 pan. Warm tortillas. Place ¼ cup cheese in each tortilla and roll up. Lay close together in dish and spread the rest of the meat -sauce mixture over tortillas. Sprinkle with more cheese if desired. Bake or microwave until heated through and cheese inside enchiladas is melted.

Enchilada Sauce:
1 stick oleo
½ cup flour
1 pint tomato juice
3 cups water

1 teaspoon salt
3 tablespoons chili powder
pepper

Melt oleo, stir in flour. Add rest of ingredients, heat till thickened. Divide into 3 parts. (Should be about 1 pint apiece.) Freeze for use in recipe above.

Jolene Unruh

Golden Turkey Casserole

1 chicken flavored bouillon cube
1¼ cups boiling water
¼ cup butter or margarine
¼ cup chopped onion
¼ cup chopped green pepper
¼ cup all purpose flour
1 teaspoon salt
¼ teaspoon pepper

3 cups diced cooked turkey
2 cups cooked rice
¼ cup chopped pimiento
2 tablespoons grated Parmesan
  cheese
¼ cup cornflakes crumbs
1 tablespoon butter or margarine,
  melted

Dissolve bouillon cube in boiling water; set aside to cool. (1¼ cups turkey broth or chicken broth may be substituted for bouillon.) Melt ¼ cup butter in a medium skillet. Add onion and green pepper; saute until tender. Add flour, stirring until smooth; cook 1 minute, gradually add bouillon stirring constantly until thickened and bubbly. Stir in salt and pepper. Combine turkey, rice, pimiento, Parmesan cheese, and sauce; mix well. Spoon into a greased 1½ quart casserole dish. Combine cornflakes crumbs and 1 tablespoon melted butter, mixing well. Sprinkle on top of casserole. Bake, uncovered at 350 for 30 minutes.

Arlene Giesel Koehn   Makes 6 servings

Turkey Enchiladas

½ cup chopped onion
4 ounces green chilies
3 tablespoons butter
½ cup taco sauce
1 cup sour cream
¼ teaspoon chili powder

2½ cups turkey
2 cups grated cheese
2 tablespoons flour
10 flour tortillas
1 cup turkey broth

Combine onion, chilies, and 1 tablespoon butter. Microwave 1 minute. Add taco sauce, ¼ cup sour cream, and chili powder. Stir in turkey and ½ cup cheese. Divide mixture into tortillas, place seam side down in a greased 9 by 13 pan.

Microwave rest of butter, blend in flour. Slowly stir in turkey broth. Microwave 2 to 3 minutes till thickened, stirring every minute. Add the rest of the sour cream and green chilies, pour over the top of the enchiladas.

Bake a 325 degrees for 45 minutes. Then add the rest of the cheese and bake until melted.

Cherylyn, Mrs. Mike Unruh

Cider Baked Turkey Breast

1 (5-6 pound) turkey breast
1½ cups apple cider
¼ cup soy sauce

Sauce:
2 tablespoons cornstarch
½ cup apple cider

Place turkey breast, skin side up, in a large pan. Bake at 450 degrees for 30 minutes (uncovered) or until skin is crisp. Combine 1½ cups cider and soy sauce; pour over turkey. Cover and bake at 325 degrees until done. Baste turkey frequently with cider mixture in pan. Combine cornstarch and ½ cup cider, stirring well; stir in pan drippings. Return to oven and bake uncovered until sauce is thickened. Transfer turkey to serving platter. Serve with sauce.

Arlene Giesel Koehn   Yield: 12 to 16 servings

Marinated Turkey Fillets

2 cups white wine
1 cup peanut oil
1 cup soy sauce

garlic powder
turkey fillets

Marinate for at least 48 hours, shaking every 6 hours or less. Grill on slow fire for 18 minutes on both sides.

Julie Nightengale

Stuffed Turkey Breast

½ cup (1 stick) butter
¾ cup chopped onion
½ cup chopped celery
2 teaspoons poultry seasoning
½ teaspoon salt
¼ teaspoon pepper
½ cup milk

2 eggs slightly beaten
2 cups dry corn bread stuffing
2 cups coarse dry whole wheat
    bread crumbs
5 pound turkey breast, thawed
¼ cup (½ stick) of butter

Melt ½ cup butter in large skillet. Saute onion and celery until tender, about 8 minutes. Remove from heat. Stir in spices. Add milk and eggs. Mix well. Gently toss with corn bread and whole wheat crumbs. Preheat oven to 325 degrees. Loosen the skin of the turkey breast by gently pushing hand between skin and flesh. Leave about an inch of skin attached around the edge to hold the stuffing in place. Place the stuffing between the flesh and the skin. (Place remaining stuffing in buttered casserole. Bake uncovered 30 to 35 minutes at 325 degrees.) Place stuffed breast on rack in roasting pan. Brush with melted butter. Bake uncovered, basting frequently 3 to 3 ½ hours. When turkey breast reaches desired degree of brown, tent roasting pan with foil to prevent further browning. Let rest 15 minutes before carving. Also could use Stove Top dressing if desired.

Carolyn, Mrs. Wayne Holdeman

Roast Turkey in Foil

Turkey
salt and pepper

1 stick melted butter
2 teaspoons Kitchen Bouquet

Rub turkey cavity with salt and pepper. Fill the bird loosely with stuffing. Truss. Rub turkey with salt and pepper. Brush with mixture of melted butter and Kitchen Bouquet. Wrap tightly in foil. In 350-degree oven, roast breast side down for first hour. Turn turkey breast side up for remaining roasting time, allowing 22 minutes per pound. Remove foil during the last half-hour and baste bird every 10 minutes with butter mixture and drippings.

Arlene Giesel Koehn

Roast Turkey

Wash turkey with cold water and dry. Rub outside of thawed turkey with melted margarine. Sprinkle salt and poultry seasoning while you rub. Fold wings back and tuck under turkey. Add stuffing at this time to cavity if you so desire. It is corn bread stuffing, isn't it?! Tuck drumsticks under band of skin at tail or tie with heavy string, then tie to tail. Place turkey, breast side up, in roasting pan. Do not cover. Roast in 350 degree oven until golden. Then place a tent of foil loosely over turkey and seal off edges. When turkey is ⅔ done, release the legs.

Timetable For Roasting Turkey (for best results use a meat thermometer):

6-8 pounds, 3 to 3½ hours

8-12 pounds, 3½ to 4½ hours

12-16 pounds, 4½ to 5½ hours

16-20 pounds, 5½ to 6½ hours

20-24 pounds, 6½ to 7 hours.

185 degrees for all weights.

Jerry Ratzlaff

P.S. Janice's dressing recipe will follow.

Sage Dressing

I never make it the same twice, but I will try to tell you how I usually do it, guessing at some of the amounts!

1 stick margarine	onion salt
poultry seasoning	chopped onions
garlic salt	salt and pepper
chopped celery	bread and corn bread
broth	

In a large kettle, melt margarine. Saute celery and onions in margarine - any amount - the more the better! I usually use 2 onions and probably 6 to 8 long pieces of celery. Then add seasonings - to taste - and broth. You can make broth by cooking the turkey giblets, use bouillon, or canned broth. The amount isn't important, but you will probably want at least 1½ quarts. Then you can break up your corn bread and bread, (I like to leave it out overnight to dry) and add it to the broth mixture until it takes up the moisture, but isn't too dry. Try it, it isn't hard!

Janice, Mrs. Jerry Ratzlaff

Cajun Catfish

6 skinned and dressed catfish
(½ pound each)
½ cup tomato sauce
2 tablespoons chopped parsley

1 (0.7 ounce) package Italian
dressing mix
2 tablespoons vegetable oil
2 tablespoons Parmesan cheese

Wash and dry fish. Combine ingredients and mix well. Brush fish inside and out with sauce. Place in lightly greased 13 by 9 baking pan. Cover and refrigerate at least 30 minutes. Bake at 350 degrees for 30 to 35 minutes. Then broil fish 4 inches from heat for 2 minutes, or until lightly crisp and browned. I use fillets instead of whole catfish.

Cherylyn, Mrs. Mike Unruh

Salmon Croquettes

1 large can flaked salmon
1 onion finely chopped
juice of 2 lemons
salt and pepper to taste

2 large eggs, slightly beaten
1 cup milk
3½ cups crumbled saltine crackers

Mix all ingredients reserving 1¾ cups cracker crumbs. Chill mixture for several hours. Shape into patties and roll in remaining cracker crumbs until completely covered. Cook over medium heat until crispy. Remove to absorbent paper to drain. May be served with a medium white sauce. Serves 6-8. I remember my mother, Mary Giesel, making these. I thought they were great.

Arlene Giesel Koehn

Salmon Loaf with Shrimp Sauce

2 one pound cans of salmon
¼ cup finely minced onion
¼ cup chopped parsley
¼ cup lemon juice
½ teaspoon salt
½ teaspoon pepper

½ to 1 teaspoon ground thyme
2 cups coarse cracker crumbs
about ½ cup milk
4 eggs, well beaten
¼ cup butter, melted
shrimp sauce

Drain salmon, saving liquid. Flake salmon into bowl, and add onion, parsley, lemon juice, seasonings and cracker crumbs; mix lightly. Add salmon liquid plus enough milk to make 1 cup; add eggs and melted butter. Mix lightly. Spoon into greased 2 quart loaf pan or casserole. Bake in moderate oven (350 degrees) 1 hour or until loaf is set in center.

Shrimp Sauce: heat a can of frozen condensed cream of shrimp soup according to directions on label. Add ¼ cup milk, stir until smooth. Spoon onto hot salmon loaf.

Arlene Giesel Koehn   Makes 8 servings

Almost Pizza

1 pound lean ground beef
6 cups thinly sliced potatoes,
   lightly salted
1 eleven ounce can condensed
   nacho cheese soup
1 cup milk
1 (10¾ oz.) can condensed tomato
   soup

½ cup chopped onion
1 teaspoon sugar
½ teaspoon ground oregano
3 to 4 ounces pepperoni, thinly sliced
1 large green bell pepper, cut
   into thin rings
2 cups (8 oz.) shredded mozzarella
   cheese

Brown ground beef; drain. Place sliced potatoes in well-greased 13 x 9 x 2 inch baking pan. Sprinkle ground beef over potatoes. Combine cheese soup and milk in small saucepan. Over medium heat, stir until heated through. Pour over meat. Mix tomato soup, onion, sugar, and oregano, and spoon over cheese mixture. Top with pepperoni slices. Cover with foil, and bake in 350 degree oven, 1 to 1 ¼ hours. Remove casserole from oven; arrange green pepper rings on top, then sprinkle with shredded cheese. Turn off oven heat, and return casserole to oven, uncovered for an additional 20 to 30 minutes. Serve immediately. Serve with a green salad, bread sticks, or french bread, and cold Pepsi.

Edna Giesel   Yield: 8 to 10 servings

Crazy Pizza

Batter:
1 cup flour
1 teaspoon salt
1 teaspoon oregano

⅛ teaspoon pepper
2 eggs
⅔ cup milk

Heat oven to 425 degrees. In skillet, brown 1 ½ pound beef and season. Drain and set aside. Slightly grease and flour a 14x12 inch pizza pan. In a small bowl, combine flour, salt, oregano, pepper, eggs, and milk. Pour batter into pan, tilting pan so batter will cover bottom. Arrange topping of meat, ¼ cup chopped onion, and 14 ounce can of mushroom (optional). Bake at 425 degrees for 25 to 30 minutes until pizza is deep golden brown. Drizzle with one cup pizza sauce, 1 cup mozzarella cheese. Return to oven for 10 to 15 minutes.

LeAnne Holdeman

Little Pizzas

1 can refrigerator biscuits
5 tablespoons pizza sauce

pepperoni or ham
1 cup mozzarella cheese

Place biscuits on greased cookie sheet, make depression in center of each biscuit. Cut meat into tiny pieces. Put 1 teaspoon sauce and a tablespoon of meat on each. Bake at 400 degrees for 15 minutes. Sprinkle cheese on each one and heat in oven until cheese is melted. Enjoy!

Holly Koehn

Crispi Crust Pizza

3 cups flour
1 tablespoon vegetable oil
1 tablespoon quick-rise or
    instant yeast

1 teaspoon salt
1 cup lukewarm water
½ teaspoon sugar

Mix together all ingredients. Knead by hand for 3 minutes. Shape and put in bowl. Cover and let rise until double in volume. Punch down; divide into 2 equal pieces and shape into round balls for 12" pizzas, or shape into one ball for a 16" pizza. Let dough rest 4 minutes. Roll out approximately 12" or 16" diameter.

Spray Crispi Crust pizza pan lightly with vegetable oil and wipe off excess. Place dough on pan or pans, and let rise for 10 to 15 minutes. Add sauce, meat and/or other toppings and cheese. Place on bottom rack in COLD oven; turn oven to 500 degrees, and bake for 20 minutes or until cheese begins to brown.

Jolene Unruh

German Pizza

1 pound ground beef
½ medium chopped onion
½ green pepper, diced
1½ teaspoon salt, divided
½ teaspoon pepper
6 medium potatoes, peeled and
    finely shredded

3 eggs beaten
⅓ cup milk
2 cups shredded cheddar or
    mozzarella cheese

Brown ground beef with onion, green pepper, ½ teaspoon salt and pepper. Remove meat mixture from skillet and drain. Reduce heat to low. Melt butter; spread potatoes over butter and sprinkle with remaining salt. Top with beef mixture. Combine eggs and milk; pour over all. Cook, covered, until potatoes are tender, about 30 minutes. Top with cheese and heat until cheese is melted. Cut into wedges or squares to serve.

Charmaine Wedel　　　　　　　　　　　　　　　　　　Yield: 4 to 6 servings

Pizza Pockets

Brown hamburger with onion, salt and pepper. Roll out refrigerator biscuits, spread with 1 tablespoon pizza sauce, add hamburger, top with cheese. Roll up and bake at 400-425 degrees until brown. Serve.

Jul Nightengale

Mexican Pizza

1 package corn muffin mix
1 can beans, mashed
1½ cups shredded cheese
½ pound ground beef
½ package taco seasoning mix

1 cup tomato sauce
3 tablespoons each chopped green
pepper and onion
2 tablespoons hot salsa

Make corn bread according to package instructions only decrease milk to ¼ cup. Spread evenly in well buttered pizza pan. Bake 20 minutes at 400 degrees. Cool slightly. Brown hamburger, add mashed beans, and seasoning mix. Spread on crust. Top with ½ of cheese. Mix sauce, onions, peppers, and hot salsa, spread over meat mixture. Top with remaining cheese. Bake at 350 degrees for 15 minutes. Garnish with lettuce and tomato if desired.

LeAnne Nichols

Pizza

1 tablespoon yeast
2¼ cups warm water
3 tablespoons sugar

1 cup shortening
½ tablespoon salt
6 cups flour

Dissolve yeast and sugar in warm water. Add shortening, salt and flour. Let rise for 30 minutes. Press onto 3 cookie sheets for thin crust, smaller pans for thick. Prick with a fork. Let rise a bit and then bake at 450 degrees for 10 minutes.

Sauce:

1 (10¾ oz.) can tomato puree
¼ teaspoon oregano
¼ teaspoon basil
¼ teaspoon black pepper
⅛ teaspoon garlic powder

⅛ teaspoon onion powder
2 teaspoons Parmesan cheese
½ teaspoon salt
¼ teaspoon MSG or Accent

Mix together and add 1 can mushroom soup. Spread on crust. Sprinkle with a bit more Parmesan cheese. Top with grated cheese and meat toppings. Bake until cheese bubbles. These freeze terrific before baking the second time.

Debby, Mrs. Jerry Ensz

Pizza Loaf

1 pound ground beef
¼ cup mushrooms
½ cup minced onions
salt and pepper to taste

Bread Dough:
portion for 1 bread or frozen
    bread dough
1 cup diced cheddar cheese

½ teaspoon oregano
½ teaspoon garlic salt
8 ounce tomato sauce
¾ cup chopped ripe olives (optional)

¾ cup shredded mozzarella cheese

Saute beef, mushroom, and onion until meat is browned. Mix in spices. Add tomato sauce, simmer about 30 minutes, covered. Stir in ripe olives, if desired; cool. Prepare bread dough through first rising. Punch down and roll 15 by 12 inch rectangle. Place filling down center of dough using ⅓ of width. Sprinkle meat with cheddar then mozzarella cheese. Make diagonal cuts 1 and ½ inches apart down each side of dough, cutting to ½ inch of filling. Bring strips of dough over filling to center, crisscrossing each side. Seal overlapping strips with drop of water. Place on greased baking sheet, brush with melted butter, and bake at 350 degrees about 30 to 40 minutes until browned. Serve warm.

Note: You may let filled log rise a short time. You do not want too much bread in proportion to the filling.

We like it just as well, if not better, rolled as for cinnamon rolls.

Valerie, Mrs. Roger Holdeman

Stuffed Pizza

½ pound sausage
½ pound hamburger
3⅓ cups Bisquick
¾ cup cold water

3 cups shredded mozzarella
    cheese (12 oz.)
1 (15½ oz.) jar pizza sauce
pizza toppings of your choice

Brown sausage and beef, drain and set aside; grease a 13 x 9" baking dish; heat oven to 450 degrees. Mix Bisquick and water to make dough. Divide into 2 parts, one slightly larger; roll larger portion into 16 x 14" rectangle and line pan. Sprinkle with 1 cup cheese, cover with ¾ cup sauce; add meat mixture and other toppings. Cover with 1 ½ cup cheese. Roll remaining dough for top crust, seal edges and make slits for steam. Spread crust with remaining sauce and sprinkle with cheese. Bake at 375 degrees for 22-25 minutes or until crust is golden.

LeAnne Nichols

Yield: 8-10 servings

Jolene's Tasty Pizza

Crust:

1 tablespoon yeast
1 tablespoon sugar
¾ cup warm water
⅓ cup butter flavored Crisco

½ teaspoon salt
¼ cup whole wheat flour
1¾ cups white flour

Meat and Sauce Mixture:

2 pounds hamburger, may use
   part sausage, browned
1 can cream of mushroom soup
1 can tomato soup
1 green pepper, chopped

chopped onion to taste
¼ teaspoon ground red pepper
½ teaspoon oregano
1½ teaspoon Italian seasoning
½ teaspoon salt

Other Ingredients:

Velveeta cheese
Colby or cheddar cheese

Mozzarella cheese
Pepperoni slices

Preheat oven to 350 degrees. Mix yeast and sugar and dissolve in water. Stir in remaining ingredients. Let bowl rest 5 minutes in warm water. Spread in 2 ungreased pizza pans, making an edge. Prick with fork; Bake 10-15 minutes. Combine meat (drained) and sauce mixture, if to thick add water. Place thin slices of Velveeta cheese on crust, spread meat mixture over cheese. Add shredded Colby or cheddar, then sprinkle freely with mozzarella and top with pepperoni. Bake 10-15 minutes, or until crust is crunchy.

Finette Giesel Koehn

Taco Pizza

pizza crust (your choice)
1 pound ground beef
1 can refried beans
chopped onion to taste
1 teaspoon taco seasoning

shredded mozzarella cheese
shredded lettuce
diced tomato
shredded cheddar cheese

Pre-bake crust 8-10 minutes. Mix cooked beef, refried beans, onion and taco seasoning. May add tomato juice if needed. Spread mixture over baked crust, sprinkle with mozzarella cheese and bake another 10 minutes or until done. Top with shredded lettuce, diced tomato and cheddar cheese. Serve!

Jolene Unruh

Pop-up Pizza

1½ pounds ground beef
1 cup chopped onion
1 cup chopped green pepper
1 garlic clove, minced
½ teaspoon oregano
dash of salt

½ cup water
⅛ teaspoon Tabasco sauce
1⅔ cup tomato sauce
1 envelope spaghetti sauce mix
6 (8 oz.) sliced mozzarella or
  Monterey jack cheese

Heat oven to 400 degrees, brown beef, drain; stir in onion, green pepper, garlic, oregano, salt, water, hot sauce, tomato sauce, and sauce mix; simmer 10 minutes stirring occasionally.

Popover Batter:
1 cup milk
1 tablespoon oil
2 eggs

1 cup flour
½ teaspoon salt
½ cup Parmesan cheese

In small bowl, combine milk, oil, and eggs; beat 1 minute at medium speed. Add flour and salt; beat 2 minutes at medium speed or until smooth; Pour hot meat mixture into 13 x 9 inch pan; top with cheese slices. Pour batter over cheese, covering completely; sprinkle with Parmesan cheese. Bake at 400 degrees for 25 to 30 minutes or until puffed and deep golden brown. Serve immediately.

Valerie, Mrs. Roger Holdeman   Yield: 10 servings

Upside down Pizza

2 pounds hamburger
¼ cup onion
6 ounces tomato juice
1 envelope spaghetti sauce mix
1½ cup mozzarella cheese, grated

1 (8 oz.) can refrigerator
  crescent rolls
2 tablespoons butter, melted
⅓ cup Parmesan cheese
sour cream

Cook hamburger with onions, add tomato juice and spaghetti sauce mix. Spread meat mixture into a 9 x 13" baking dish; layer cheese and sour cream over meat. Top with crescent rolls and brush with butter. Sprinkle with Parmesan cheese. Bake at 375 degrees for 20-30 minutes. Note; may use 1 pint pizza sauce, in place of tomato juice and spaghetti sauce.

Betty, Mrs. Gordon Unruh   Yield: 8-10 servings

Barbeque Sauce for Grilled Chicken

1 cup oleo	1 cup water
4 teaspoons salt	2 tablespoons Worcestershire sauce
2 tablespoons onion salt	½ teaspoon pepper
4 tablespoons lemon juice	2 teaspoons sugar

Heat all ingredients until oleo melts; brush chicken with sauce while grilling. For well done chicken place chicken (after grilling) in oven , pouring left over sauce over chicken. Bake at 325 degrees 30-60 minutes.

Joyce, Mrs. Leland Koehn

Meat Sauce (for corn chips)

1-1½ pounds hamburger	¼ chopped onion
¼ chopped green pepper	

Brown hamburger, add taco seasonings to taste, ketchup, water and 1 pint pinto beans. Let simmer. Put this over chips, add cheese, lettuce and hot sauce to taste. Note: I make this in large batches and can, process at 10 pounds pressure for 10 minutes. This is very handy for a quick meal.

Sophie Giesel Koehn

Mornay Sauce

2 tablespoons butter	⅛ teaspoon nutmeg
2 tablespoons flour	salt to taste
1 cup chicken, veal or fish stock	dash pepper

Melt butter over low heat; stir in flour. Cook over low heat, stir until smooth and bubbly. Remove from heat; gradually stir in stock, bring to boil; boil 1 minute. Blend in seasonings, stir in 1 cup cream, ⅛ teaspoon cayenne pepper; heat, stirring constantly. Add 1 cup diced sharp cheddar cheese, Parmesan or Swiss cheese. Glamorize meats, fish and eggs.

Wilma Giesel

Marinade for Steak

1 package (6 oz.) Good Seasons
   zesty Italian dressing mix
¼ cup (extra virgin) olive oil
⅓ cup tarragon wine vinegar

½ teaspoon meat tenderizer
   (optional)
3-4 pound beef chuck roast or
   thick sirloin

Combine marinade ingredients, pour small amount to cover bottom of a 9 x 13" pan. Place beef in pan, top with remaining marinade. Pierce generously, with fork, turn meat and pierce, cover; refrigerate for 8 hours or over night, piercing and turning meat often. Before cooking let beef come to room temperature. Grill over hot coals, 6 minutes per side for medium rare cuts 1" thick. 8-9 minutes per side for thicker cuts. Serve with sliced tomatoes and sweet onions.

Carolyn, Mrs. Wayne Holdeman

Fish Sauce

For broiled, baked, or fried fish.

Cucumber Sauce: combine 1½ cups chopped cucumber, 1 tablespoon vinegar, 1 teaspoon salt in a bowl; let stand 10 minutes, drain; add 2 tablespoons each, chopped pimiento, chopped green pepper, 1 tablespoon horseradish, ½ teaspoon paprika, dash of Tabasco, 1 tablespoon lemon juice, and 1 cup mayonnaise; blend together and chill.

Betty Giesel Martens

Tarter Sauce

Combine 1 cup mayonnaise, ¼ cup pickle relish, ½ teaspoon grated onion, and 2 teaspoons prepared mustard; chill.

Betty Giesel Martens

Fresh Tartar Sauce

½ cup mayonnaise or salad dressing
¼ cup chopped sweet pickles

few drops red-pepper seasonings

Combine all ingredients in a small bowl. Cover and chill at least 1 hour to blend flavors.

Arlene Giesel Koehn   Yield: ¾ cup

Shrimp Batter

1 egg
1¼ cup flour
1 tablespoon baking powder
1 cup ice water

1 teaspoon salt
1 teaspoon paprika
1 teaspoon garlic salt

Dip shrimp into batter and place on rack to drain excess batter. Deep fat fry.

Deanna Giesel

Dip and Bake Mixture

4 cups dry bread crumbs
½ cup cooking oil
1 tablespoon salt

2 teaspoons paprika
1 teaspoon celery seed
1 teaspoon pepper

Mix all ingredients well. To use, cut fish in serving size pieces, drain well, then dip in the mixture on both sides. Place on a well greased cookie sheet and bake. This mixture will do for chicken and pork chops also.

Mornie Giesel Unruh

VEGETABLES & FRUITS

Cajun Red Beans and Rice

1 pound dried red beans
3 cups chopped onions
1 cup chopped green pepper
1 cup chopped fresh parsley
1 tablespoon garlic salt
¼ teaspoon dried oregano
1 teaspoon red pepper

1 tablespoon Worcestershire sauce
1 teaspoon pepper
1½ teaspoons hot sauce
1 (8 oz.) can tomato sauce
1 pound sausage
hot cooked rice

Sort and wash beans; place in large Dutch oven. Cover with water 2" above beans, let soak overnight. Cook and simmer 45 minutes. Stir in next 10 ingredients. Continue to cook 1 hour. Brown sausage and drain; add to bean mixture, partially mashing beans. Cover and simmer 45 minutes, adding more water if necessary. Serve over rice.

Jana, Mrs. Robert Nichols

Maple Baked Beans

1 pound dry navy beans
4 quarts water, divided
6 slices bacon cut in pieces
1 medium onion, chopped
1 cup maple syrup
½ cup ketchup

½ cup barbecue sauce
5 teaspoons cider vinegar
1 teaspoon prepared mustard
1 teaspoon salt
½ teaspoon pepper

Sort and rinse beans; place in a 4 quart Dutch oven. Cover with 2 quarts water. Bring to a boil, reduce heat and simmer for two minutes; remove from heat. Cover and let stand for 1 hour. Drain and rinse beans, cover with remaining water. Bring to a boil, reduce heat and simmer 40-45 minutes, or until almost tender. Drain and reserve liquid. In a 2½ quart casserole or bean pot, combine beans with all remaining ingredients. Bake covered at 300 degrees for 3 hours or until tender. Stir occasionally, adding reserved bean liquid if necessary.

Charmaine Wedel

Savory Baked Beans

1 (16 oz.) can pinto beans
2-3 tablespoons brown sugar
¼ teaspoon mustard

1 teaspoon beef bouillon
salt and pepper to taste

Combine all ingredients in well greased baking dish. Cover. Bake 1 hour 350 degrees.

Jana, Mrs. Robert Nichols   3-4 servings

Old Settlers Baked Beans

½ pound ground beef
½ pound bacon, diced
1 medium onion, chopped
⅓ cup sugar
½ cup brown sugar
¼ cup ketchup
¼ cup barbeque sauce
1 tablespoon prepared mustard

½ teaspoon pepper
½ teaspoon chili powder
1 can (16 oz.) pork and beans, undrained
1 can (16 oz.) kidney beans, rinsed and drained
1 can (16 oz.) northern beans, rinsed and drained

In a large skillet, cook beef, bacon, and onion until meat is done and onion is tender. Drain; combine all remaining ingredients, except beans. Add to meat mixture; mix well. Stir in beans. Place in a greased 2½ quart casserole. Bake uncovered 1 hour at 350 degrees.

Jana, Mrs. Robert Nichols

8-10 servings

Pinto Beans

1 quart canned pinto beans
⅔ cup ketchup
¾ cup brown sugar

1 small onion, chopped
4-5 slices bacon

Cook bacon with onion; drain. Add ingredients together, and simmer for 1-1½ hours.

David L. Unruh

Broccoli Casserole

2 packages frozen broccoli
2 eggs, slightly beaten
1 cup rolled cracker crumbs
1 cup grated cheese

2 tablespoons onion, chopped
1 cup mayonnaise
1 can cream of mushroom soup
salt to taste

Cook broccoli and drain. Place on bottom of casserole dish. Mix remaining ingredients together, except cracker crumbs and cheese. Put cracker crumbs on last. Bake at 400 for 20 minutes.

Arlene Giesel Koehn.

Broccoli Casserole

2 packages chopped broccoli
½ onion, chopped
2 tablespoons butter
2 cups cooked rice

1 can mushroom soup
1 can cream of celery soup
1 small jar cheese whiz

Brown onion in butter. Add soups. Add rice and broccoli. Stir in cheese whiz. Bake 1 hour at 350 degrees.

Janice, Mrs. Jerry Ratzlaff

Broccoli Casserole

12 slices bacon, diced
12 green onions, chopped
2 stalks celery, diced
2 boxes wild rice and mushroom mix

2 packages frozen broccoli
1 can sliced mushrooms
1 (8 oz.) jar cheese whiz

Cook bacon until crisp. Saute onions and celery in bacon drippings until soft. Cook rice according to package directions, drain; add cooked broccoli and remaining ingredients, mix. Place in a 9 x 13 baking dish, bake at 350 degrees for 20 minutes or until hot and bubbly.

Mark Koehn

Savory Stuffed Cabbage

8 large cabbage leaves
1 pound ground beef
¼ cup chopped onion
1 teaspoon salt

1 can tomato soup
1 cup cooked rice
1 egg, slightly beaten
¼ teaspoon pepper

Cook cabbage leaves in salted water a few minutes to soften; drain. Mix 2 tablespoons soup with remaining ingredients. Divide mixture on cabbage leaves; fold in sides; roll up and secure with toothpicks. In skillet, place rolls seam down; pour soup over, cover; simmer 40 minutes. Stir occasionally. Spoon sauce over roll to serve.

Janice, Mrs. Jerry Ratzlaff   4 servings

Cauliflower and Carrots with Wild Rice

2 cloves garlic, minced
1 tablespoon butter or margarine,
   melted
1¾ cups water
½ cup uncooked wild rice
2 teaspoons chicken-flavored
   bouillon granules
½ teaspoon salt

½ teaspoon onion salt
½ cup uncooked long-grain rice
1 cup cauliflower flowerets
2 medium carrots, scraped and
   shredded
3 green onions, thinly sliced
2-3 tablespoons whipping cream

Saute garlic in butter in a large saucepan. Add water and next 4 ingredients. Bring to a boil; cover, reduce heat, and simmer 25 minutes. Add rice, cover and simmer 20 minutes. Add cauliflower; cover and simmer 10 minutes or until rice is tender and liquid is absorbed. Stir in carrots, green onions, and cream. Cook until mixture is thoroughly heated.

Arlene Giesel Koehn   Yield: 6-8 servings

Terrific Cauliflower

1 medium head cauliflower
¼ teaspoon salt
⅛ teaspoon pepper
1 (8 oz.) carton sour cream

1 cup (4 oz.) shredded sharp
    Cheddar cheese
1 tablespoon sesame seed, toasted

Remove large outer leaves of cauliflower. Break cauliflower into flowerets. Bring a small amount of water, ¼ teaspoon salt and ⅛ teaspoon pepper to a boil in a large saucepan; add cauliflower, cover and cook 8-10 minutes or until tender; drain. Arrange half of cauliflower in a 1-quart baking dish. Spread ½ cup sour cream over cauliflower. Sprinkle with ½ cup cheese and 1½ teaspoons sesame seeds. Repeat layers. Bake at 350 degrees for 10-15 minutes.

Arlene Giesel Koehn   Yield: 4-6 servings

Carrot Cheese Casserole

3 cans sliced carrots

1 pound cheese slices

Layer carrots and cheese slices, ending with carrots.

Sauce:
¾ cup oleo
1 large onion, chopped
¾ cup flour

3 cups milk
½ teaspoon dry mustard
¾ teaspoon seasoning salt

Brown onions slightly in oleo; add flour, mustard and seasoning salt. Stir well and add milk. Cook till bubbly. Pour over carrots and sprinkle buttered bread crumbs on top. Bake until bubbly, 30-45 minutes at 350 degrees. This can be refrigerated over night, and then bake.

Shirley, Mrs Arden Penner

Marinaded Carrots

2 pounds carrots
1 small green pepper, chopped
1 medium onion, chopped
1 can tomato soup
½ cup oil
1 cup sugar

¾ cup vinegar
1 teaspoon prepared mustard
1 teaspoon Worcestershire sauce
½ teaspoon salt
¼ teaspoon pepper

Slice carrots and cook until barely tender. Mix remaining ingredients, and pour over drained carrots. Marinate at least 6 hours.

Arlene Giesel Koehn

Nutty Carrots

1½ pounds carrots, scraped and
    cut into julienne strips
1½ cups water
½ teaspoon salt
¼ cup butter, melted
1 teaspoon salt

¼ teaspoon coarsely ground pepper
¼ teaspoon grated lemon rind
2 tablespoons lemon juice
2 teaspoons honey
½ cup coarsely chopped walnuts

Combine carrots, water and ½ teaspoon salt in a heavy saucepan. Bring to a boil; cover, reduce heat, and simmer 15 minutes or until carrots are tender. Drain well. Set aside, and keep warm. Combine butter, 1 teaspoon salt, pepper, lemon rind, lemon juice, and honey in a small saucepan, and stir well. Cook over medium heat until mixture is thoroughly heated, stirring constantly. Pour sauce over carrots. Add chopped walnuts, and toss gently.

Arlene Giesel Koehn   Yield: 6-8 servings

Corn Pot Luck Special

1 (16 oz.) can creamed style corn
1 (16 oz.) can whole kernel corn
1 (8 oz.) carton sour cream

1 box jiffy cornbread mix
1 stick melted oleo

Combine all ingredients; pour into lightly greased 9 x 13 pan and bake uncovered for 45 minutes at 350 degrees.

Carolyn, Mrs. Wayne Holdeman

King Style Scalloped Corn

1 can (16 oz.) cream style corn
1 cup cracker crumbs
½ cup chopped celery
¼ cup chopped onion
⅔ cup shredded cheese

1 teaspoon salt
2 eggs, beaten
¼ teaspoon paprika
2 tablespoons melted oleo
1 cup milk

Combine all ingredients. Place in a 1½ quart casserole. Bake at 350 degrees for 50-55 minutes.

Betty Giesel Martens   10-12 servings

Baked Cheesy Green Beans

1 (10 oz.) package frozen green beans
1 can cream of celery soup
1 (5 oz.) jar bacon and cheese spread
1 (3½ oz) can French fried onions
3 slices crisply fried bacon, crumbled

Cook beans according to package directions; drain. Combine soup and cheese spread. Toss beans with soup mixture; place in 6-cup casserole. Top with onions and bacon. bake in 325 degree oven for 30 minutes.

Arlene Giesel Koehn   Yield 6 servings

Green Beans in Sour Cream Dressing

1 onion, thinly sliced
3 cans Blue Lake beans, drained
1 can water chestnuts
1 tablespoon salad oil
1 tablespoon vinegar
coarsely ground pepper to taste
salt to taste
1 cup sour cream
½ cup mayonnaise
1 teaspoon lemon juice
¼ teaspoon dry mustard
1 tablespoon horseradish

Place onion over beans in container. Drain water chestnuts; slice. Place over onion. Add oil, vinegar, pepper, and salt; refrigerate for 1 hour or longer. Drain well. Mix remaining ingredients and salt. Add to bean mixture; mix well. Refrigerate for at least 12 hours before serving.

Arlene Giesel Koehn

Green Beans and Sour Cream

3 tablespoons oleo
2 tablespoons flour
½ tablespoon grated onion
1 teaspoon salt
¼ teaspoon pepper
1 cup sour cream
2 cans or 1 quart green beans, drained
¾ cup American cheese
½ cup corn flakes crumbs

Cook together oleo, flour, onion, salt and pepper. Add sour cream and mix with green beans. Place in a greased 1½ quart casserole; top with cheese, and sprinkle corn flake crumbs over cheese.. Bake at 350 degrees for 30 minutes.

Betty Giesel Martens

Goldenrod Beans

1½ pound fresh green beans	2 tablespoons all-purpose flour
2½ cups water	½ cup evaporated milk
½ teaspoon salt	½ teaspoon salt
3 hard-cooked eggs	⅛ teaspoon pepper
1½ tablespoons butter or margarine	2 tablespoons mayonnaise

Cut beans into 1½-inch pieces. Combine beans, water and ½ teaspoon salt in a heavy saucepan; bring to a boil. reduce heat, cover, and simmer 30-35 minutes or until tender. Drain, reserving ½ cup bean liquid; set beans aside and keep warm. Slice eggs in half; remove yolks. Press yolks through a sieve, and set aside. Chop egg whites, and set aside. Melt butter in a heavy saucepan over low heat; add flour, stirring until smooth. Cook 1 minute, stirring constantly. Gradually add milk and reserved bean liquid; cook over medium heat, stirring constantly, until thickened and bubbly. Stir in ½ teaspoon salt, pepper, mayonnaise, and egg whites. Place beans in a serving dish; pour sauce over top. Sprinkle egg yolks over sauce.

Arlene Giesel Koehn   Yield: 6 servings

French Fried Onion Rings

Slice 2 large onions into ¼" slices. Beat 1 egg white, ¾ cup water, 2 teaspoons lemon juice, and 1 tablespoon cooking oil, until frothy. Add 1 cup flour, 1 ½ teaspoon baking powder, and ½ teaspoon salt. Beat all together until smooth. Dip rings in batter and fry and drain.. In the summertime when the little garden produced more onions then what the folks needed, Mother would fix these French Fried Onions. They are real crunchy and good flavored. My notes say I got this recipe from her in 1984. I don't know how many years old the recipe was by that time.

Jennie, Mrs. Calvin Unruh

Baked Potatoes with Topping

Topping:

2½ pounds hamburger	¼ cup green pepper (chopped)
½ cup chopped onion	½ tablespoon chili powder

Brown hamburger and onion, add green pepper and chili powder and simmer. Add: ¾ cup catsup, ½ cup tomato juice, ¼ cup water, ½ cup oatmeal, ½ tablespoon salt, ¾ teaspoon pepper, 2 tablespoons brown sugar, 1½ teaspoon Worcestershire sauce, 2½ slices cheese. Simmer until oatmeal disappears. Serve over baked potatoes, top with bacon bits, grated cheese, diced tomatoes, green onions and lettuce. Add dressing. Dressing: Miracle Whip, Vinegar, Sugar, Sour Cream, Seasoned Salt. Mix according to taste.

Karen, Mrs. Rick Penner

Cheese Potatoes

4 large potatoes
1 cup sour cream
1 onion (diced)

1 teaspoon salt
1 can cream of mushroom soup
1 pound grated cheese

Boil potatoes, cool and grate. Combine all ingredients and put in the crockpot. Dot the top with butter and sprinkle a little paprika. Cook on low 4 to 6 hours.

Elaine, Mrs. Bruce Unruh   Yield: 8 servings

Delicious Potatoes

2 pounds frozen hash brown
   potatoes
1 to 2 cups shredded longhorn
   style cheese
¾ cup sour cream
½ cup melted margarine

2 tablespoons dried onion or
   ¼ cup minced onion
2 cans cream of chicken soup
2 cups crushed corn flakes
¼ cup melted margarine
salt and pepper

Let potatoes thaw. Place in a greased 2 quart casserole. Salt and pepper the potatoes if desired. Add or sprinkle with onion. Mix together the cheese, chicken soup, sour cream, ½ cup melted margarine; pour over potatoes, mix. Top with crushed corn flakes that have been mixed with ¼ cup melted margarine. Bake at 350 for 45 minutes.

Bernice Lorenzen

French Onion Soup Potatoes

6 medium size potatoes
1 package French onion soup

1 stick butter

Slice potatoes, thin, place into a 9 x 13" pan. Melt butter and drizzle over potatoes. Sprinkle onion soup over top. Cover with foil and bake at 350 degrees for 1 hour.

Julie Nightengale

Holiday Potatoes

4 pounds potatoes, cooked
1 cup chopped onion
¼ cup butter
1 can cream of celery soup

1 pint dairy sour cream
1½ cups shredded cheese
½ cup corn flakes, crushed
1 teaspoon butter

Grate potatoes, add cheese and set aside; cook onion in butter; stir in soup and sour cream. Pour over potatoes and cheese and mix. Blend corn flakes with butter, spread over top. Bake at 350 degrees for 1 hour. May be refrigerated over night before baking.

Marisa Giesel Wedel

Make Ahead Mashed Potatoes

5 pounds potatoes
2 (3 oz.) packages cream cheese,
  softened
1 cup sour cream

2 teaspoons onion salt
¼ teaspoon pepper
2 tablespoons butter

Cook peeled and sliced potatoes in salted water until tender; drain and mash smooth. Add cream cheese, sour cream, salt, pepper, and butter; beat until light and fluffy. Cool. Cover and place in refrigerator. May be used anytime within 2 weeks. To use, place desired amount in a greased casserole, dot with butter, and bake at 350 degrees about 30 minutes. Freezes well.

Arlene Giesel Koehn

Oven Fried Potatoes

4 large baking potatoes, unpeeled
¼ cup vegetable oil
1-2 tablespoons Parmesan cheese
½ teaspoon salt

¼ teaspoon garlic powder
¼ teaspoon paprika
⅛ teaspoon pepper

Wash unpeeled potatoes and cut lengthwise into 4 wedges. Place skin side down in a 13 x 9" baking dish. Combine remaining ingredients; brush over potatoes. Bake at 375 degrees for 1 hour, brushing with oil cheese mixture at 15 minute intervals. Turn potatoes over for last 15 minutes.

Renee Koehn

Yield: 4 servings

Potato-broccoli-cheese Bake

2 tablespoons butter or margarine
2 tablespoons all-purpose flour
2 cups milk
1 (3 oz.) package cream cheese,
  cubed
½ cup shredded Swiss cheese
1 teaspoon salt
⅛ teaspoon ground nutmeg

⅛ teaspoon pepper
1 (16 oz.) package frozen shredded
  hash brown potatoes, thawed
1 (10 oz.) package frozen chopped
  broccoli, cooked and drained
¼ cup dry bread crumbs
1 tablespoon melted butter or
  margarine

Melt 2 tablespoons butter in a heavy Dutch oven over low heat; add flour and cook 1 minute, stirring constantly. Gradually add milk; cook over medium heat, stirring constantly, until thicken and bubbly. Add cream cheese, Swiss cheese, salt, nutmeg, and pepper; cook over low heat, stirring constantly, until cheese melts. Add potatoes , and stir well. Spoon one-half of potato mixture into a lightly greased 9-inch square baking dish; spread broccoli evenly over potatoes. Spoon remaining potatoes over broccoli layer. Cover and bake at 350 degrees for 35 minutes. Combine bread crumbs and 1 tablespoon melted butter, stirring to coat bread crumbs; sprinkle over casserole, bake, uncovered an additional 10-15 minutes.

Arlene Giesel Koehn

Yield: 8 servings

Roasted Potatoes

6 baking potatoes
¼ cup margarine, melted
1 teaspoon sweet basil
1 teaspoon salt

2 tablespoons dried bread crumbs
½ cup shredded low fat Mozzarella
cheese

Peel potatoes and place in cold water. Place one potato at a time on a wooden spoon, large enough to cradle it. Slice down at ⅛ inch intervals across potato. Return potatoes to cold water. When ready to roast, dry potatoes and place in a greased 8 x 8" pan. Combine oleo, basil, and salt, brush over potatoes. Bake at 425 degrees for 35 minutes. Sprinkle with crumbs and cheese. Continue to bake for additional 10 minutes or until done.

Betty, Mrs. Gordon Unruh

Scalloped Potatoes

½ cup finely chopped onion
2 tablespoons flour
1 teaspoon salt
¼ teaspoon pepper

4 cups pared, thinly sliced potatoes
3 tablespoons butter or margarine,
divided
2 cups milk

Combine onion, flour, salt and pepper. Place ⅓ potatoes in greased 2 quart baking dish. Sprinkle with ½ flour mixture; dot with 1 tablespoon spoon butter. Repeat with ⅓ potatoes, ½ flour mixture and 1 tablespoon butter. Top with ⅓ potatoes and 1 tablespoon butter. Pour milk over to barely cover potatoes. Bake covered at 325 degrees for 45 minutes. Uncover baking dish and bake 30 minutes longer or until potatoes are tender.

Jackie Koehn   6-8 servings

Scalloped Potatoes

3 tablespoons margarine
1 small onion, chopped
3 tablespoons flour
1 teaspoon salt
1½ cup milk

1 cup cheddar cheese, shredded
5 medium potatoes, peeled and
thinly sliced
¼ teaspoon paprika

Preheat oven to 375 degrees. In 2 quart saucepan over medium heat, in hot margarine, cook onion until tender, about 5 minutes. Stir in flour and salt until blended; cook 1 minute. Gradually stir in milk and cook , stirring constantly, until mixture thickens slightly. Remove saucepan from heat; stir in ¼ cup shredded cheese. In shallow 2 quart casserole, arrange half potato slices; pour ½ of the sauce on top. Sprinkle with half of the remaining cheese; repeat. Sprinkle with paprika. Bake covered 45 minutes. Uncover and bake 15 minutes longer or until potatoes are tender.

Pat, Mrs. Mitchell Unruh

Sliced Baked Potatoes

4 medium even potatoes
1 teaspoon salt
2-3 tablespoons melted butter
2-3 tablespoons chopped fresh
   herbs such as parsley, chives,
   thyme or sage or 2-3 tablespoons
   dried herbs of your choice

4 tablespoons grated Cheddar cheese
1½ tablespoons Parmesan cheese

Peel or scrub potatoes. Cut potatoes into thin slices but not all the way through. Put potatoes in baking dish Fan them slightly. Sprinkle with salt and drizzle with butter. Sprinkle with herbs. Bake at 425 degrees for 50 minutes. Remove from oven. Sprinkle with cheeses. Bake an additional 10-15 minutes until lightly browned, and cheeses are melted.

Carolyn, Mrs. Wayne Holdeman

Layered Sweet Potato Casserole

6-8 medium sweet potatoes
¾ cup packed brown sugar
¼ cup butter

1 can whole cranberry sauce
½ cup orange juice

Boil sweet potatoes in jackets until done; peel and cut in slices. Place half the slices in a layer in buttered casserole. Add half the brown sugar; dot with half the butter. Add a layer of cranberry sauce. Repeat layers; pour orange juice over top. Bake at 350 degree oven until heated through.

Arlene Giesel Koehn

Maple-glazed Sweet Potatoes and Apples

3 pounds sweet potatoes, peeled, cut
   crosswise into ¼ inch rounds
1¾ pounds tart green apples, peeled,
   halved, cored, cut into ¼ inch slices

¾ cup pure maple syrup
¼ cup apple cider
¼ cup unsalted butter, cut in pieces
½ teaspoon salt

Preheat oven to 375 degrees. In 13 x 9 inch glass baking dish, alternate potato and apple slices in rows, packing tightly. Combine remaining ingredients in heavy saucepan and bring to a boil over high heat. Pour hot syrup over potatoes and apples. Cover dish tightly with foil and bake 1 hour. Uncover casserole. Reduce temperature to 350 degrees. Bake until potatoes and apples are tender and syrup is reduced to thick glaze, basting occasionally, about 45 minutes. Let stand 10 minutes.

Arlene Giesel Koehn

8 servings

Mushroom Almond Rice

1 cup uncooked rice
1 cup chopped onion, or to taste
4 tablespoons butter, divided
2 cups beef bouillon

¼ teaspoon pepper
½ cup sliced almonds
1 small can mushrooms

Cook onions and rice in 2 tablespoons butter till onions are tender and rice is golden. Add bouillon and pepper. Stir well. Heat to boiling, cover pan, reduce heat and simmer 15 minutes, till rice is done. Saute almonds and mushrooms in 2 tablespoons butter. Add to rice. Toss and serve. I got this recipe from one of my dear Gallup friends. I serve this with pork or chicken.

Michelle, Mrs. Richard Ensz   6 servings

Rice Pilaff

¼ cup oleo
¾ cup chopped onion
1 cup chopped celery
1 cup raw rice
1 envelope Lipton chicken noodle
   soup mix

2½ cups water
1 teaspoon salt
¼ teaspoon sage
¼ teaspoon pepper
¼ teaspoon thyme

In skillet heat oleo and saute onion, celery, and rice until rice is golden brown. Stir in remaining ingredients. Cover and simmer on low heat for 20 minutes. Remove from heat and let stand 10 minutes before lifting lid.

Jul Nightengale; Donna, Mrs. Donavan Nikkel

Mexican Fried Rice

1 stick margarine
1 large onion chopped
2 cups rice
1 bell pepper (diced)

1½ teaspoon garlic salt
1½ teaspoon cumin
1½ teaspoon oregano
4 cups chicken broth

Melt margarine. Brown rice, onion, pepper and spices until golden brown. Add broth and simmer until done (about 30 minutes).

LeAnne Nichols

Sauerkraut

1 quart sauerkraut, rinse jar with ½ cup water	1 pound wieners, sliced into small pieces
1 head cabbage, shredded	

Simmer kraut and cabbage slowly until fresh cabbage changes to color of kraut. Add wieners and serve.

Soon after we were married in 1951, we visited Grandma Carrie. I marveled, how she could fix a meal in her small kitchen, an old time cook stove, few cabinets, and small work table. Going back and forth to her small pantry for supplies. She prepared sauerkraut for us that day, using the above recipe, with one exception; she used 1 quart home canned sausage in place of the wieners.

Jennie, Mrs. Calvin Unruh

Squash Casserole

2 pounds Zucchini, sliced	1 small onion, chopped
1 tablespoon melted margarine	salt and pepper to taste
1 can cream of chicken soup, undiluted	8 ounces sour cream
½ cup melted margarine	2 tablespoons chopped pimiento
	1 (8 oz.) package stuffing mix

Cook squash and onion until tender in a small amount boiling water; drain. Season with salt and pepper and 1 tablespoon margarine. Stir in sour cream, soup and pimiento. Combine ½ cup margarine and stuffing mix, stirring until well blended. Combine half stuffing mix and squash mixture. Spoon into a 2 quart casserole. Top with remaining stuffing mix. Bake at 375 degrees for 30 minutes.

Janice, Mrs. Jerry Ratzlaff

Squash Cheese Casserole

5 cups diced raw summer squash, zucchini or yellow	1 (8 oz.) sour cream
	2 cups shredded cheese
1 small onion, chopped	salt and pepper to taste
1 can cream of celery soup	buttered crumbs

Cover squash and onion with water; cook until tender, drain. Mix soup, seasonings, sour cream, and cheese. Add squash, stir; pour into buttered casserole and top with buttered crumbs. Bake 45 minutes at 350 degrees.

Betty Giesel Martens

Serves 10

Squash Casserole

2 pounds squash	3 tablespoons brown sugar
2 eggs	1 teaspoon salt
½ medium onion, chopped	1½ cups shredded cheddar cheese
6 tablespoons margarine	Round Butter crackers, crushed
½ cup milk	butter or margarine

Cook squash in a small amount water until tender; drain well and mash. Saute onion in margarine, add squash, beaten eggs, milk, brown sugar, and salt to onions, mix well. In a buttered 2-quart casserole, place a layer of 10 crushed crackers, 1 layer of squash mixture, 1 layer of cheese. Repeat the layers; top with cracker crumbs and dots of butter. Bake uncovered for 45 minutes, at 350 degrees. Can be frozen.

Arlene Giesel Koehn   Yield: 8-10 servings

Squash and Dressing

1 stick oleo	1 box Stove Top dressing

Melt butter and mix with dry dressing; reserve 1 cup and spread remaining mix in bottom of a 9" x 13" baking dish. 2 cups yellow squash, 1 small onion, 1 can cream mushroom soup, 1 cup sour cream. Steam squash and onion until tender; mix together with soup, and sour cream. Add to dressing mix, place reserved dressing mix on top. Sprinkle with cheese. Bake at 350 degrees for 30 minutes.

Cherylyn, Mrs. Mike Unruh

Fried Tomatoes

Slice tomatoes into ¼ inch slices; dip into seasoned flour (salt, pepper and paprika) then into beaten egg, cover both sides with cracker crumbs. Saute in margarine, about 10 minutes. Serve.

Betty, Giesel Martens

Company Vegetables

24 oz. package mixed vegetables	½ teaspoon pepper
(cauliflower, broccoli, carrots)	1½ cups Swiss American cheese
1½ can cream of mushroom soup	4 oz. can French Fried onions
¾ cup sour cream	

Mix all ingredients, except ¾ cup cheese and onions. Bake covered at 350 degrees for 30 minutes. Sprinkle remaining cheese and onion on top. Return to oven and bake for 5 minutes.

Serena Amoth

Vegetable Bake

1 (16 oz.) package frozen California
    Blend vegetables
1 large onion, chopped
4 tablespoons butter
1 (4 oz.) can mushrooms or
    fresh sliced

1 can cream of chicken soup
1 cup sour cream
1 cup cheddar cheese, grated
1 cup slivered almonds
1½ cup croutons

Thaw vegetables. In large skillet, saute onion and mushrooms in butter, over medium heat. Remove from pan, add vegetables to skillet, cover and stir frequently, about 10 minutes. Remove from heat. Add onion and mushrooms, soup and sour cream, cheese and almonds. Place in greased 9" x 13" pan. Sprinkle croutons over top. Bake at 350 degrees until hot and bubbly.

Arlene Giesel Koehn

Vegetable Casserole

1 pound process cheese
2 hard cooked eggs, chopped
1 cup mayonnaise
2 (16 oz.) cans mixed vegetables,
    drained

1 (16 oz.) can English peas, drained
1 cup chopped celery
1 cup finely chopped onion
1 (8 oz.) package cornbread dressing
    with herbs

Freeze cheese before grating. In large bowl combine cheese, eggs, and mayonnaise together. Add mixed vegetables, peas, celery, and onion; blend well. Pour into a 3 quart casserole and top with cornbread dressing. Bake at 325 degrees for 30-40 minutes.

Arlene Giesel Koehn   Yield: 10-12 servings

Vegetable Variety

1 can cut green beans, drained
1 can mixed vegetables, drained

1 can cream of chicken soup

Combine all ingredients, mixing well. Place in a 8" x 8" greased dish. Top with crushed potato chips and dot with butter. Bake in 350 degree oven for 45 minutes.

Mornie Giesel Unruh

Batter for French Fried Vegetables

1 egg yolk, well beaten
⅜ cup milk
½ cup sifted flour

1 tablespoon melted butter
salt and pepper to taste
1¼ teaspoon baking powder

To well beaten egg yolk add milk and melted butter. Mix and sift in flour and baking powder. Beat until thoroughly mixed, and smooth. Stir in salt and pepper.

Arlene Giesel Koehn

Carnation Three Minute Cheese Sauce

1⅔ cup carnation milk
½ teaspoon salt
1 teaspoon dry mustard

1 tablespoon steak sauce
2 cups grated process American
  cheese

Simmer Carnation, salt, mustard and steak sauce in saucepan over low heat, just below boiling (about 2 minutes). Add cheese; stir over low heat until cheese melts, 1 minute longer.

Arlene Giesel Koehn

Sauce for Baked Potatoes

1 pound Velveeta cheese
2 cans cheddar cheese soup
3 pounds ground beef, browned

2 cans chili beans
1 pound cheddar cheese
8 oz mild picante sauce

Make a white sauce: melt 1 stick oleo, and stir in ½ cup flour, blending until smooth, add 6 cups milk. Cook until thickened and comes to a boil. Mix all ingredients together, place in a crock pot and simmer until ready to serve. Serve over baked potatoes.

Carol, Mrs. Gary Koehn   Yield: 15-20 servings

Topping for Cooked Vegetables

A special topping for cooked vegetables or casseroles can be made by crushing ½ cup herb-seasoned stuffing mix with 2 tablespoons melted butter; top dish with this mixture and sprinkle with 1 cup shredded cheese.

Arlene Giesel Koehn

Blackberry Delight

1 cup blackberries
1 cup cantaloupe, cubed
1 cup honeydew, cubed
1 cup watermelon, cubed

1 cup grapes, seedless
3 bananas, sliced
1 tablespoon powdered sugar

Mix all fruits together in a bowl; chill for 2 hours. Sprinkle sugar over fruit before serving.

Arlene Giesel Koehn

Candied Apples

12 apples, peeled and quartered
¼ cup water

1½ cups sugar
½ cup red hot candies

Mix all ingredients together and cook over low heat until apples are tender. Mix 3 tablespoons cornstarch and ¼ cup water, stir until smooth, add to apples and continue to cook until clear. Serve hot or chilled.

Deloris, Mrs. Isaac Unruh, Jr.

Delicious Fruit Bowl

1 large apple, diced
2 cups seedless grapes
2 tangerines, diced
1 orange, diced
½ cup raisins
2 bananas, sliced

1 cup candied cherries, chopped
¾ cup coconut, grated
1 cup strawberries, diced
2 tablespoons sugar
1 cup walnuts, chopped
½ cup pecans, chopped

Combine all fruits; add coconut and nuts. Sprinkle with sugar. Chill 2 hours before serving.

Arlene Giesel Koehn   Serves 6

Gingered Fruit Compote

1 tablespoon cornstarch
1 tablespoon sugar
⅛ teaspoon ground ginger
1 cup pineapple or orange juice

1 cup fresh blueberries
1½ cups fresh strawberries
1½ cups fresh pineapple chunks
1 cup fresh sliced peaches

Combine first 3 ingredients in a small saucepan; gradually add pineapple juice, stirring until smooth. Bring mixture to a boil over medium heat; boil 1 minute, stirring constantly. Remove from heat, and cool. Combine fruit in a large bowl. Pour sauce over fruit; toss gently. Chill.

Arlene Giesel Koehn   Yield: 8 servings

Hot Fruit Casserole

1 (25 oz.) can apple sauce
⅓ cup butter
¾ cup dark brown sugar
1 (16 oz.) can pears
1 (20 oz.) can pineapple
1 (16 oz.) can peaches

1 (6 oz.) jar maraschino cherries
1 (16 oz.) can purple plums
2 bananas
½ cup chopped nuts
3 tablespoons brown sugar

Melt butter and sugar. Add applesauce, and blend well. Cut up canned fruit and drain, and remove seeds from plums. Slice bananas and add whole maraschino cherries (drained) to other fruit. Place fruit in a 3 quart baking dish and top with applesauce mixture. Sprinkle with remaining 3 tablespoons brown sugar and nuts. Bake at 300 degrees for 1 hour.

Arlene Giesel Koehn

Serves 12-15

Layered Ambrosia

3 cups orange sections
1 cup pink grapefruit sections
½ cup flaked coconut

1 (8 oz) can unsweetened crushed
    pineapple, undrained
3 tablespoons honey

Arrange half of orange sections in a glass bowl; top with grapefruit sections, ¼ cup coconut, pineapple, and remaining orange sections. Drizzle with honey, and sprinkle with remaining ¼ cup coconut. Cover and chill 8 hours.

Arlene Giesel Koehn

Pluma Moos

½ cup raisins
1½ cups prunes

2½ cups water

Simmer over low heat, for 30 minutes. Remove fruit from liquid, reserve liquid, add water if necessary to equal 1½ cups. Make a paste using the 1½ cup liquid, 1¼ cup sugar, 2½ tablespoons cornstarch, 2½ tablespoons flour, ¼ teaspoon salt, ¼ teaspoon cinnamon, ⅓ cup milk and ⅓ cup cream. Bring to a boil, stir constantly; cook until sauce thickens, remove from heat and let cool 10 minutes. Slowly add 3 cups buttermilk and prunes and raisins. Cool and serve. This recipe comes from my friend Ormah.

Arlene Giesel Koehn

Pluma Moos (Cold)

¾ cup raisins
6 dried prunes, pitted
⅓ cup sugar
1½ cups water
1 cup milk

½ cup heavy cream
⅛ cup plus 1 tablespoon flour
¼ teaspoon salt
¼ teaspoon cinnamon
¼ teaspoon ground star anise, optional

Cover fruits with water. Stir in sugar and bring to boil. Reduce heat; cover and simmer until fruit is tender, about 10 minutes. Mix milk, cream, flour, salt and spices, blending well. Stir mixture into fruit, cook over low heat, stirring constantly until bubbly and slightly thickened. Chill overnight. Stir to blend before serving.

Edna Giesel   Makes about 3½ cups

Poached Apples and Pears with Berry Sauce

4 cups apple, or apple raspberry juice
1 cup finely chopped strawberries
   or raspberries
2 slices lemon
1 1-inch cinnamon stick

½ teaspoon vanilla
2 whole golden or red delicious
   apples, peeled
2 whole Bosc pears, peeled

Combine apple juice, berries, lemon slices, cinnamon stick, and vanilla. Bring to a boil over high heat, reduce to a simmer, add apples and pears, cover and cook 12 minutes. or until done. Remove apples and pears with a slotted spoon and set aside in a covered dish to keep warm. Continue cooking the juice and berries until liquid is reduced to a thick sauce, about 25 minutes. Divide fruit among 4 plates and drizzle the sauce over each serving.

Arlene Giesel Koehn   Serves 4

Scalloped Pineapple

Drain 1 (20 oz.) can chunk pineapple and layer in a casserole. Grate ¼ pound cheddar cheese and sprinkle over pineapple. Mix together ½ cup sugar and ½ cup flour, sprinkle over cheese. Pour reserved pineapple juice over all. Bake 325 degrees for 1 hour. Delicious served with ham.

Valetta, Mrs. John Koehn

Topping Just for Fruit

1 (8 oz.) carton sour cream
¼ cup orange juice
¼ cup flaked coconut

¼ cup chopped walnuts
3 tablespoons peach, apricot,
   or peach preserves

Combine all ingredients; stir well. Chill 2-3 hours. Serve with assorted fruit.

Arlene Giesel Koehn   Yield: 1¼ cups

Nutty Fruit Dressing

1 (7 oz.) jar marshmallow cream
⅓ cup pineapple juice
1 teaspoon almond extract

2 teaspoons lemon juice
1 cup salted peanuts, coarsely
  chopped

Combine first 4 ingredients; mix well. Stir in peanuts. Chill well. Stir before serving. Serve over assorted fresh fruits.

Arlene Giesel Koehn

Yield: 1⅓ cups

TIP: To give prunes a new flavor, soak them in pineapple or other juice instead of plain water. Allow them to stand as usual, until plump and soft.

Arlene Giesel Koehn

BREADS

Broccoli Cornbread

1 box frozen broccoli
1 box Jiffy cornbread mix
1 medium onion, chopped
4 eggs, beaten
1 stick butter, melted

½ cup milk
1 cup cheese(cheddar), grated
4 tablespoons sugar
½ teaspoon salt

Mix all ingredients together. Place in 8x8 baking dish. Bake at 375 degrees for 25 minutes, or until done.

Shana Koehn

Cornbread

1½ cups corn meal (preferably white)
1½ cups flour
6 teaspoons baking powder

½ teaspoon salt
½ cup shortening
1 egg
Milk to make a stiff dough

Beat one minute. Grease pan and bake at 450 degrees until brown. (Sprinkle sugar on top).

Jul Nightengale

Mom's Corn Bread

1 cup flour
1 cup yellow cornmeal
2 teaspoons baking powder

2 teaspoons sugar
1 cup liquid (½ cream and ½ milk)

Mix and pour in 9x9 inch greased pan, sprinkle top with sugar. Bake for 20 minutes in 400 degree oven.

Deloris, Mrs. Isaac Unruh, Jr.

Bread Stuffing

12 cups bread, cubed and toasted
¼ cup butter, melted
¾ cup finely chopped onion
1½ cup chopped celery

1 tablespoon salt
1 tablespoon sage(scant)
1 teaspoon pepper
1 tablespoon poultry seasoning(scant)

Saute onion in butter, stir in some bread crumbs, stirring to prevent excessive browning. Place in a large bowl, add celery, salt, sage, pepper and poultry seasoning. Mix in enough hot water to moisten dry crumbs. Place stuffing in 12 pound turkey.

Coreen Holdeman

Chicken Dressing

6 cups bread crumbs	dash of pepper
1 teaspoon salt	1¼ teaspoon sage
11 oz. can condensed cream of chicken soup	2 tablespoons onion (chopped)
	½ cup melted margarine

Mix well. Stuff chicken or arrange on other type of meat.

Nancy, Mrs. Kenneth Unruh

Corn Bread Dressing

Make and bake a 9"x13" pan of cornbread. Set aside. Cook one chicken, debone, and save broth.

Sauté:

¾ to 1 stick oleo	1 small onion, chopped
½ to 1 cup chopped green onion	1 cup fine chopped celery

In a large bowl mix:

crumbled corn bread	2 teaspoons sage
½ box crushed saltine crackers	salt and pepper to taste
6 raw eggs	2½ to 3 cups broth
3 or 4 boiled eggs, chopped fine	cut up chicken pieces

Bake at 250 degrees until hot.

Kathy Wedel

Turkey Dressing

1 loaf of bread	1 teaspoon poultry seasoning
1 quart milk	1 apple
2 cups sugar	½ cup (approx.) raisins

Bring milk to boil. Mix while hot with rest of ingredients.

Sophie Giesel Koehn

Turkey Dressing (Microwave)

1 box stove top dressing	1½ to 2 cups boiling water

Add 2 teaspoons chicken bouillon and seasoning mix that comes in the stove box dressing to boiling water. Stir until dissolved. 1 jar pimientos (small), one half cup celery, diced, one half onion, diced, one egg beaten well. Mix all together and fill cavity of turkey. Put the turkey in a browning bag and microwave, allowing about 8 minutes per pound. Then let set 15 minutes before carving. Delicious and juicy. Never salt meat before cooking.

Carolyn, Mrs. Wayne Holdeman

Banana French Toast with Blueberry Topping

No-stick cooking spray
¾ cup skim milk
¾ cup (1 medium) banana, sliced

2 egg whites
¼ teaspoon nutmeg
8 slices whole wheat bread

Blueberry Topping:
1 tablespoon cornstarch
¼ teaspoon cinnamon
½ cup water

2 tablespoons honey
2 cups frozen blueberries

Heat oven to 425 degrees. Spray 15x10x1 inch baking pan with cooking spray. In blender container or food processor bowl with metal blade, combine milk, banana, egg whites and nutmeg. Blend until smooth. Pour into shallow bowl or pie pan. Dip bread slices in egg mixture; place in sprayed pan. Pour any remaining mixture over bread slices. Bake at 425 degrees for 12 minutes. Turn and bake an additional 10 minutes or until golden brown. Meanwhile, in small saucepan combine cornstarch, cinnamon, water and honey; blend well. Stir in blueberries. Cook over medium heat until mixture boils and thickens, stirring constantly. Serve over French toast.

Arlene Giesel Koehn 4 servings

French Toast

3 eggs, beaten
1¼ cups cream
⅛ teaspoon salt

2 tablespoons sugar
¼ teaspoon cinnamon
½ teaspoon vanilla

Blend ingredients, grease skillet lightly only once, then dampen bread on both sides in liquid and fry to light brown on both sides. The cream helps to keep the bread from sticking to the skillet. Serve with your favorite syrup.

Coreen Holdeman

French Toast or Fried Bread

6 slices of bread
1 cup milk
1 egg, slightly beaten
1 teaspoon vanilla

¼ teaspoon salt
2 tablespoons sugar
1 teaspoon cinnamon

Combine and blend all ingredients except bread. Dip bread in mixture, soak it well. Cook on a well greased griddle. Brown both sides. Serve with jelly, syrup, or hot apple sauce, sprinkled with cinnamon. Grandma Mornie gave me this recipe when I was twelve years old. Daddy (Allen) was ill and was on a special diet. Grandma Mornie made me a cookbook with simple recipes. I cherish this cookbook today.

Kathy Wedel

Vanilla French Toast with Slivered Almonds

1 cup slivered almonds	2 eggs
½ cup apple juice	2 egg whites
2 tablespoons honey	2 teaspoons vegetable oil
1½ teaspoons vanilla extract	8 slices whole-grain bread

Preheat oven to 325 degrees. Place nuts on a baking tray and toast in the oven until golden brown, about 10 minutes. Remove and set aside. In a small saucepan, bring the apple juice to a boil over high heat. Reduce to a simmer and add the honey. Stir to melt. Add the vanilla extract and remove from heat. Cool to room temperature. In a large bowl, whisk together the eggs and egg whites. Add the apple-honey mixture and whisk to combine. Warm a large skillet over medium heat. Add one teaspoon of the oil and when hot, dip a slice of bread into the egg mixture and drop it into the pan. Add enough slices to fill the skillet with one layer. Cook for about four minutes per side, or until golden brown. Repeat with each slice of bread, adding oil as needed. Remove the toast to a baking pan and cook 6 minutes in the oven, or until the toast looks puffy. Top with toasted almonds, and serve with maple syrup.

Arlene Giesel Koehn   Serves four

Crepes

This recipe was given to me by a friend from France.

2 cups flour	5 eggs

Mix together and add: 4 cups milk and one third cup oil. Let rest 1 hour. Fry in a large skillet. Serve with your choice of syrup or fruit.

Jackie Koehn

Crullers Roll Kuchen

½ cup sweet cream	1 teaspoon salt
½ cup milk	1 teaspoon sugar
2 eggs	3½ - 4 cups flour
1 teaspoon baking soda	

Beat eggs, add cream and milk. Sift dry ingredients together and add to liquid. Use just enough flour so that dough can be rolled but is still soft. When well mixed, let stand 2 hours. Punch down, roll out ⅜ inch thick and cut into oblong strips 2x7 inches. Cut 2 slashes through strip crosswise to aid in frying. Fry in deep fat (365 degrees) until light brown on both sides. Yield: 3½ dozen. If a sweet cruller is preferred, add ½ cup sugar to mixture. These are good served with watermelon.

Betty Giesel Martens

Buttermilk Pancakes

2 cups flour
1½ teaspoon soda
2 eggs
a little sugar (optional)

2 teaspoons salt
2 cups buttermilk
¼ cup oil

Mix dry ingredients in a bowl. Make a well in the center and put buttermilk, oil and eggs in well. Blend well. Bake on hot griddle. (I was given this recipe by my Aunt Jerry Dirks, before I was married—it's the only one that works for me!) You may want to use whole wheat flour so your pancakes will stay with you longer.

Janice, Mrs. Jerry Ratzlaff

Light and Fluffy Pancakes

2 eggs
3 tablespoons oil
1¾ cup milk
1½ teaspoons salt

2 tablespoons sugar
2 tablespoons baking powder
2 cups flour

Beat eggs. Stir in oil and milk. Beat in dry ingredients. Bake in oiled electric skillet at 375 degrees, till bubbles appear on tops of pancakes. Turn. Whole wheat flour may be substituted for some of the white flour.

Jolene Unruh

Mom's Pancakes

1½ cup flour
1 tablespoon baking powder
1½ tablespoons sugar
1 rounded teaspoon soda
scant teaspoon salt

1 egg
¾ cup buttermilk
¾ cup milk
2 tablespoons oil

Stir dry ingredients together. Slightly beat egg and add to dry mixture along with buttermilk, milk and oil. Fry on hot griddle. Makes approximately 12. (Of course, no one can make pancakes like Mom).

Jana, Mrs. Robert Nichols

Quick Mix

(I use for pancakes.)

10 cups flour	4 teaspoons salt
1¼ cups powdered milk	2 cups vegetable shortening
⅓ cup baking powder	

Blend to cut in shortening. Store in an airtight container at room temperature for up to 2 weeks. To keep longer, store in refrigerator or freezer.

Pancakes: 2 cups mix, 2 teaspoons sugar. Add 1 beaten egg and 1¼ cup water. Bake on preheated griddle. One reason I like this mix is because it has powdered milk in the ingredients, so when you mix it you just need to add water.

Elaine, Mrs. David Unruh

Club Soda Waffles

2 cups biscuit mix	½ cup oil
1 egg, beaten	1⅓ cups club soda

Mix ingredients together, pour in waffle maker and enjoy!

Arlene Giesel Koehn

Angel Biscuits

Angel biscuits are so named because they rise more than the traditional biscuit due to the addition of yeast. They're lighter and airier— like a roll.

2 packages dry yeast	¼ cup sugar
¼ cup warm water (105 to 115 degrees)	1 tablespoon baking powder
2 cups buttermilk	1 teaspoon baking soda
5 cups all-purpose flour	1 teaspoon salt
	1 cup shortening

Combine yeast and warm water; let stand 5 minutes. Add buttermilk to yeast mixture, and set aside. Combine all remaining ingredients except shortening in a large bowl; cut in shortening with a pastry blender until mixture resembles coarse meal. Add buttermilk mixture, stirring with a fork until dry ingredients are moistened. Roll dough to ½ inch thickness; cut with a 2½ inch biscuit cutter. Place on lightly greased baking sheets. Cover and let rise in a warm place (85 degrees), free from drafts, for 1 hour. Bake at 450 degrees for 10 to 12 minutes or until browned. Yield: 2 dozen. Note: Biscuits can be made ahead and frozen. Before freezing biscuits, bake 10 minutes; cool. Place biscuits in freezer bags, and freeze. To prepare biscuits for serving, remove from freezer; place biscuits on lightly greased baking sheets, and let thaw. Bake at 450 degrees for 5 minutes or until thoroughly heated.

Arlene Giesel Koehn

Daisy Biscuits

Separate one package refrigerator biscuits. Using a kitchen scissors, make 5 small cuts around the edge of each biscuit, cutting about halfway to center. Make a depression in the center of each biscuit with your thumb. Spoon ½ teaspoon of your favorite jam into each thumb print. Bake according to package directions.

Charmaine Wedel

Soft-As-Cloud Sour Cream Biscuits

1 cup all-purpose flour
2 teaspoons baking powder
1 teaspoon sugar
¼ teaspoon baking soda

¼ teaspoon salt
½ cup commercial sour cream
¼ cup half and half

Combine first 5 ingredients; stir well. Combine sour cream and half and half; add to flour mixture, stirring with a fork until dry ingredients are moistened. Turn dough out onto a lightly floured surface, and knead lightly 4 or 5 times. Roll dough to ½ inch thickness, and cut with a floured 2 inch biscuit cutter. Place biscuits on an ungreased baking sheet; bake at 425 degrees for 8-10 minutes.

Arlene Giesel Koehn   Yield: 10 biscuits

Quick Mix

(I use for biscuits.)

Mix together:
8 cups flour
⅓ cup baking powder
2 teaspoons salt

8 teaspoon sugar (optional)
(I use ¼ cup)

With pastry blender cut in 1 cup shortening until the mixture resembles coarse meal. Store in airtight, covered container. The mixture will keep on the shelf or for longer storage keep in the refrigerator or freezer. To make biscuits: Add ⅓ cup milk for every cup of mix. This mix can be made into pancakes, waffles, dumplings, etc. (I like to use this best of all for biscuits. Also for shortcake. For shortcake I add a little more sugar, a little more milk, so it's thin enough to spread. Also spread it out thin in the pan. Then sprinkle sugar on top. Put sugared fresh or frozen fruit on top after it has been baked. For more calories, cool whip could go over top.)

Elaine, Mrs. David Unruh

"Beginner's Rolls"

Put 4 tablespoons yeast in 1 cup warm water. Scald 2 cups milk. Pour milk into mixer bowl. Add 2 sticks oleo and stir to melt. Add 1 cup ice cold water, 1 cup powdered potato flakes, 1 tablespoon salt and 1¼ cups sugar. Stir while beating 3 eggs. Add eggs to mixer - then add yeast. Add 6 cups flour and beat till smooth. Continue adding flour till you have a soft dough. "Call Mom to check it."

Let rise once - punch down. Let rise again and form rolls. Bake at 350 degrees. Butterhorns - 10 minutes and check. Cinnamon rolls - 15 minutes and check.

Melissa, Mrs. Jason Koehn

Butterhorns

1 cake yeast	1 teaspoon salt
½ cup sugar	1 cup warm water
3 eggs	4½ - 5 cups flour
½ cup melted margarine	

Bind yeast with 1 tablespoon sugar and warm water. Add beaten eggs. Add rest of ingredients. Put in refrigerator overnight. Use for doughnuts, cinnamon rolls, any others.

Glaze:

1 pound powdered sugar	1 teaspoon vanilla
1 tablespoon melted butter	1 package gelatin

Soften gelatin in ¼ cup cold water. Dissolve in ½ cup boiling water. Add butter and vanilla. Then add powdered sugar gradually.

LeAnne Nichols

Butterhorns

2 cups lukewarm water	1 cup melted oleo
2 packages yeast	2 teaspoons salt
2 tablespoons sugar	6 eggs
1 cup sugar	9-10 cups flour

Blend yeast with 2 tablespoons sugar and water. Add beaten eggs. Add rest of ingredients. Put in refrigerator overnight. Roll as for pie dough and shape into crescents. Dip in melted oleo. Let rise 3 hours. Bake at 350 degrees about 15 minutes or until light brown.

Donna, Mrs. Quinn Schmidt

Dinner Rolls

1 cup milk
⅓ cup shortening
⅓ cup sugar
2 eggs

1 package yeast
3-5 cups flour
butter or margarine for spreading

Place milk, shortening and sugar in pan. Heat and stir until shortening is almost melted (125 degrees). Mix 2 cups flour and yeast, add milk mixture. Stir in eggs. Mix with electric mixer on low for 30 seconds. Mix on high for 3 minutes. Stir in more flour a little at a time until dough is moderately stiff. Knead 6-8 minutes. Cover and let rise until double (1 - 1½ hours). Punch down and divide in 2 parts and let rest 10 minutes. Roll out on a floured surface in a circle and cut into 12 pie shaped pieces. Spread with butter. Start with the wide end and roll to the point. Place on greased cookie sheet (point side down). Let rise until double (35 minutes). Bake at 350 degrees for 8-10 minutes or until golden.

Jeffrey D. Jenkins and Darla J. Jenkins, grandchildren of Nathan Giesel   Makes 24

Easy Yeast Rolls

4½ to 5 cups flour
2 packages yeast
1 cup milk
½ cup oil

¾ cup water
¼ cup sugar
1 teaspoon salt

Put 2 cups flour in large mixing bowl; add yeast and mix. Combine the rest of ingredients, except flour, in saucepan and heat to 110 degrees. Add to flour and yeast, beat 3 minutes. Stir in remaining flour. Let rise 10 minutes. Shape into cinnamon rolls or dinner rolls. Allow to rise 30 minutes. Bake at 350 degrees for 20 to 30 minutes. (Less time for dinner rolls) Let dough rise for only 30 minutes, it will fall while baking if allowed to rise longer.

Coreen Holdeman

Golden Dinner Rolls

2 packages dry yeast	1 tablespoon sugar

Disolve in ½ cup warm water. Beat together:

¾ cup lukewarm potato water	2 eggs, slightly beaten
½ cup mashed potatoes	¼ cup soft shortening
½ cup sugar	¼ cup soft butter or oleo
1½ teaspoons salt	2 cups sifted flour

Add yeast mixture and beat well. Stir in 2 cups sifted flour, all at once. Turn out onto kneading table and knead in an additional ½ cup flour. Place dough in well greased bowl, and let rise till very doubled. Punch down. Cut dough ball into fourths. Roll each fourth into a small circle. Cut each circle into 8 pie shaped wedges. Roll each wedge into a rope and tie into rosettes. Allow to double once more. Bake in 400 degrees oven, 8 to 10 minutes, just till golden brown. Brush roll tops with melted butter after removing from oven. This recipe makes nice cinnamon rolls also.

Finette Giesel Koehn

Instant Miracle Rolls

2 packages yeast	1 cup shortening
½ cup warm water	2 cups lukewarm buttermilk
5 cups unsifted, self-rising flour	(buttermilk must be lukewarm
¼ cup sugar	for rolls to rise)
1 teaspoon soda	

Dissolve yeast in warm water and set aside. Mix flour, sugar and soda. Cut in shortening. Add buttermilk, yeast and mix. Place desired amount of dough on floured surface, roll out and cut with biscuit cutter. Let rise in warm room 10 to 15 minutes. Bake 350 degrees for 15 minutes. This can be made up and kept in air-tight container in the refrigerator for a week to 10 days.

Arlene Giesel Koehn

Makes about 32 rolls

Refrigerator Rolls

2 eggs	1 cup warm mashed potatoes
⅔ cup shortening	1½ cups warm water
1½ teaspoons salt	7½ cups flour
⅔ cup sugar	¾ tablespoon instant dry yeast

Blend the eggs, sugar, shortening, salt, mashed potatoes and water together. Put the instant yeast in sifter with the flour. Put in about ½ of the flour and mix with a hand mixer. Mix and knead till all of the flour has been put in. Refrigerate immediately or let rise twice and bake. If putting in the refrigerator, it may need to be punched down once after it's been in for a few hours. This won't damage the yeast. When getting it out to work with, it works best to leave it at room temperature for several hours to let it warm up and rise, this makes it more pliable to work with. The dough should be just a little cooler than your hand, not cold. If you would like to use the dough right away in the morning, put in a warm oven (so your hand can touch the grates without feeling hot.) This will speed it up a lot. Can be used for cinnamon rolls or buns. This recipe comes from Jennie, but I revised it to use instant yeast.

Elaine, Mrs. David Unruh

Working Girl Rolls

1 package yeast	1 egg
2 cups warm water	¼ cup oil
¼ cup sugar	4 cups self-rising flour

Dissolve yeast in warm water and set aside. Mix sugar, egg and oil. Add flour alternately with yeast mixture. Drop by spoonfuls into greased muffin pans. Bake at 425 degrees for 10-15 minutes.

Charmaine Wedel

Bun Recipe

5 cups water	2 dessert spoons salt
1 cup sugar	2 packages yeast
1 cup lard (preferred)	13 cups flour

Grandma Mornie said she used to make these into coffee cakes and buns before she went to bed. She let them rise all night, then baked them in the morning.

Donna, Mrs. Quinn Schmidt

Raisin Buns

2 tablespoons yeast in 1 cup warm
  water
2½ cups warm water plus about 1
  cup powdered milk (Sometimes
  I use potato water)
3 eggs
3½ teaspoons salt
1 teaspoon cinnamon

½ to 1 cup chopped walnuts
1 cup raisins
1 cup sugar
¾ cup shortening, part butter
  if you like
10-10½ cups flour, just enough
  to make a soft dough

Mix well. Let rise 10 minutes and punch down. Let rise again and punch down. Put in pans, let rise. Bake at 350 degrees until brown. When done, brush top with glaze of 1 teaspoon sugar and some cream or milk.

Sophie Giesel Koehn

Zwieback

2 tablespoons yeast, dissolved in 1
  cup warm water
2 cups warm water
¾ cup powdered milk
2-3 teaspoons salt

1/6 cup sugar
¾ cup shortening (I use part oleo
  and part Crisco)
7 to 7½ cups flour

Dough should be somewhat softer than for bread. Let stand for 10 minutes and punch down. Let rise 30 minutes and punch down. Let rise 30 minutes and put in pan. Pinch off a piece of dough and pinch off another piece about the same size and put on top of the first piece. Press your thumb on top so the top piece stays in place. (I bake them at 400 degrees for about 15 to 18 minutes. I like them brown.) Adjust heat to your oven. Juanita says this is my recipe, I've used so many years I don't remember. I had to learn to bake zwieback after I got married as Jonas was used to having them fresh for supper on Saturday evening with milk of course. Not me, as I do not drink milk.

Sophie Giesel Koehn

French Bread

4 cups potato water
2 packages yeast

1 cup water (for yeast)
2 tablespoons sugar

Dissolve yeast in water. Add:
¼ cup lard
¼ cup sugar

12 cups flour
2 teaspoons to 2 tablespoons salt

Punch down every 15 minutes for 1½ hours. Roll as for jelly roll. Let rise 1 hour or until double. Bake 20 minutes at 400 degrees.

JoEtta Koehn

French Bread

¼ cup warm water
1 teaspoon sugar
1 package yeast
1 teaspoon salt

2 tablespoons sugar
1½ tablespoons oleo
1 cup boiling water
3 to 3½ cups flour

In a small bowl, mix ¼ cup water, 1 teaspoon sugar, and yeast. Let rise while mixing rest of dough. In large bowl of electric mixer, dissolve salt, 2 tablespoons sugar, and oleo in boiling water. Beat in slowly 1 cup flour. When cooled down, add 1 cup flour and yeast mixture. Beat well. Finish adding flour by hand with spoon. Set in warm place to rise. Beat dough down every 10 minutes with spoon, for 6-7 times. Turn out on floured board. Press out ½ inch thick, roll up like jelly roll and pinch edges. Place on greased baking sheet seam side down. Slash top 3 or 4 times. Let rise 30 minutes to 1 hour. Bake 20 minutes at 400 degrees.

This is my standby fast bread recipe—the one I make when it's already 9 o'clock in the morning and there are men coming for dinner! I usually double it and bake both loaves together on a sheet cake pan—that seems to work best for me. You can also quadruple it.

Michele, Mrs. Richard Ensz

French Bread

2½ cups boiled water
2 teaspoons salt

4 tablespoons sugar
4 tablespoons shortening (I use oil)

Mix and cool 2 packages of yeast and 2 teaspoons sugar dissolved in ½ cup warm water. If using instant yeast, mix 2 tablespoons yeast in 2 cups flour and omit the water. Mix in approximately 6½ cups of flour (including 2 cups). Work down 5 times every 10 minutes. Roll out as for cinnamon rolls. Bake at 400 degrees for 20 minutes. For whole wheat bread, use two cups whole wheat flour in place of two cups white.

Beulah, Mrs Dennis Unruh   Makes 4 loaves

Grandma Carrie's White Bread

2 cups warm water
2 teaspoons salt

4 teaspoons sugar
2 tablespoons lard

Put first 3 ingredients in bowl. Sprinkle 1 package yeast over. Add lard and 6 cups flour(more or less). Let rise 2 or 3 times. Bake at 325 degrees 40-50 minutes. Grandma Carrie's bread turned out better than mine does. Grandma had some grandchildren over one evening for supper. She had baked this recipe of bread. Guess we were a hungry bunch. She ran out. she laughed and said that was the first time that had happened to her. She sure was a good grandma.

Beulah, Mrs. Dennis Unruh   Makes 3 loaves

Honey Whole Wheat Bread

1¾ cups warm water	2 packages yeast
½ cup honey	2 eggs, beaten
2 teaspoons salt	6 cups whole wheat flour
½ cup oil	

All ingredients should be room temperature. Mix water, honey and yeast. Let rest for a few minutes. Add eggs, oil, salt and four cups flour. Beat at medium speed for 5 minutes. Add remaining flour and knead with mixer at low speed for another 5 minutes. Bake at 350 degrees for 30 minutes.

Zella Fay Unruh   Makes 3 loaves

Mock French Bread

Since I don't bake nice bread, I devised this method to save my face. If you let the bread thaw and rise real slowly all the time, it'll turn out fine grained and white. But if it rises too fast, such as in summertime heat, the results will give you a yellow heavy loaf.

3 loaves Rhoades frozen bread loaves. Let rise in refrigerator overnight in sealed bag to thaw. Grease large cookie sheet, 10½ x 15½. Grease bread too. Gently squeeze out loaves into long, narrow shape. Do not pull or stretch. Place 2 loaves on one end of the long side. Place third loaf on other end across the width. Let rise until doubled in cold oven. Lightly slash diagonally across the loaves. Starting from a cold oven, bake at 350 degrees for 30 minutes. So, now you know my secret for homemade Bread.

Jennie, Mrs. Calvin Unruh

Pillow Bread

3 cups flour	2 tablespoons yeast
¾ teaspoon salt	1 beaten egg
4 tablespoons sugar	1 cup warm water

Use medium size bowl. Mix dry ingredients together, including yeast, if using instant yeast. Beat egg with fork and mix with water. Add to dry ingredients and mix well. Let rise until doubled. Place dough on floured work surface. Pat out with floured hands. Roll out dough to ¼ inch thick. Quickly cut vertically and horizontally with pizza cutter, making pillows of dough approximately 1 ½x2 inches. Melt one stick oleo and cool slightly. Grease 2 loaf pans. Dunk pillows in melted oleo. Place in pans until evenly filled. Let rise till doubled. Bake 20-30 minutes at 350 degrees. Turn upside down over serving plate.

For a breakfast food or dessert, pillows could also be dipped in cinnamon and sugar after dipping in Oleo.

Jolene Unruh

Rye Bread

1 package dry yeast	2 tablespoons oil
1 cup warm water	2 tablespoons molasses or brown sugar
1 cup milk scalded and cooled	2 cups fine rye flour
1 tablespoon salt	1 egg

Dissolve yeast in warm water. Add all other ingredients. Beat until smooth. Slowly blend in 4½ cups white flour. Knead 5-10 minutes. Allow to rise. Punch down and divide into 2 loaves. Place into 4½" x 8½" pans. Let rise until double in size. Bake at 350 degrees for 35-40 minutes. Butter tops after removing from oven.

I started baking rye bread because our church is required to make it annually for our local nursing home gift day. We like it just as well as whole wheat and it has a finer texture.

Betty Giesel Martens

Whole Wheat Bread

2 packages or 2 tablespoons active dry yeast	2 cups stirred Groth Farms whole wheat flour
½ cup warm water (110 degrees)	1 beaten egg
2 tablespoons white sugar	6½ -7 cups Hudson Cream-Short
3 cups hot water (150 degrees)	Patent white flour, divided
⅓ cup shortening	1 tablespoon Carey salt
⅓ cup brown sugar	

Soften active dry yeast in ½ cup warm water with 2 tablespoons white sugar. Combine hot water, brown sugar, salt, shortening and whole wheat flour; mix 2 minutes. Stir in the softened yeast and the beaten egg. Beat well, add 2 cups white flour and mix well. Let this mixture rest 10 minutes. Add enough remaining flour to make a moderately stiff dough. Turn out on a lightly floured surface, knead until smooth and satiny (10-12 minutes). Shape dough in a ball and place in a lightly greased bowl, turning once to grease surface. Cover with plastic wrap or lid. Let rise in warm (85 degrees) place until double. Punch down. Cut into four portions and shape each into a smooth ball. Cover with clean, damp linen towel; let rest 10 minutes. Shape into loaves; place in 4 greased 8½ x 4½ x 2½ inch loaf pans. Let rise until double, covered with damp towel in (95 degrees) place. Bake in preheated 400 degree oven for 10 minutes, reduce temperature to 350 degrees and continue baking for 25 minutes. Remove from pans; cool on wire racks.

Dawn Giesel Dyck   Makes 4 loaves

Whole Wheat Bread

Step I: Mix 3½ cups (150 degrees) hot water with ⅓ cup brown sugar, 1 tablespoon salt, ⅓ cup softened shortening, 2 cups whole wheat flour. Beat 2 minutes. Step II: Add 2 tablespoons instant yeast, 1 egg, 2 cups white flour and beat. Then let rest 10 minutes. Step III: Add 4½-5 cups white flour, knead 8 minutes. Shape dough in a ball in a lightly greased bowl. Cover; let rise in 85 degrees place until double. Punch down. Cut into 4 portions, shape into a smooth ball; cover with a damp cloth; let rest 10 minutes. Shape into loaves; place in 4 greased 8½ x 4½ x 2½ loaf pans. Let rise till double in 95 degrees place. Bake at 350 degrees for 30-35 minutes.

Betty Giesel Martens   Yield: 4 loaves

Flour Tortillas

2 cups flour
1 teaspoon salt
½ teaspoon baking powder
¼ cup shortening
water

Mix flour, salt and baking powder together. Cut in shortening. Add enough water to make a dough. Knead a few times and shape into balls. Cover and let set 15 minutes. Roll each ball as thin as you can, and fry in a skillet without any grease. (Teflon is good.)

Jackie Koehn

Apple-Carrot Bread

1½ cups peeled, shredded apples
½ cup shredded carrots
¼ cup butter
1 teaspoon lemon juice
2 eggs, beaten
½ cup honey
2 cups whole wheat flour
1 teaspoon baking soda
1 teaspoon baking powder
½ teaspoon salt
½ cup chopped pecans

In a large bowl, blend first six ingredients and beat one minute at medium speed of Electric mixer. Add remaining ingredients and beat an additional 3 minutes. Bake in oiled 9x5 loaf pan for 1 hour at 350 degrees. Cool on wire rack, remove from pan and refrigerate.

John C. Jenkins, Jr., Grandson of Nathan Giesel

Blue Ribbon Date Walnut Loaf

2 cups chopped dates
1 cup chopped walnuts
⅓ cup shortening
1 cup boiling water
⅓ cup cold water
¾ cup firmly packed brown sugar

1 well beaten egg
1 teaspoon vanilla extract
2 cups all-purpose flour
1 teaspoon baking powder
1 teaspoon soda
1½ teaspoons salt

Combine dates, walnuts, and shortening in a large mixing bowl. Add boiling water, stirring just until shortening melts. Stir in cold water. Add sugar, egg, and vanilla, mixing well. Combine dry ingredients, and add gradually to date mixture, beating well. Pour mixture into a greased 9x5x3 inch loaf pan. Bake at 350 degrees for 1 hour and 15 minutes or until loaf tests done. Cool in pan 10 minutes; remove from pan and cool on a wire rack.

Arlene Giesel Koehn

Yield: 1 loaf

Cranberry Bread

This is a delicious breakfast bread.

2 cups flour
1 egg, beaten
½ teaspoon salt
2 tablespoons melted shortening
or butter
½ teaspoon baking soda

1 cup sugar
1 cup fresh or frozen cranberries,
coarsely ground
1½ teaspoon baking powder
Juice and grated rind of 1 orange
½ cup walnut meats, coarsely chopped

Preheat oven to 325 degrees. Mix dry ingredients together very well in a large mixing bowl. Put the juice and grated rind in a measuring cup and add enough boiling water to make ¾ cup liquid. Add to the dry mixture. Add egg and shortening or oil and mix just enough to moisten flour mixture. Add cranberries and nut meats. Bake in a greased loaf pan 60-70 minutes. Store 24 hours before cutting.

Arlene Giesel Koehn

Makes 1 loaf (10 Servings)

Poppy Seed Bread

1½ cup milk
1½ teaspoon vanilla
1½ teaspoon almond flavoring
1½ teaspoon butter flavoring
1 cup and 2 tablespoons oil
3 cups flour

3 eggs
2¼ cups sugar
3 tablespoons poppy seed
½ teaspoon salt
1½ teaspoons baking powder

Combine milk, eggs, vanilla, almond and butter flavorings and mix well. Add remaining ingredients and stir well. Bake in 2 greased loaf pans for 1 hour at 350 degrees. Remove from oven and let set for 5 minutes.

Glaze:
¼ cup orange juice
1 teaspoon vanilla
1 teaspoon almond flavoring

1 teaspoon butter flavoring
1 cup powdered sugar

Combine the above and pour over top. (I take the bread out of the pans and then brush on the glaze).

Zella Fay Unruh

Pumpkin Ribbon Bread

Filling:
2 (3 oz.) packages cream cheese, softened
⅓ cup sugar

1 egg
1 tablespoon flour
2 teaspoons grated orange peel

Bread:
1 cup cooked pumpkin
2 eggs
½ teaspoon salt
½ teaspoon cinnamon
1 teaspoon baking soda

½ cup oil
1½ cups sugar
½ teaspoon cloves
1⅔ cups flour
1 cup chopped pecans

For filling, beat cream cheese, sugar, and flour together in small bowl. Add egg; mix to blend. Stir in orange peel; set aside. Make bread by combining pumpkin, oil and eggs in large bowl. Add sugar, salt, cloves, cinnamon, flour, baking soda and pecans. Mix to blend. Pour ¼ of batter into two greased and floured 7½ x 3½ x 3 inch loaf pans. Carefully spread cream cheese mixture over batter. Add remaining batter, covering filling. Bake at 325 degrees for 1½ hours or until bread tests done with pick.

Melissa, Mrs. Jason Koehn

Rhubarb Bread

1⅓ cup brown sugar
⅔ cup vegetable oil
1 beaten egg
1 teaspoon vanilla
1 cup buttermilk
2½ cups flour

¾ teaspoon salt
1 teaspoon baking soda
½ teaspoon cinnamon
1½-2 cups finely diced rhubarb
½ cup chopped nuts

Mix together sugar and oil; blend in egg, vanilla and milk. In separate bowl, combine flour, salt, cinnamon and baking soda; add to moist ingredients. Stir in rhubarb and nuts. Divide batter between two well-greased 8x4 inch loaf pans. Bake at 350 degrees for about 45 minutes or until bread tests done with toothpick. Turn out onto rack to cool.

Pat, Mrs. Mitchell Unruh

Strawberry Nut Bread

1 cup butter
1½ cups sugar
1 teaspoon vanilla
¼ teaspoon lemon extract
4 eggs
3 cups all purpose flour

1 teaspoon cream of tartar
½ teaspoon soda
1 cup strawberry jam
½ cup sour cream
½ cup broken walnuts
1 teaspoon salt

Cream butter, sugar, vanilla and lemon extract together in large bowl until light and fluffy. Add eggs 1 at a time, beating well after each addition. In another bowl, sift together flour, salt, cream of tartar and baking soda; set aside. In small bowl, stir together jam and sour cream. Add alternately with dry ingredients. Beat until well combined. Stir in nuts. Divide batter among 2 9-inch greased and floured loaf pans. Bake 350 degrees 50 minutes. Cool in pans for 10 minutes. Remove from pans to cooling racks. Make spread by combining ingredients, 1 package softened cream cheese and 2 tablespoons jam.

Jul Nightengale

Cinnamon Rolls

1½ package yeast
¼ cup warm water
1 cup milk
½ cup sugar

1 teaspoon salt
1 tablespoon shortening
2 cups flour
2 eggs

Dissolve yeast in ¼ cup warm water, let stand in warm place till light. Heat milk, add sugar, salt and shortening. Add 2 cups flour and beat. Add eggs and beat. Add yeast, (stir) and 2-3 cups additional flour. Set bowl in pan of warm water to rise. Cover; when puffed, divide in half and roll to a 10" x 14" rectangle. Spread with butter; sprinkle with brown sugar, cinnamon, and nutmeg. Roll and cut into 1 inch slices. Let rise in warm place. Bake at 375 degrees for 15 to 20 minutes. Spread with icing.

Barbara Jean, Mrs. John Jenkins

Mom's Cinnamon Rolls

2 cakes or 2 tablespoons yeast
1 tablespoon sugar
1 cup lukewarm water
1 cup milk
3 eggs

8 tablespoons oleo
1 cup sugar
1½ teaspoons salt
8 cups flour
1 cup cold water

Dissolve yeast and 1 tablespoon sugar in lukewarm water. Scald milk, add oleo, sugar and salt. Add 1 cup cold water to cool scalded mixture. Add 2 cups flour to make a batter. Add yeast and beaten eggs; mix well. Add remaining flour. Knead and place in greased bowl. Cover and set in warm place. Let rise 1 hour. Knead again and let rise until doubled in bulk. Punch down and make cinnamon rolls or dinner rolls.

Barbara, Mrs. Ervin Koehn

Mom's (Matilda) Cinnamon Rolls

½ cup warm water (to dissolve
  yeast in)
2 packages yeast
1 cup scalded milk
2 rounded tablespoons margarine
  (or butter)

½ cup sugar
1 teaspoon salt
2 eggs
flour to make a soft dough

Put yeast in water, set aside. Heat milk, pour over margarine, sugar and salt. Add 2 cups flour to the milk mix, and beat. Add eggs, beat again. Add yeast and stir. Add more flour, and knead until it is smooth, but still very soft (about 2-3 cups additional flour). Let rise once in warm place (about 2 hours). Punch down. Let rest 10 minutes. Roll out dough to about a 10x14 inch rectangle. Put melted butter, brown sugar, cinnamon, and nutmeg (also chopped nuts or raisins if desired) over rolled out dough, roll up and cut. Place slices cut side down in a greased pan, and let rise again in warm place till all puffed up. Makes 30. Bake at 375 degrees for 15-25 minutes. Ice with powdered sugar frosting while rather warm. These rolls were often given to grandchildren on their birthdays—and we all enjoyed being in Mom's kitchen on roll making day!

Bernice, Mrs. Leland Lorenzen and Barbara, Mrs. John Jenkins

Cream Cheese Stollen

¼ cup warm water

1 package yeast

¾ cup milk (heated)

½ cup oleo

Combine warm milk and oleo with yeast mixture. Add:

2 cups flour

⅓ cup sugar

½ teaspoon salt

Beat with mixer until smooth. Then add:

1 egg

1¾-2 cups flour

Knead 5-10 minutes and let rise till double in bulk.

Filling:

2 packages cream cheese, softened

½ cup sugar

1 egg

2 teaspoons vanilla

dash of salt

Divide dough into two portions and roll out ⅛ inch thick. Spread ½ of filling on each dough portion. Roll dough to meet in the middle, tuck in the ends. Snip top of dough with scissors. Bake at 350 degrees for 25-30 minutes. When bread is cooled, drizzle with icing.

Icing:

2 cups powdered sugar

2 tablespoons cornstarch

2 tablespoons butter

2 teaspoons vanilla

Combine powdered sugar and cornstarch. Add other ingredients and enough water and cream to make a glaze. This makes a delicious breakfast bread.

Cherylyn, Mrs. Mike Unruh

Flaky Cherry Rolls

2 packages dry yeast

¼ cup warm water

1 cup milk

1 egg

2 tablespoons sugar

1 teaspoon salt

3-3½ cups flour

2 sticks oleo

1 can cherry pie filling

Dissolve yeast in ¼ cup warm water; let stand 3-5 minutes. Stir well and then stir in milk, egg, sugar, salt and flour. Roll out on floured surface to approximately 14x10 inches. Slice oleo onto ⅔ of the dough; fold the unbuttered ⅓ over onto buttered surface and then fold remaining buttered surface over top (the oleo is all inside). Roll the dough out again to 14x10 inches and refold as you have just done without rebuttering surface. Repeat the process 3 or 4 times. Roll ¼ inch thick and cut dough into 3 inch squares. Place 1 tablespoon of pie filling on each square. Fold into a triangle and pinch edges together. Place on greased baking sheet and let rise 30 minutes. Bake at 425 degrees for 10 minutes. Frost with a thin powdered sugar icing.

Note: These resemble the cherry rolls found in the grocery store except they're homemade and men just love them fresh out of the oven for break!

Donna, Mrs. Donavon Nikkel

Pineapple Rolls

2 cups milk
½ cup oleo
⅓ cup sugar
1 tablespoon salt

2 packages yeast
¼ cup water (to mix yeast.)
2 well beaten eggs

Scald milk, add sugar, salt, oleo. Cool. Add yeast, eggs and 6 cups flour (soft dough). Let rise once or twice. Roll out and spread with oleo. Roll up and cut. Place on cookie sheet. Make an indentation in middle. While dough is rising, thicken one 8¼ oz. can of crushed pineapple with 1 tablespoon flour and 1 tablespoon sugar. Let cool. When rolls are cut, place 1 teaspoon of pineapple mixture on each roll. Let rise and bake in 350 degree oven 15 to 20 Minutes. Makes 2½ -3 dozen.

Beulah, Mrs. Dennis Unruh

Quick Cinnamon Twists

Using refrigerator biscuits, dip each biscuit in melted butter, then in sugar-cinnamon mixture. Twist once and place on baking sheet. Sprinkle all twists with brown sugar and bake according to biscuit directions. This is a favorite quickie for unexpected company.

Louise Wedel

Red - Hot Cinnamon Rolls

¼ cup warm water
1 package active dry yeast
¼ cup instant potato flakes
hot water (see below)
⅓ cup margarine

¼ cup sugar
2 teaspoons salt
2 eggs
3¾ cups all-purpose flour, divided

Dissolve yeast in warm water. Add enough hot water to potato flakes so mixture measures one cup. In mixer bowl, combine potato mixture, margarine, sugar, salt, eggs and 1½ cups flour. Blend ingredients, then add yeast and beat at medium speed two minutes. By hand, stir in remaining 2¼ cup flour. Turn dough onto floured surface and knead until smooth and easy to handle. Place in greased bowl; cover and allow to rise until doubled. Punch down; roll into an 11x15 inch rectangle. Distribute filling evenly over dough (filling will be stiff). Roll as for jelly roll; cut into twelve pieces. Place in well-greased 13x9x2 inch baking pan. Flatten rolls slightly and let rise until almost doubled. Bake in 350 degrees oven 15 to 20 minutes. While warm, frost with your favorite frosting.

Filling:

Prepare while dough is rising
¾ cup unsifted confectioners sugar
¼ cup finely chopped pecans
¼ cup soft margarine

⅓ cup red-hot candies, crushed
1 teaspoon cinnamon

Mix ingredients together with tines of a fork until blended. Set aside. Note: To crush red-hots, place several teaspoons of candies at a time in a plastic Ziploc bag. Place on a cutting board and crush with a small hammer.

Edna Giesel   Yield: one dozen rolls

Sweet Rolls

2 packages yeast
1 tablespoon sugar
1 cup luke warm water
1 cup milk
1 cup cold water

3 eggs, beaten
1 stick oleo
1 cup sugar
2 teaspoons salt
8 cups flour

Dissolve yeast and 1 tablespoon sugar in lukewarm water. Scald milk and oleo, sugar and salt. Add 1 cup cold water and cool to lukewarm. Add 2 cups flour to make batter. Add yeast and beaten eggs; beat well. Add remaining flour, a cup at a time. Mix well. Put in greased bowl. Cover and set in warm place. Let rise 30 minutes, then knead down. Let rise again till double in bulk. Punch down and use for dinner rolls, cinnamon rolls, coffee or bierocks. Excellent for freezing.

Deloris, Mrs. Isaac Unruh, Jr.

Sweet Roll Dough

Mix together:
⅔ cups powdered milk
½ cup sugar

2 teaspoons salt
½ cup instant potato flakes

Add:
3 cups hot water
¾ cup shortening or oleo

4 beaten eggs

Dissolve 2 tablespoons yeast in ¾ cup water. Add to lukewarm liquid mixture. Gradually add 10-12 cups flour. Knead 5 minutes. Put in lightly greased bowl. Let rise twice, then put in pans. Let rise. Bake in 375 degree oven for 10-12 minutes.

Valerie Koehn

Cranberry Coffee Cake

Perfect for the holidays!

¾ cup margarine, softened
1½ cups sugar
3 eggs, room temperature
1½ teaspoons almond extract
3 cups all-purpose flour
1½ teaspoons baking powder

1½ teaspoons baking soda
¾ teaspoon salt
1½ cups sour cream
1 (16 oz.) can whole-berry
    cranberry sauce
½ cup chopped nuts

Glaze:

¾ cup powdered sugar
1 tablespoon warm water

½ teaspoon almond extract

In large bowl, cream margarine and sugar until light. Add eggs, one at a time, beating thoroughly after each addition. Beat in almond extract.

Sift together flour, baking powder, baking soda and salt. Add to creamed mixture alternately with sour cream, beating well after each addition. Spoon one-third of batter into greased and floured Bundt or other 12 cup tube pan. Distribute one-third of cranberry sauce over batter. Repeat layers two more times, ending with cranberry sauce. Sprinkle nuts over top. Bake at 350 degrees one hour or until cake tests done. Cool in pan 5 minutes. Remove from pan and cool on wire rack. Drizzle glaze over top. Serve warm or cooled. Makes 20 servings. To make glaze, blend powdered sugar, extract and water in small bowl until smooth.

Carolyn, Mrs. Wayne Holdeman

Breakfast Bubbles

1 (24 oz.) package frozen
    dinner rolls
¾ stick or 6 tablespoons butter
    or margarine
1 (3 oz.) package butterscotch
    pudding mix (not instant)

½ cup brown sugar
1 tablespoon ground cinnamon
½ cup nuts or raisins (optional)

Butter bundt pan or angel food cake pan. Thaw rolls till they can be cut with a knife. Cut into halves or fourths. Place rolls in pan. Melt butter; combine with pudding mix, brown sugar, cinnamon and nuts or raisins, if using. Dab mixture over top of rolls, letting mixture fall around rolls. Leave on counter to rise overnight. Drizzle with cream or canned milk before baking. Bake at 350 degrees for 25 minutes or till done. Turn upside down onto serving plate. Serve warm. Vanilla pudding may be used in place of butterscotch pudding.

Jolene Unruh

Breakfast Cakes

Preheat oven to 350 degrees.

Crumbs:

18 tablespoons flour
1½ teaspoons baking soda
1½ teaspoons cinnamon

¾ cup brown sugar
6 tablespoons butter or margarine

Mix together and set aside.

Cake:

6 egg whites
2 cups sugar
3 cups flour
2 teaspoons baking powder

1 cup Crisco
6 egg yolks
1 cup milk
½ teaspoon salt

Beat 6 egg whites till stiff. Let set. In a separate bowl, beat together Crisco, sugar, and the egg yolks. Add 1½ cups flour and beat again. Add the milk and beat. Add the rest of the flour, baking powder and salt. Beat together and then fold in the egg whites. Divide into three 9 inch cake pans and sprinkle the crumbs on top. Bake for 30-45 minutes.

Janice, Mrs. Jerry Ratzlaff   Makes three 9 inch cakes

Breakfast Danish

2 cups Bisquick
⅔ cup milk
2 tablespoons sugar

2 tablespoons butter
Your choice of jam

Stir together Bisquick and sugar. Crumble with butter. Stir in milk. Spread biscuits on pan; top with jam. Bake 8-10 minutes at 400 degrees. Glaze.

Jana, Mrs. Robert Nichols   Makes 8 small servings

Butterquick Coffee Cake

2 cups flour
1 cup sugar
3 teaspoons baking powder
1 teaspoon salt

⅓ cup butter
1 egg
1 cup milk

Beat hard 2 minutes and spread ½ mixture in greased 9x13 inch pan. Sprinkle on ½ topping. Repeat.

Topping:

½ cup sugar
½ cup chopped nuts

1 teaspoon cinnamon

Bake at 350 degrees for 25 minutes.

Marisa Giesel Wedel

Caramel Dumplings

Dumplings:

Mix together:

¼ cup sugar
1½ tablespoons butter
¼ teaspoon salt

1½ tablespoons baking powder
¾ cup flour
¼ cup milk

Sauce:

¾ cup brown sugar
1 cup water

1 tablespoon butter

Heat sauce hot and add dumplings. Cook 15 minutes and don't lift lid. I use my electric skillet with the temperature on 250 to 300 degrees

Jackie Koehn

Crunchy Pecan Ring

¾ - 1 cup chopped pecans
¾ cup firmly packed brown sugar
½ cup butter or margarine

¼ cup maple syrup
2 (10 oz.) cans refrigerated flaky
  biscuits

Combine first 4 ingredients in a saucepan; cook over low heat until butter melts. Spoon ¼ of mixture into a lightly greased 10 inch bundt pan. Separate biscuits and arrange in pan standing each on edge and slightly overlapping. Spoon remaining brown sugar mixture over biscuits. Bake at 375 degrees for 30 minutes. Cool in pan 3 minutes. Invert onto a serving plate and serve immediately.

Carolyn, Mrs. Wayne Holdeman   Yield: 10 inch coffee cake

New England Blueberry Coffee Cake

1½ cups flour
½ cup sugar
1 tablespoon baking powder
1 teaspoon cinnamon
½ teaspoon salt

1½ cups fresh blueberries
1 egg
½ cup milk
¼ cup butter or margarine, melted

In a large mixing bowl combine flour, sugar, baking powder, cinnamon and salt. Gently fold in blueberries. In a small bowl, whisk together the egg, milk and butter. Add to the flour mixture and stir carefully. Spread into a greased 8x8 inch pan. Combine all topping ingredients and sprinkle over batter.

Topping:

¼ cup butter or margarine, melted
¾ cup brown sugar

1 tablespoon flour
½ cup chopped walnuts or pecans

Bake at 425 degrees for 20-25 minutes or until top is light golden brown. Serve warm or at room temperature.

Wonderful with mid-morning coffee or with ice cream as a dessert!

Jana, Mrs. Robert Nichols   Yield: 12 servings

Sour Cream Coffee Cake

Prepare about 2 hours before serving, or a day ahead.

¾ cup California walnuts, finely
   chopped
1½ teaspoons ground cinnamon
   sugar
¾ cup butter or margarine

3 cups all-purpose flour
1½ cups sour cream
3 eggs
1½ teaspoons baking soda
1½ teaspoons vanilla extract

Preheat oven to 350 degrees. In small bowl; combine walnuts, cinnamon and ¾ cup sugar. Grease 10 inch tube pan. In large bowl with mixer at medium speed, beat butter or margarine with 1¼ cups sugar until light and fluffy. Add flour and remaining ingredients and beat at low speed until blended, constantly scraping bowl with rubber spatula. Increase speed to medium; beat 3 minutes, occasionally scraping bowl. Spread half of batter in pan; sprinkle with half of nut mixture; spread evenly with remaining batter and sprinkle with remaining nut mixture. Bake 60 minutes to 65 minutes until cake pulls away from side of pan. Cool cake in pan completely on wire rack.

Arlene Giesel Koehn   Makes 12 Servings

Swedish Tea Wreath

1½ cups milk, scalded
½ cup shortening
½ cup sugar
2 teaspoons salt

2 cakes or packages yeast
½ cup lukewarm water
2 well beaten eggs
7-8 cups flour

Combine milk, shortening, sugar and salt. Cool to lukewarm. Add yeast softened in water. Add eggs; mix well. Add flour gradually; beat smooth. Knead on floured surface until smooth and elastic. Place in greased bowl; cover and let rise until double. Punch down. Divide into 2 parts and roll in ½ inch rectangles. Brush with melted shortening. Sprinkle each with mixture of ¼ cup sugar, 1 tablespoon cinnamon and ½ cup raisins. Roll. Shape in circle on greased baking sheet. Snip at 1½ inch intervals. Cover and let rise until double. Bake at 350 degrees for 35 minutes. Glaze.

Mary, Mrs. Lee Giesel   Makes two wreaths

Raised Doughnuts

2 cups scalded milk	9¼ cups flour
½ cup butter	1½ teaspoons salt
1½ cups thin mashed potatoes	¾ cup sugar
2 eggs	1½ packages yeast

Makes a real soft dough. Work down once and let rise again. Then cut the doughnuts and let rise about 45 minutes. Fry in deep fat.

Glaze:

2 pounds powdered sugar	2 tablespoons sweet cream
2 tablespoons corn starch or flour	vanilla
¼ pound butter	

Add warm water to make a paste, dip hot doughnuts in and drain.

Mornie Giesel Unruh

Southern Snowballs

2 eggs	pinch of salt
½ cup sugar	2 teaspoons baking powder
1 cup sweet milk	1 teaspoon vanilla

Add cocoa for chocolate snowballs. Enough flour to make a soft batter so they will drop from a teaspoon.

Use a ¾ teaspoon of dough for a snowball. Push off the spoon into hot fat. Fry like doughnuts. Put a tablespoon sugar in a paper bag and shake. I used to fix these in a hurry for school lunches.

Sophie Giesel Koehn

Sopapillas

2 cups flour	2 tablespoons shortening
1 tablespoon baking powder	¾ cup ice water
1 teaspoon salt	oil (for frying)
1 teaspoon sugar	

Sift all dry ingredients together; cut in shortening until mealy, work in water gradually to form a pastry-like dough. Turn out on lightly floured board and knead until smooth. Place in bowl, cover and let rise one hour. Roll ⅛ inch thick, cut into squares and fry in hot fat (370 degrees), turning after they puff. Use a slotted spoon and gently throw the hot fat on each one until they puff. Drain on paper towels and serve immediately. Serve with honey.

Coreen Holdeman

Tortilla and Sopapilla Dough

4 cups flour
1½ teaspoons salt
3 teaspoons baking powder
4 tablespoons shortening

oil
honey
cinnamon sugar

Mix together flour, salt and baking powder. Add shortening; stir until mixture resembles pie dough. Add warm water until dough is soft and pliable. (Sealing dough in container for several hours makes it easier to work with.) For tortillas, pinch off dough in 2 inch balls; flatten and roll thin to 8 inch diameter. Heat oil in skillet; brown tortilla, turning once when top of tortilla bubbles.

To make sopapillas, roll out one-quarter of dough to ⅛ inch thickness; cut into 2 inch squares. Deep fry a few at time, turning each piece until light brown. Drain on paper towels. Repeat with remaining three-quarters of dough. Serve with honey or cinnamon sugar. Dough will keep in refrigerator for 2 days.

Carolyn, Mrs. Wayne Holdeman

Bran Muffins

1¼ cups flour
1 tablespoon baking powder
½ teaspoon salt
½ cup sugar

1½ cup All-Bran cereal
1¼ cup skim milk
1 egg
¼ cup vegetable oil

Sift together flour, baking powder, salt and sugar; set aside. Measure cereal and milk into large mixing bowl. Stir to combine. Let stand 2 minutes or until cereal softens. Add egg and oil. Beat well. Add flour mixture, stirring only until combined. Spoon batter evenly into twelve 2½ inch muffin pan cups coated with cooking spray. Bake at 400 degrees about 18 minutes. Low-fat muffins: Use 2 tablespoons sugar, 1 tablespoon vegetable oil, and substitute 2 egg whites for 1 egg. These are really good!

Ronda, Mrs. Kenny Giesel

Cinnamon Muffins

1½ cup flour
⅓ cup honey
2 teaspoons baking powder
½ teaspoon salt

½ teaspoon cinnamon
1 beaten egg
½ cup vegetable oil
½ cup milk

Mix egg, oil, milk and honey together. Add dry ingredients. Stir just enough to moisten. Fill greased muffin pan ⅔ full. Bake at 350 degrees for 20-25 minutes.

Joyce, Mrs. Leland Koehn

Graham Gems

Grandma Carrie always made "Graham Gems" when we were growing up.

¼ cup sugar
¼ teaspoon salt
½ cup all purpose flour
2 teaspoons baking powder
1 cup whole wheat flour

1 cup milk
2 tablespoons sour cream
1 beaten egg
butter or margarine
honey

In a mixing bowl, stir together first five ingredients; make a well in center. In another bowl, combine milk, sour cream and egg, stirring just until blended. Add to dry ingredients. Mix. Pour into muffin cups. Bake at 425 degrees for 15 to 20 minutes, or until lightly browned. Yield: 12 muffins. Eat with butter and honey. This was a favorite, they could be served with any meal or as a snack.

Mornie Giesel Unruh

Pumpkin Spice Muffins

½ cup canned pumpkin
½ cup milk
1 egg
2 cups biscuit mix

¼ cup sugar
½ teaspoon ground nutmeg
½ teaspoon ground cinnamon
½ teaspoon ground ginger

Streusel Topping:
1 tablespoon biscuit mix
2 tablespoons sugar
¼ teaspoon ground cinnamon

2 teaspoons butter or margarine,
  softened

In a mixing bowl, combine pumpkin, milk and egg with a fork. Combine dry ingredients; add to mixing bowl and stir just until moistened. Spoon into 12 well-greased muffin cups. Combine streusel ingredients; sprinkle over muffins. Bake at 400 degrees for 15 minutes or until golden brown. Serve warm.

Charmaine Wedel   Yield: 1 dozen

Quick Date Muffins

1 egg
2 cups buttermilk baking mix
⅓ cup sugar
¾ - 1 cup plain yogurt

2 tablespoons oil
½ teaspoon cinnamon
¾ cup chopped dates

Streusel Topping:
⅓ cup buttermilk baking mix
⅓ cup brown sugar

2 tablespoons margarine
½ teaspoon cinnamon

Beat egg in bowl. Add remaining ingredients, except dates. Stir until moistened. Fold in dates. Pour ¼ cup batter into 12-15 greased muffin cups. Combine streusel ingredients with a fork until crumbly and sprinkle on top of muffins. Bake at 400 degrees 15-18 minutes. This is another recipe from my Mom. They're easy and good!

Michele, Mrs. Richard Ensz

Rhubarb Muffins

1¼ cup brown sugar   1 egg
½ cup oil

Combine and beat till blended. Stir in:
1 cup buttermilk   ½ walnuts
1½ - 2 cups rhubarb

Mix together:
2½ cups flour   1 teaspoon baking powder
1 teaspoon soda   ½ teaspoon salt

Add to rhubarb mixture. Stir till blended. Fill muffin tins ⅔ full.

Topping:
½ cup sugar (small amount   1½ teaspoon cinnamon
   brown sugar)   1 tablespoon melted butter

Mix together and put a small dab on top of each muffin and press down. Bake 20 minutes at 400 degrees.

Jul Nightengale   Makes 20-24 muffins

Sugar Muffins

2 cups flour   1 egg
3 teaspoons baking powder   ¾ cup milk
4 tablespoons sugar   ¼ cup butter (melted)
¾ teaspoon salt   2 teaspoons cinnamon
⅓ cup shortening

Mix all dry ingredients except 2 tablespoons sugar and cinnamon. Blend in shortening until mixture is coarse in texture. Beat in egg until dough is thoroughly moistened. Fill greased muffin tins ⅔ full. Bake at 450 degrees for 20 minutes. For sugar- crusted top, remove from tin as soon as muffins are baked and dip muffin tops into melted butter. Drop into a bag containing a mixture of 2 tablespoons sugar and 2 teaspoons cinnamon and shake.

Arlene Giesel Koehn   Makes 10-12 muffins

Fruit-flavor Syrup

Try this thrifty syrup on Sunday morning pancakes or waffles.

In a medium saucepan, mix one regular size of fruit-flavored gelatin (we like strawberry best) with ½ cup sugar and 2 tablespoons cornstarch. Add 1 cup water and bring to a boil while stirring. Let it boil good to thicken the cornstarch and pour into a pitcher and serve while hot. Delicious! This makes a generous amount for four or five people.

Mornie Giesel Unruh

Syrup

½ cup brown sugar   ½ cup white sugar
1 cup whipping cream

Mix and bring to a boil. Boil for one or two minutes. Serve hot over waffles, pancakes, or french toast. This keeps well for weeks in refrigerator. If you have cream that needs to used, cook into syrup and store in refrigerator.

Deloris, Mrs. Isaac Unruh, Jr.

DESSERTS

Amish Christmas Cake

1 cup chopped pecans
1 cup (2 sticks) butter
2 cups sugar
2 cups seedless raisins
2 cups water
1 teaspoon ground cinnamon

1 teaspoon grated nutmeg
1 teaspoon ground cloves
1 tablespoon grated lemon rind
3½ cups all-purpose flour
1 teaspoon baking soda
1 tablespoon grated orange rind

Preheat oven to 350 degrees. In a large deep kettle, combine the first 8 ingredients. Simmer, uncovered, over moderate heat, for 4 minutes then let cool to room temperature. Add the lemon and orange rinds and transfer to a large mixing bowl. Sift together the flour and baking soda and, using slow speed, gradually beat it into the raisin mixture. Pour the batter into an oiled and floured 10-inch tube pan. Bake for 1 hour, or until the top springs back up when touched with your finger. Let cool in the pan for 10 to 15 minutes, then tip out onto a wire rack to finish cooling. This cake freezes well and will keep, tightly wrapped in foil, for 2 weeks in the refrigerator.

Arlene Giesel Koehn   Makes 24 slices

Apple Cake

½ cup shortening
1⅔ cups sugar
2 eggs
2 cups flour
1 teaspoon baking powder

1 teaspoon soda
1 teaspoon cinnamon
1 teaspoon nutmeg
½ teaspoon salt
4 cups sliced apples

Cream sugar and shortening, add eggs and mix well. Sift dry ingredients together and stir into creamed mixture. Stir in apples (mixture will be thick). Press into greased 9x13 pan and bake at 350 degrees for 45 minutes.

Mary, Mrs. Lee Giesel

Fresh Apple Cake

This is a very moist and delicious cake. A favorite

¾ cup shortening	1 teaspoon cinnamon
2 cups sugar	1 teaspoon allspice
4 egg yolks	½ teaspoon salt
½ cup milk	2 teaspoons vanilla
1 teaspoon soda	4 egg whites, beaten stiff
1 teaspoon baking powder	4 or 5 apples diced or shredded
1 teaspoon nutmeg	3 cups flour

Cream shortening, sugar, and egg yolks. Add flour, milk, and spices. Beat good. Whip egg whites and fold in. Add apples. Bake in large loaf pan at 275 degrees for one hour. Ice with Easy Caramel Icing.

Easy Caramel Icing:

Mix together in sauce pan:

1½ cups brown sugar (packed)	4 tablespoons butter
¼ cup top milk, (does that tell you how old this recipe is?)	

Bring to a boil and boil 3 minutes

Valetta, Mrs. John Koehn

Apricot Nectar Cake

1 (18½ ounce) box lemon cake mix	1 cup apricot nectar
½ cup sugar	4 eggs
¾ cup vegetable oil	

Combine cake mix, sugar, oil, and apricot nectar together. Blend well. Add eggs one at a time, beating well after each addition. Bake 1 hour in a greased 10-inch tube pan at 325 degrees.

Glaze:

1 cup powdered sugar	Juice from 1 lemon

Mix well and spread on top of cake.

Arlene Giesel Koehn

Banana Crunch Cake

1 cup coconut
1 cup rolled oats
¾ cup packed brown sugar
½ cup all-purpose flour
½ cup chopped pecans
½ cup margarine or butter

1½ cups (2 large) very ripe
  bananas, sliced
½ cup sour cream
1 package yellow cake mix
  (Pillsbury recommended)
3 eggs

Heat oven to 350 degrees. Grease and flour 10-inch tube pan. Lightly spoon flour into measuring cup; level off. In medium bowl, combine coconut, rolled oats, brown sugar, flour and pecans. Using pastry blender or fork, cut in margarine until mixture is crumbly; set aside. In large bowl, combine bananas, sour cream and eggs; blend until smooth. Add cake mix; beat 2 minutes at highest speed. Spread ⅓ of batter into prepared pan; sprinkle with ⅓ of crunch mixture. Repeat layers twice. Bake for 50 or 60 minutes or until toothpick inserted in center comes out clean. Cool upright in pan for 15 minutes. Remove from pan; place on serving plate crunch side up.

Arlene Giesel Koehn   Makes 16 servings

Banana Nut Cake

2 cups flour
1¼ teaspoon baking powder
1 teaspoon baking soda
1 teaspoon salt
1⅔ cup sugar
⅔ cup shortening

2 eggs
1 teaspoon vanilla
1¼ cup (3 or 4) mashed ripe bananas
⅔ cup buttermilk or sour milk
⅔ cup finely chopped nuts

Cream sugar, shortening, eggs and vanilla thoroughly. Add mashed bananas. Mix well. Add dry ingredients to creamed mixture alternately with buttermilk starting and ending with dry ingredients. Mix well after each addition but do not overbeat. Stir in nuts. Spread batter in 2 greased 9 inch layer pans or one 9x13 inch pan. (Also makes good cupcakes.) Bake at 350 degrees for 40-50 minutes.

Karen, Mrs. Rick Penner

Blueberry Cake

¼ cup flour
¼ cup sugar
3 tablespoons butter
3 cups sifted flour
1 teaspoon soda
1 teaspoon baking powder
1 cup sugar

1 cup butter or margarine
1 cup commercial sour cream
   or plain yogurt
1 cup milk
1 teaspoon vanilla
2 eggs
1 can (21 oz.) blueberry pie filling

In a small bowl combine ¼ cup flour and ¼ cup sugar; cut in 3 tablespoons butter. Grease a 12-cup fluted or Bundt pan; sprinkle ½ of above mixture in pan. In a large bowl, combine 3 cups flour; soda; baking powder; and sugar; cut in butter. Add sour cream, milk, vanilla, and eggs. Beat well. Spread ½ batter in the prepared Bundt pan. Spoon pie filling on top of batter; do not mix pie filling in batter. Add remaining batter on top of filling layer and sprinkle remaining flour-sugar mixture over top of cake. Bake at 325 degrees for 50-60 minutes or until cake tests done. Cool in pan 10-15 minutes; turn out on wire rack to complete cooling. Sprinkle with confectioners' sugar or top with vanilla glaze. Variations; Cherry, raisin, apricot, or pineapple pie filling may be used in place blueberry.

Arlene Giesel Koehn

Carrot Cake

Makes three 9-inch layers or 1 large oblong.

3 cups flour (whole wheat or regular)
2 cups sugar (may substitute 1
   cup of honey)
2 teaspoons salt

2 teaspoons baking powder
   (increase to 3 tsp if using
   whole wheat flour)
1½ teaspoons baking soda

Sift above ingredients together.

Beat:
4 eggs in a mixing bowl.

Add:

1 teaspoon black walnut flavoring
1½ cups of oil (Mazola,
   Sunflower, etc.)

2 cups grated carrots
1 cup black walnuts

Beat these ingredients together real well, then add the dry ingredients above and beat well. Bake at 375 degrees for at least 30 minutes. I find it takes a little longer when using whole wheat flour.

John and Barbara Jenkins

Caramel Filled Butter Pecan Cake

1 cup shortening
2 cups sugar
4 eggs
3 cups cake flour
2½ teaspoons baking powder
½ teaspoon salt

1 cup milk
1 teaspoon almond extract
1 teaspoon vanilla extract
Caramel filling
Butter cream frosting
1 cup chopped pecans

Cream shortening, gradually add sugar, beating well. Add eggs, one at a time, beating well after each addition. Combine dry ingredients, add to creamed mixture alternately with milk. Add flavorings, mix well. Grease three 9-inch round cake pans, line with wax paper; grease wax paper. Pour batter in prepared pans, bake at 375 degrees 22-25 minutes. Cool on wire racks. Spread caramel filling (below) between layers and on top of cake. Spread butter cream frosting (below) on sides of cake. Press chopped pecans into frosting on sides of cake.

Caramel Filling:

3 cups sugar, divided
¾ cup milk
1 egg, beaten

pinch of salt
½ cup butter or margarine, cut up

Sprinkle ½ cup sugar in a large heavy saucepan. Place over medium heat and cook, stirring constantly until sugar melts and syrup is light golden brown. Combine remaining ingredients. Stir this mixture into hot caramelized sugar. (The mixture will lump, becoming smooth with further cooking.) Cook over medium heat stirring often, until a candy thermometer registers 230 degrees. (15-20 minutes.) Cool 5 minutes. Beat with a wooden spoon to almost spreading consistency.

Yield: 2½ cups

Butter Cream Frosting

½ cup butter or margarine (softened)
3 cups powdered sugar

2-3 tablespoons half and half
½ teaspoon vanilla

Beat together until light and fluffy. This makes a big, beautiful, delicious cake. Allow plenty of time to make the filling. It's worth the effort and almost fool-proof.

LeAnne Nichols

Chocolate Cake

1 package chocolate cake mix, mix as directed on the package

Mix the following and pour over top of cake mixture:

1 package (8 ounces) cream cheese,   1 egg
    softened   **1 teaspoon vanilla**
1½ cups sugar

Mix well. Dribble over cake mixture which has been put in a sheet cake pan. Last, sprinkle 1 cup of chocolate chips over top and bake all at 350 degrees for 20 minutes.

Deloris, Mrs. Isaac Unruh, Jr.

Chocolate Upside Down Cake

Part 1:

1 cup flour   **2 teaspoons baking powder**
¾ cup sugar   **¼ teaspoon salt**
2 tablespoons cocoa

Mix together thoroughly.

Add:
½ cup milk

Stir well.

Add:
2 tablespoons melted butter   **½ cup chopped nutmeats**
1 teaspoon vanilla

Pour into greased and floured pan.

Part 2:

½ cup white sugar   **½ cup brown sugar**
2 tablespoons cocoa

Mix thoroughly and sprinkle over batter. Pour 1 cup cold water over the top. Bake 30 to 35 minutes in a moderate oven (350 degrees). Leave in pan until ready to serve.

Elma Giesel Koehn by Louise Wedel

Chocolate Zucchini Cake

½ cup margarine, softened
½ cup vegetable oil
1¾ cup sugar
2 eggs
1 teaspoon vanilla
½ cup sour milk
2½ cups unsifted flour

4 tablespoons cocoa
½ teaspoon baking powder
1 teaspoon soda
½ teaspoon salt
½ teaspoon cinnamon
2 cups shredded zucchini

Topping:
1 cup chocolate chips
½ cup chopped nuts

2 tablespoons sugar

Cream margarine, oil and sugar. Add eggs, vanilla and sour milk. Beat well. Mix all dry ingredients and add to creamed mixture. Beat well. Stir in zucchini. Pour into 15¼ x 10¼ inch jelly roll pan. Sprinkle with topping. Bake at 350 degrees for 30-35 minutes.

Pat, Mrs. Mitchell Unruh

Moist Chocolate Cake

2 eggs
1 cup Wesson oil
1 cup buttermilk
1 cup hot water with 2 teaspoons
    soda

1 teaspoon vanilla
2½ cups flour
1 teaspoon baking powder
5 tablespoons cocoa
2 cups sugar

Sift all dry ingredients. Then combine all ingredients. Beat 2 or 3 minutes. Bake in 17x12x2 inch pan. Bake at 350 degrees for 30 minutes or until done.

Icing for moist chocolate cake:
1 cup brown sugar
1 cup sugar

½ cup cream
1 teaspoon vanilla

Combine sugars and cream. Boil until soft ball, then add vanilla. Cool and put on cake.

Ronda, Mrs. Ryan Wedel

Light as a Cloud Coconut Cake

Cake:

4 egg yolks	2½ cups all-purpose flour
2 whole eggs	1 tablespoon baking powder
1 ½ cups sugar	1 teaspoon vanilla
½ cup butter or margarine, cut up	½ cup chopped black walnuts or
1 cup hot milk	toasted walnuts or pecans

Frosting:

1 ¾ cups sugar	½ teaspoon cream of tartar
½ cup water	1 teaspoon vanilla
3 egg whites	2 cups shredded fresh coconut

Preheat oven to 350 degrees. Grease and flour three 9-inch round cake pans. To make the cake: In a large mixing bowl, beat the egg yolks, whole eggs and sugar with an electric mixer of at least 5 minutes or until light and fluffy. Stir the butter or margarine pieces into the hot milk until the butter has melted. Combine the flour with the baking powder. Add ½ cup of the flour mixture into the egg mixture, beating slowly. Add half the hot milk mixture, 1 cup of the flour mixture, then the remaining hot milk, beating after each addition. Add the remaining flour mixture and the vanilla. Beat well. Fold in the nuts. Pour the batter into the prepared pans. Bake the layers in the 350 degree oven for 12 to 15 minutes or until a wooden toothpick inserted in the centers comes out clean. Cool for 5 minutes in the pans. Remove the cakes from the pans and cool completely on wire racks. To make the frosting: In a medium saucepan, combine the sugar with the water. Bring the mixture to boiling and boil for 2 minutes or until it is syrupy and the sugar dissolves. (Undissolved sugar will make the frosting grainy.) Make sure to scrape down the sides of the saucepan and stir in a figure-eight motion. In a large mixing bowl, beat the egg whites with the cream of tartar with an electric mixer until foamy. Slowly pour the hot sugar syrup into the egg whites, beating constantly at the highest speed for 4 to 6 minutes or until the frosting is stiff enough to spread. Use a rubber spatula to guide the egg whites toward the beaters and scrape down the sides of the bowl to make sure that the frosting is evenly mixed. Beat in the vanilla. The finished frosting should be smooth and fluffy, and hold stiff peaks. Place a cake layer on a cake plate; spread with about 1 cup frosting and sprinkle with ⅓ cup of coconut. Repeat with remaining layers. Frost the sides of the cake and sprinkle with the remaining coconut. Store cake in the refrigerator up to 24 hours.

Arlene Giesel Koehn

Crumb Cake

"Dee-licious," you'll say when you try this recipe for old-fashioned crumb cake. Serve it when still slightly warm.

1½ cup sugar (half or all brown)	2 teaspoons baking powder
¾ cup shortening (part butter)	½ teaspoon salt
2 cups flour	1 teaspoon cinnamon

Mix together into crumbs as you mix pastry for pie. Take out a small cupful of crumbs for topping. Break into remainder of crumbs 2 eggs, then add ¾ cup milk. Beat until well blended. Pour into greased and floured pan and then sprinkle over top of batter the crumbs you have left. Bake in moderate oven about 25 minutes.

Nancy, Mrs. Kenneth Unruh

Date-cherry Cake

1 pound chopped dates	8 oz. medium candied cherries (whole)
(2 boxes chopped)	2 slices candied green pineapple
1 pound pecans (4 cups) cut-up	(chopped)

Mix this all together and dredge with 1 cup plain flour.

Beat with mixer:

1 cup sugar	½ teaspoon baking powder
4 whole eggs	

Pour this over first mixture and mix well. Bake in foil-lined loaf pans 1½ to 2 hours at 250 degrees. Remove from loaf pan at once and peel foil from cake.

Arlene Giesel Koehn

Easy Red Velvet Cake

1 box yellow cake mix	½ cup Crisco oil
1 small instant vanilla pudding	4 eggs
mix	3 teaspoons cocoa
1 cup water	1 (1 oz.) bottle red food coloring

Combine dry ingredients. Add oil, water, coloring and eggs. Mix thoroughly, pour into oiled and floured cake pans. If you have 3 pans, bake 20-25 minutes at 350 degrees. If you have 2 pans, bake about 35 to 40 minutes. Use 8 or 9-inch pans.

Cream Cheese Icing:

8 oz. package cream cheese	2 teaspoons vanilla flavoring
1 box confectioners sugar	1 cup chopped pecans (optional)
1 stick margarine	

Combine first 4 ingredients. Mix until smooth. Add pecans. Frost cake.

Louise Wedel

Earthquake Cake

1 cup pecans
1 cup coconut
1 box German Chocolate cake mix
8 oz. package cream cheese

½ cup margarine
1 pound confectioners sugar
1 teaspoon vanilla

Grease bottom of 10x14 inch pan. Preheat oven to 350 degrees. Mix pecans and coconut and spread in bottom of pan. Prepare cake mix as directed on box and pour over coconut and pecans. Mix together the remaining ingredients and spoon over cake batter evenly. Bake 45 to 50 minutes.

Betty, Mrs. Gordon Unruh; Jana, Mrs. Robert Nichols

Fruit Cake

¼ cup light corn syrup
1⅓ cups walnuts
1⅓ cups pecan halves
2¼ cups gum drops
1½ cups dates (halved)

2¼ cups maraschino cherries,
    candied cherries, candied
    pineapple
½ cup coconut
½ cup flour

Mix fruit and nuts and toss all with the flour.

Cake batter:
1 cup shortening
1 cup sugar
½ teaspoon almond flavoring
5 eggs
1½ cups sifted flour

1 teaspoon baking powder
¾ teaspoon salt
½ teaspoon cinnamon
¼ teaspoon cloves
⅓ cup cherry juice

Cream the shortening, sugar and almond flavoring. Add the eggs and beat until light and fluffy. Sift together the flour, baking powder, salt, cinnamon and cloves. Alternate flour mixture and cherry juice, then pour over fruit and mix well. Grease and line bottom and sides of a 10 inch tube pan with wax paper. I put mine in two bread pans. Bake in slow oven at 275 degrees for 2½ hours or until tooth pick comes clean when tried in cake. Have a pan of water on bottom shelf of oven while baking. Cool in pan, wrap and store. If you do not want a large cake, cut the recipe in half. I usually make this and the wafer fruit cake for Christmas. Peppernuts and raisin buns are a must for Christmas. I revised this recipe many years ago as I did not like the candied citrus.

Sophie Giesel Koehn

German Chocolate Cream Cheese Cake

1 German chocolate cake mix, prepared as directed on box

Pour into a 15x10 inch pan.

8 oz. cream cheese	**1 egg**
1½ cups sugar	**1 teaspoon vanilla**

Beat together and pour on top of cake, swirl with knife. Sprinkle over top:
1 cup chocolate chips

Bake at 350 degrees for 30 minutes.

Shirley, Mrs. Arden Penner

Gopher Hill Cake

1 cup dates, cut fine	**¾ cup shortening**
1¼ cup boiling water	**2 teaspoons cocoa**
1 teaspoon soda	**2 eggs**
1 cup sugar	**1½ cups flour**

Soak dates in water and soda. Mix together the rest of the ingredients well and add date mixture. Pour into greased glass pan.

Cover with:

½ cup sugar	**½ cup nuts**
1 package chocolate chips	

Bake at 325 degrees for 50 minutes.

Arlene Giesel Koehn

Heath Candy Bar Cake

Crumble and reserve 1 cup for topping:

2 cups brown sugar	**1 stick butter or oleo**
2 cups flour	

Mix together:

1 egg	**1 teaspoon vanilla**
1 cup buttermilk or sour milk	**¼ teaspoon salt**
1 teaspoon soda	

Add to crumb mixture and put in 9x13 inch pan. Combine reserved crumbs and
4 or 5 Heath candy bars (crumbled)

Sprinkle over top of cake and bake 30 minutes at 350 degrees.

Elaine, Mrs. Bruce Unruh; Jul Nightengale

Hickory Nut Cake

This cake is delicious!

Cake:

2 cups sugar
⅔ cup butter
3 eggs
⅛ teaspoon salt
2 teaspoons baking powder

2½ cups all-purpose flour
1 cup milk
1 teaspoon vanilla extract
1 cup hickory nuts, chopped

Penuche frosting:

½ cup butter
1 cup packed brown sugar
¼ cup milk or cream
2 cups powdered sugar

1 teaspoon vanilla extract
½ cup chopped hickory nuts,
   if desired

For cake: cream together sugar and butter. Add eggs and beat on medium speed of mixer for 2 minutes. Mix salt, baking powder and flour together lightly with fork. Alternate adding flour mixture and milk to sugar mixture. Mix well. Stir in vanilla and nuts. Pour into greased and floured 9x13 inch pan (cake can also be made in 8 inch layer pans.) Bake at 325 degrees for 45 to 50 minutes. Cool. For frosting; melt butter in a medium saucepan. Add brown sugar and boil 2 minutes. Add milk and bring to a boil. Remove from heat; cool to lukewarm. Beat in sugar and vanilla. If desired, add chopped hickory nuts. Frost cake.

Arlene Giesel Koehn   Makes 16 servings

Ho Ho Cake

German chocolate cake mix

Mix and bake in 10x15 inch sheet pan as directed on box. Cool.

5 tablespoons flour
1½ cups milk
1 cup sugar

1 cup Crisco
1 teaspoon vanilla

Mix flour with milk and cook till thick. Cool. Add the sugar, Crisco and vanilla and beat 8-10 minutes. Spread on cake.

Chocolate Icing:

One stick oleo, melted
4 tablespoons cocoa
3 cups powdered sugar

2 teaspoons hot water
1 egg
1 teaspoon vanilla

Mix and spread on cake while frosting is still warm. Add milk if frosting is too thick. Best if frosting can be poured on the filling, because it's hard to spread. (This is a Gallup recipe.)

Dawn Giesel Dyck

Honey Bun Cake

1 yellow cake mix with pudding
4 eggs
⅔ cups vegetable oil
⅓ cup water

8 oz. carton sour cream
½ cup firmly packed brown sugar
1 teaspoon cinnamon
⅔ cup chopped pecans

Glaze:
1 cup sifted powdered sugar
2 tablespoons milk

½ teaspoon vanilla

Combine first five ingredients in a mixing bowl, beat at medium speed with an electric mixer until smooth. Set aside. Combine brown sugar, cinnamon and pecans; set aside. Pour half of batter in a greased and floured 9x13 inch pan. Sprinkle half of sugar mixture over batter. Repeat layers. Gently swirl batter with a knife. Bake at 350 degrees for 30-35 minutes or until a toothpick inserted in center comes out clean. Remove from oven. Drizzle glaze over cake and cool.

Connie, Mrs. Marlon Giesel and Charmaine Wedel

Hummingbird Cake

3 cups all purpose flour
2 cups sugar
1 teaspoon baking soda
1 teaspoon salt
1 teaspoon ground cinnamon
3 well beaten eggs

1 cup vegetable oil
1½ teaspoons vanilla extract
8 oz. can crushed pineapple,
 undrained
1 cup chopped pecans
2 cups chopped bananas

Combine first five ingredients in large mixing bowl. Add well-beaten eggs and oil, stirring until dry ingredients are moistened. Do not beat. Stir in vanilla, pineapple, 1 cup pecans and bananas. Spoon into 3 greased 9 inch floured cake pans. Bake at 350 degrees for 25 to 30 minutes or until wooden pick comes out clean. Cool for 10 minutes in pans. Remove from pans and cool completely. Spread frosting between layers and on top and sides of cake. Sprinkle ½ cup chopped pecans on top.

Cream Cheese Frosting:
8 oz. package cream cheese
½ cup butter, softened

16 oz. package confectioners sugar
1 teaspoon vanilla extract

Combine cream cheese and butter, creaming well. Add:
½ package sugar

Blend well. Stir in vanilla. Add remaining sugar. Stir until frosting reaches spreading consistency.

Carolyn, Mrs. Wayne Holdeman

Maple-nut Cake

Creamy caramel frosting tops this flavorful cake that's good to the last crumb.

½ cup shortening	¼ teaspoon salt
¾ cup brown sugar	3 teaspoons baking powder
½ cup granulated sugar	1 cup milk
3 egg yolks	3 egg whites, beaten stiff
½ teaspoon maple flavoring	½ cup chopped walnuts
2½ cups cake flour	

Thoroughly cream shortening and sugars. Add egg yolks and flavoring; beat until fluffy. Sift together flour, salt and baking powder. Add sifted dry ingredients alternately with milk. Fold in nuts and stiffly-beaten egg whites. Bake in two greased 9 inch layer cake pans in moderate oven, 350 degrees, for 30 minutes. Frost with Caramel Frosting.

Caramel Frosting:

2 cups brown sugar	½ cup milk
½ cup butter	4 cups powdered sugar

Combine brown sugar, butter, milk, heat to boiling. Cook over low heat 3 minutes. Cool. Stir in powdered sugar; beat thoroughly. Spread on cake. Decorate with nut halves.

Mornie Giesel Unruh

Milky Wonder Cake

6 regular size or 13 individual size Milky Way candy bars	2½ cups all-purpose flour
	½ teaspoon baking soda
2 sticks butter, divided	1¼ cups buttermilk
2 cups sugar	1 teaspoon vanilla
4 eggs	1 cup chopped nuts

Frosting:

3 regular sized Milky Way candy bars	2 cups confectioners sugar
1 stick butter	1 to 2 tablespoons milk

In heavy saucepan over low heat, or in microwave, melt candy bars with 1 stick of the butter, stirring frequently until smooth. Remove mixture from heat and allow to cool. Beat remaining 1 stick butter and sugar until light and fluffy. Add eggs 1 at a time, mixing well after each addition. Stir together flour and baking soda and add to batter alternately with buttermilk, mixing just until dry ingredients are moistened. Blend in cooled Milky Way mixture, vanilla and nuts. Turn into a greased and floured Bundt pan or 10 inch tube pan. Bake in 350 degree oven 1 hour and 20 minutes, or until top springs back when lightly touched with finger tips and wooden pick inserted in center comes out clean. (Top will be quite dark). Cool 10 minutes before removing from pan and cooling on wire rack. To make frosting: In saucepan over very low heat, or in microwave, melt candy bars and butter. Gradually beat in confectioners sugar. Thin to desired consistency with milk, spread over cake.

Arlene Giesel Koehn

'Mounds' Cake

½ cup cocoa
2 cups sifted flour
2 cups granulated sugar
1 teaspoon salt
½ cup Oleo
1½ teaspoons baking soda

¾ cup milk
¾ teaspoons baking powder
½ cup milk
3 eggs, unbeaten
1 teaspoon vanilla

Put first seven ingredients in mixing bowl. Beat two minutes. Add baking powder, milk, eggs, and vanilla. Beat two minutes. Pour into two 8 inch square pans which have been greased and floured. Bake for 30-35 minutes. Cool on cake rack for 10-15 minutes. Remove from pans and slit each layer horizontally.

Filling:

1 cup sugar
1 cup milk

30 marshmallows
14 ounces coconut

Put sugar, milk and marshmallows in pan over low heat. Stir constantly until marshmallows melt. Remove from heat and add coconut. Stir well and spread between layers of cake.

Icing:

4 tablespoons cocoa
1½ cups sugar
7 tablespoons milk
2 tablespoons shortening

2 tablespoons oleo
1 tablespoon corn syrup
¼ teaspoon salt
1 teaspoon vanilla

Mix all ingredients except vanilla. Bring slowly to boil, stirring constantly. Boil one and one-half minutes. Remove from heat and cool. Add vanilla and beat until thick enough to spread. (If it thickens too much, add a few drops of milk). Spread over top and sides of cake.

Arlene Giesel Koehn

Oatmeal Chocolate Chip Cake

1¾ cup boiling water
1 cup uncooked oatmeal
1 cup brown sugar
1 cup sugar
½ cup butter or margarine, softened
3 eggs

1¾ cups flour
1 teaspoon baking soda
1 teaspoon cocoa
¼ teaspoon salt
1 package (12 oz.) chocolate chips
¾ cup chopped walnuts or pecans

In mixing bowl, pour water over oatmeal; let stand 10 minutes. Add sugars and butter, stirring until the butter melts. Add eggs, one at a time, mixing well after each addition. Sift flour, soda, cocoa and salt together. Add to batter; mix well. Stir in 1 cup chocolate chips. Pour into greased 9x13 inch pan. Sprinkle top of cake with nuts and remaining chips. Bake at 350 degrees for about 40 minutes. Makes 12 servings. Cake is best served warm. A chocolate lovers delight!

Jana, Mrs. Robert Nichols

Orange Slice Cake

1 cup butter or oleo	1 pound chopped dates
2 cups sugar	1 pound chopped orange slice candy
4 eggs	2 cups chopped nuts
1 teaspoon soda	1 cup coconut
½ cup buttermilk	1 cup fresh orange juice
3½ cups all-purpose flour	2 cups powdered sugar

Cream butter and sugar; add eggs, beat well after each. Dissolve soda in buttermilk and add to creamed mixture. Put flour in large bowl and add fruit, candy and nuts. Stir until coated with flour. Add creamed mixture and work with hands. Put in pan of your choice. Will rise about 1 to 1½ inches. Bake at 250 degrees for 2½ to 3½ hours, depending on pan. Combine orange juice and powdered sugar and pour over hot cake. I use a meat fork to poke holes in the cake so the juice can soak in. Age cake in refrigerator for at least one week.

Ronda, Mrs. Ryan Wedel

Prune Cake with Butterscotch Frosting

Cake:

2 cups all purpose flour	¼ tespoon ground nutmeg
1 teaspoon baking soda	½ cup (1 stick) butter, room
½ teaspoon baking powder	temperature
1 cup sugar	1 cup prune juice
2 eggs	1 cup coarsely chopped pitted prunes
½ teaspoon salt	1 teaspoon cinnamon
¼ teaspoon ground cloves	

Frosting:

1 cup firmly packed golden	¼ cup milk
brown sugar	1 cup powdered sugar
5 tablespoons butter	

For cake: Preheat oven to 350 degrees. Butter 9x13 inch baking pan. Combine flour, baking soda and baking powder in medium bowl. Using electric mixer, beat sugar and butter in large bowl until light and fluffy. Mix in eggs, cinnamon, salt, cloves and nutmeg. Add dry ingredients to butter mixture alternately with prune juice, beginning and ending with dry ingredients. Mix in prunes. Transfer batter to prepared pan. Bake until cake is brown and tester inserted in center comes out clean, about 30 minutes. Cool cake in pan on rack. (Can be prepared 1 day ahead. Cover and store at room temperature.) For frosting: Stir sugar and butter in heavy medium saucepan over medium-low heat until melted and smooth. Add milk and bring mixture to boil, stirring constantly. Boil without stirring until thick, swirling pan occasionally, about 3 minutes. Cool to lukewarm. Add powdered sugar and beat until thickened. Spread frosting over cooled cake. (Can be prepared 8 hours ahead, let stand at room temperature.)

Arlene Giesel Koehn   16 servings

Peter Paul Cake

1 chocolate cake mix

Filling:

1 cup evaporated milk
1 cup sugar
½ cup oleo

20 large marshmallows
¾ pound coconut

Frosting:

¾ stick oleo
⅓ cup evaporated milk

¼ cup cocoa
1 box powdered sugar

Prepare cake mix according to directions on box. Bake in 2 layers. Cool. Split to make 4 layers. Put filling between layers. Filling: Boil milk, sugar and oleo for 5 minutes, then add marshmallows and coconut. Cool. Frosting: Melt oleo, evaporated milk and cocoa. Add powdered sugar. Beat well. Frost top and sides of cake. This cake is better if served 1-3 days after baking. Tastes like a Mounds candy bar. This is our family's favorite Birthday Cake. Especially Dad's!

LeAnne Nichols

Poppy Seed Cake with Orange Glaze

Cake:

2¾ cups sugar
1 cup corn oil
3 large eggs
1½ teaspoons vanilla extract
1 teaspoon almond extract

3 cups all purpose flour
2 tablespoons poppy seeds
1½ teaspoons baking powder
½ teaspoon salt
1½ cups milk

Glaze:

1 cup powdered sugar
¼ cup orange juice

¼ teaspoon almond extract

For cake: Preheat oven to 350 degrees. Grease and flour 12 cup Bundt pan. Using electric mixer, beat first 5 ingredients in large bowl to blend. Mix flour, poppy seeds, baking powder and salt in medium bowl. Stir dry ingredients alternately with milk into sugar mixture, beginning and ending with dry ingredients. Pour batter into prepared pan. Bake until tester inserted near center comes out clean, about 50 minutes. Cool cake in pan on rack 10 minutes. Meanwhile, prepare Glaze: Whisk all ingredients in small bowl to blend. Turn out cake onto rack. Spoon glaze over warm cake. Cool cake completely. Slice and serve.

Arlene Giesel Koehn   Makes 8 servings

Poppy Seed Cake

1 white cake mix   3 tablespoons poppy seed

Prepare cake mix as directed, except use whole eggs and substitute milk for water. Add poppy seed, frost and enjoy.

Deloris, Mrs. Isaac Unruh, Jr.

Pound Cake

1 cup butter	4 eggs
2 cups sugar	1 cup milk
3 cups sifted cake flour	1 teaspoon vanilla
3 teaspoons baking powder	½ teaspoon almond extract
½ teaspoon salt	

Cream butter and sugar until light and fluffy (10 minutes with mixer). Add eggs one at a time, beating well after each. Sift flour with baking powder and salt. Add alternately with milk and flavorings, beating after each addition until smooth. Pour batter into 3 greased and floured 9 inch pans. Bake at 350 degrees for 25-30 minutes. Cool in pans for 10 minutes. Remove from pans and finish cooling on racks.

Caramel Icing:

1 teaspoon vanilla	1 cup cream
3 cups sugar	1 tablespoon light Karo syrup
1 cup milk	1 stick oleo

Melt sugar in heavy pan over low heat, shaking pan as sugar melts. Heat until melted to a golden syrup, stirring constantly, to equal ½ cup. Combine and cook all ingredients, except oleo, to soft ball. Remove from heat, add oleo and beat until creamy and of spreading consistency. Freezes well.

Arlene Giesel Koehn

Pumpkin Cake

4 eggs, beaten	2 teaspoons baking powder
1⅔ cups sugar	2 teaspoons cinnamon
1 cup oil	1 teaspoon soda
2 cups pumpkin	1 teaspoon salt
2 cups flour	

Mix first 4 ingredients together, then add the remaining ingredients. Pour in a large cookie sheet. Bake at 350 degrees for 25 minutes.

Frosting:

3 ounces cream cheese	2 cups powdered sugar or more
½ cup oleo	to the consistency you want
1 teaspoon vanilla	

Fonda, Mrs. Gareth Eicker

Perfect Spice Cake

2¼ cups sifted cake flour
1 teaspoon baking powder
1 teaspoon salt
1 teaspoon cinnamon
¾ teaspoon baking soda
¼ teaspoon cloves
dash pepper

¾ cup butter
1 cup sugar
¾ cup brown sugar, firmly packed
1 teaspoon vanilla
3 eggs
1 cup buttermilk
Date-Nut Filling and Frosting

Sift dry ingredients. Cream butter and sugars till light and fluffy. Add vanilla. Add eggs, one at a time, beating after each addition. Add dry ingredients alternately with buttermilk; beat well. Pour into two 9 inch greased and floured cake pans. Bake at 350 degrees for 30 minutes or till done. Cool. Spread Date-Nut Filling between layers and frost.

Date-Nut Filling:

8 oz. package (1½ cups) dates, chopped
½ cup orange juice

1 teaspoon grated orange peel
¼ cup walnuts, chopped

In saucepan, combine dates and orange juice. Cook and stir till dates are tender and mixture is thick, about 2 or 3 minutes. Add grated orange peel. Cool. Add chopped walnuts.

Cream Cheese Whip Frosting:

2 unbeaten egg whites
¾ cup brown sugar, firmly packed
¾ cup sugar
1½ teaspoon light corn syrup or
    ¼ teaspoon cream of tartar

⅓ cup cold water minus 2 tablespoons
dash salt
1 teaspoon vanilla
1 package (3 oz.) cream cheese

Combine all ingredients, except vanilla and cream cheese over boiling water. Cook beating constantly about 7 minutes. Remove from heat, add vanilla and softened cream cheese blending thoroughly. Frost cake.

Arlene Giesel Koehn

Red Devils Food Cake

2 cups sugar
¾ cup shortening, or ½ cup
    butter and ¼ cup shortening
2 eggs
1 cup sour milk, or 1 cup sweet
    and 1 teaspoon vinegar

1 teaspoon vanilla
2½ cups sifted all purpose flour
2 teaspoons baking soda
1 teaspoon salt
½ cup cocoa
1 cup boiling water

Cream fat and sugar. Add unbeaten eggs one at a time. Beat well after each addition. Add vanilla to milk. Alternate milk with flour which has been sifted with salt, soda, and cocoa. Beginning with flour and ending with flour, dividing milk in thirds and flour in fourths. Add boiling water all at once. Stir until well combined. Bake at 350 degrees until done. This is a large, moist 3 layer cake.

Icing:

4 tablespoons cocoa
3½ tablespoons melted butter

dash of salt
¼ cup water

Bring to boil. Let set 5 minutes. Mix in powdered sugar and vanilla. Add cream or milk as needed.

Sophie Giesel Koehn

Red Velvet Cake

2 cups sugar
1 cup butter
2 eggs
1 tablespoon vinegar
1 tablespoon cocoa
2½ cups flour

½ teaspoon salt
1½ teaspoons soda
1 teaspoon vanilla
2 ounces red food coloring
1 cup buttermilk

Cream sugar, butter and eggs. Beat until fluffy. Make paste from cocoa and vinegar, add to sugar and butter mixture. Sift flour, add salt and soda. Sift again, add to mixture. Add food coloring, vinegar and buttermilk. Beat well. Bake at 350 degrees for 25 minutes.

Topping:

2 (3 oz.) packages cream cheese
2 cups confectioners sugar

3 tablespoons melted butter
1 teaspoon vanilla

Mix till soft.

Theresa, Mrs. Melvern Ratzlaff

Refrigerator Coconut Cake

1 box white cake mix	1 (8 oz.) carton sour cream
½ teaspoon baking powder	1½ cups coconut
2 cups sugar	2 cups Cool Whip

Add baking powder to cake mix. Make cake mix by directions. Make into two 8 inch layers. Split both layers after they are cooled. Blend together the sugar, sour cream and coconut. Chill. Spread all but 1 cup of sour cream mixture between 4 layers. Blend remaining sour cream mixture with cool whip and frost cake. Sprinkle extra coconut on top of cake if desired. Seal in airtight container and refrigerate for 3 days before serving.

Cherylyn, Mrs. Mike Unruh

Snicker Cake

1 regular chocolate cake mix	chocolate chips
30 caramels	nuts (optional)
1 stick butter	

Mix cake as usual. Pour ½ or a little more in a 9x13 inch pan. Bake for about 20 minutes. Melt caramels and butter in microwave and spread on baked cake. Sprinkle chips and nuts over and pour rest of cake batter on. Bake again for 12 minutes.

Julie Nightengale, Charmaine Wedel

Sour Cream Cake

1 Duncan Hines Cake Mix with	3 eggs
pudding	¾ to 1 cup water
½ cup oil	1 cup sour cream

Mix together and bake. This is scrumptious! Frost with your favorite frosting.

Jackie Koehn

Strawberry Cake

1 box cake mix, white or yellow, bake as directed

Mix:

2 boxes strawberry Jell-O	2 cups hot water

Pour over warm cake. Don't cool the Jell-O. Set cake aside to cool.

Mix:

2 cups strawberries	1 cup whipped cream or Cool Whip

Pour over cake.

Jul Nightengale

Southern Pecan Oatmeal Cake

1½ cups boiling water
1 cup quick oatmeal
1 stick margarine
1 cup brown sugar
2 eggs
1 cup white sugar

1⅓ cups flour
1 teaspoon soda
1 teaspoon cinnamon
½ teaspoon salt
1 teaspoon vanilla

Pour water over oats, add oleo and let stand until oleo is melted. Add brown sugar, white sugar, eggs and vanilla. Mix well. Sift together flour, soda, cinnamon, and salt. Add to egg and sugar mixture, mix well. Pour into greased 9x13 pan. Bake at 350 degrees 30-35 minutes.

Frosting:
¾ stick oleo
1 cup brown sugar
¼ cup cream or evaporated milk

½ cup coconut
½ cup pecans

Cook until bubbly. Spread on hot cake. Put under broiler until bubbly and slightly browned. Watch closely!

Mary, Mrs. Lee Giesel

Streusel Cake

1 box Duncan Hines butter flavored yellow cake mix

Mix according to directions. Pour into greased jelly roll pan. Sprinkle top of cake quite heavily with cinnamon sugar mixture and chopped nuts.

Cinnamon sugar mixture:
¾ cup sugar
¼ cup chopped nuts

3 teaspoons cinnamon

Swirl sugar mixture and nuts into cake batter with knife carefully. Bake in 350 degree oven for approximately 15 minutes. Remove from oven and allow to cool slightly. Drizzle with powdered sugar frosting. This is delicious when served warm!

Finette Giesel Koehn

Turtle Cake

1 package caramels
1 package German chocolate
  cake mix
½ cup margarine, softened
1½ cups water

½ cup oil
1 can (14 oz.) sweetened
  condensed milk
chopped pecans

Combine cake mix, oleo, water, oil and ½ can sweetened condensed milk in mixing bowl. Mix well. Pour half of batter into greased and floured 9x13 baking pan. Bake at 350 degrees 20-25 minutes. Melt and mix together caramels and remaining milk over low heat until smooth. Spread over baked cake layer. Sprinkle with chopped nuts. Cover with remaining batter. Return to oven and bake 25-30 minutes longer. Cool, Spread with frosting of your choice. A little goes a long way!

Mary, Mrs. Lee Giesel

Starlight Double Delight Cake

Frosting:

2 (3 oz.) packages cream cheese, softened

½ cup shortening, butter or margarine, softened

½ teaspoon vanilla extract

½ teaspoon mint flavoring (or omit and increase vanilla to 1 teaspoon)

6 cups (1½ pounds) sifted confectioners sugar, divided

¼ cup hot water

4 ounces (4 squares) unsweetened chocolate, melted

Cake:

¼ cup shortening, butter or margarine

2 cups of the chocolate frosting mixture

3 eggs

2¼ cups all purpose flour

1½ teaspoons baking soda

1 teaspoon salt

¾ cup milk

To make frosting: Cream the cream cheese with the shortening, vanilla and mint flavoring. Blend half the sugar into the creamed mixture. Add the hot water alternately with the balance of the sugar. Blend in the melted chocolate and mix until smooth. Set aside. To make cake: Combine the shortening and 2 cups of the frosting, mix thoroughly. Blend in the eggs, one at a time, and beat for 1 minute. Sift together the flour, soda and salt and add to the creamed mixture alternately with the milk, beginning and ending with the dry ingredients. Blend thoroughly after each addition. (With electric mixer, use low speed.) Pour into 2 well-greased and lightly floured 9 inch round cake pans, at least 1 ¼ inches deep. Bake in 350 degree oven for 30 to 40 minutes. (Or bake in 9x13 inch pan for 45 to 55 minutes). Cool and frost with remaining chocolate frosting.

Arlene Giesel Koehn   Serves 12

Vanilla Wafer Fruit Cake

1 pound vanilla wafers

1 pound pecans

½ pound candied cherries

½ pound candied pineapple

¾ pound gumdrops

2 eggs

½ cup powdered sugar

1 small can evaporated milk (I use a little more)

⅛ teaspoon salt

Crush vanilla wafers. Chop fruit and nuts, keeping out 4 whole cherries and 16 whole pecans for decoration. Also 2 whole slices pineapple. Mix fruit with wafer crumbs. Beat eggs well, add sugar, salt and milk to the fruit, nuts and wafers, mixing well. Let stand while putting wax paper in 2 bread loaf pans. Pack in pans and decorate. Bake at 325 degrees for 45 minutes. If I don't have enough vanilla wafers I use graham crackers. For decoration I use a few pecans. I put all the fruit in cake.

Sophie Giesel Koehn

Zucchini Cake

3 cups sugar
4 eggs
1½ cups oil
1 teaspoon vanilla
1 cup nuts
3 cups flour

½ cup teaspoon salt
1 teaspoon soda
2 teaspoons baking powder
1½ teaspoons cinnamon
3 cups zucchini

Mix sugar, eggs, oil and vanilla. Beat well. Add dry ingredients and zucchini. Mix well. Add nuts. This recipe fills a 9x13 inch pan and a 8x8 inch pan. Instead of 8x8 inch pan, I like to make 12 muffins. Frost with cream cheese frosting if desired. Very good just plain.

Bev, Mrs. Lonnie Unruh

Chocolate Filled Cupcakes

2½ cups flour
2 cups sugar
1 teaspoon baking powder
5 tablespoons cocoa
¼ teaspoon salt

2 eggs
1 cup salad oil
1 cup buttermilk
1 teaspoon vanilla

Mix altogether and add:
1 cup hot water with 2 teaspoons soda dissolved in it
Bake cupcakes 25 minutes at 350 degrees.

Filling:
½ cup sugar
1 tablespoon water
⅔ cup Crisco

⅓ cup canned milk
¼ teaspoon salt

Put this all together in bowl and beat 10 minutes. Then add:
1 teaspoon vanilla
½ cup powdered sugar

Beat until mixed. I use my cake decorator to put the filling in the cupcakes.

Shirley, Mrs. Arden Penner

Mini Cheese Cakes

Beat together:
2 packages cream cheese softened
½ cup sugar
2 eggs

Vanilla wafers
Cherry or Blueberry pie filling

In cupcake papers put 1 vanilla wafer. Pour cream cheese mixture over the top till ¾ full. Bake at 325 degrees for 25 minutes. Top with cherry or blueberry pie filling. Keep refrigerated.

Cherylyn, Mrs. Mike Unruh

Surprise Cupcakes

1 package German chocolate cake, mix as directed on box

Fill cupcake papers ⅔ full and drop 1 teaspoon filling in the top of each cupcake. Bake 25 minutes at 350 degrees. Filling, mix together:

8 ounces cream cheese (room temperature)	1 egg
	dash of salt
⅓ cup sugar	

Frosting:

⅛ cup Crisco	2½ tablespoons milk
⅛ cup cocoa	½ teaspoon vanilla
¼ teaspoon salt	1⅔ cup powdered sugar

Beat well.

Arlene, Mrs. Randy Giesel

Surprise Cupcakes

4 (1 oz.) squares semi-sweet chocolate	4 eggs
	1 cup flour
2 sticks margarine	1¼ cup sugar
½ cup chopped pecans	1 teaspoon vanilla

Melt chocolate with margarine; add pecans and set aside. Mix together lightly, without beating; eggs, flour, sugar and vanilla. Fold into chocolate mixture. Pour into greased cupcake tins, about ⅔ full. Bake in 325 degree oven 35 minutes. These need no frosting. It is important not to beat.

Mary, Mrs. Lee Giesel

Beat and Eat Frosting

1 egg white	1 teaspoon vanilla
¾ cup sugar	¼ cup boiling water
¼ teaspoon cream of tartar	

Combine unbeaten egg white, sugar, cream of tartar and vanilla in a small deep bowl. Mix well. Add boiling water and beat until mixture stands in peaks- about 5 minutes. Spread on cake.

Charmaine Wedel

Browned Butter Icing

Melt ¼ cup butter and keep over low heat until golden brown. Remove from heat. Blend in 2 cups powdered sugar, 2 tablespoons cream, 1 teaspoon cooking oil, and 1½ teaspoons vanilla. Stir in 1 tablespoon hot water. Stir until cool and of consistency to spread. If it becomes too thick to spread, warm slightly over hot water.

Sophie Giesel Koehn

Buttercream Vanilla Frosting

¼ cup butter or margarine
½ teaspoon salt
2 teaspoons vanilla

3 cups powdered sugar
¼ cup milk

Combine butter, salt, vanilla and 1 cup sugar. Add milk and remaining sugar alternately. Mix until smooth and creamy. Add sugar to thicken or milk to thin. Will frost a two layer or 9x13 inch cake.

Charmaine Wedel

Buttered Pecan Frosting

1 cup coarsely broken pecans
⅓ cup butter or margarine
3½ cups confectioners sugar,
  measured, then sifted

⅓ cup Half and Half
1 teaspoon vanilla
Butter in which pecans were sautéed

Melt butter in small saucepan. Stir in pecans and sauté over medium low heat, stirring constantly until butter is light golden and pecans are crispy (about 10 minutes.) Drain butter from pecans; set nuts aside. Mix together confectioners sugar, Half and Half, vanilla and butter in which pecans were sautéed, until creamy and of spreading consistency. Blend in nuts, then spread on the cake of your choice. Enough to frost the top of a 9x13x2 inch oblong cake.

Edna Giesel

Caramel Frosting

1 cup sugar
½ cup brown sugar

1 cup cream
1 teaspoon vanilla

Mix together, cook over medium heat, stir until consistency to spread. In memory: Heidi's favorite dessert was Angel Food cake with this frosting.

Mae Unruh, Heidi's Grandmother

Chocolate Frosting

½ cup cocoa
¼ cup Crisco
1½ teaspoons vanilla

½ cup milk
3½ cups powdered sugar

Melt Crisco, add cocoa, stir well. Add vanilla. Add milk and sugar alternately. Mix until smooth and creamy. Add sugar to thicken or milk to thin. Will frost a two layer or 9x13 inch cake.

Charmaine Wedel

Cocoa Fluff Frosting

Mix together thoroughly in mixing bowl:

1 pound powdered sugar
¼ teaspoon salt

½ cup dry cocoa

Add:

1 unbeaten egg plus enough water
  to measure ⅓ cup

1 teaspoon vanilla
⅓ cup soft butter or margarine

Blend ingredients, then beat at moderately high speed for 2 or 3 minutes. If too thick to spread easily, beat in a few drops of water. Will frost top and sides of two 8 or 9 inch layers.

Louise Wedel

Coconut Frosting

2 egg whites
1 cup white corn syrup
pinch salt

1 teaspoon vanilla
1½ cups grated coconut

Put egg whites, syrup, and salt in top of double boiler over rapidly boiling water. Beat with rotary beater until mixture forms peak. Remove from heat. Add vanilla and fold in gently. Spread on cake when cold. Sprinkle with grated coconut.

Arlene Giesel Koehn

"Decorating Icing"

⅔ cups Crisco
4 cups sifted powdered sugar

1 teaspoon almond flavoring
3 tablespoons water (or more)

Mix together well. If too thick to spread, add more water. Will cover a jelly roll size pan and still have some to decorate with. Keeps well in refrigerator.

Carol, Mrs. Gary Koehn

Delight Frosting

3 cups powdered sugar
½ cup natural flavored instant
  malted milk
6 tablespoons soft margarine

2½ tablespoons milk
1 teaspoon vanilla
3 squares (3 ounces) semi-sweet
  chocolate

Combine sugar, malted milk, butter, milk and vanilla in a large bowl. Beat with mixer until blended. Beat one minute until smooth. Makes 1⅔ cups. Spread on top of 9x13x2 inch cake. Melt chocolate over low heat or in a double boiler. Cool, spread over frosting. Refrigerate until firm.

Mornie Giesel Unruh

Fluffy Cocoa Frosting

¾ cup cocoa
4 cups powdered sugar
1 stick oleo

1 teaspoon vanilla
½ cup evaporated milk

Mix cocoa and sugar. Cream part of cocoa-sugar mixture with oleo. Blend in vanilla and half the milk. Add remaining sugar-cocoa mixture and blend well. Add remaining milk and beat to desired spreading consistency. Additional milk may be added if desired. Yield: frosting for two 9 inch layers or one 9x13 cake.

Jolene Unruh

Fudge Frosting:

2 (1 oz.) squares chocolate
1¾ cup sugar
1 tablespoon corn syrup
½ cup milk

6 tablespoons margarine
¼ teaspoon salt
1 teaspoon vanilla

Cut chocolate in pieces. Combine with sugar, syrup, milk, oleo and salt in 2 quart saucepan. Bring to full, rolling boil, stirring constantly. Boil 2 minutes. Remove from heat, cool to lukewarm. Add vanilla and beat until spreading consistency. Spread on cake.

Mary, Mrs. Lee Giesel

Lemon Cake Icing

Prepare a lemon cake according to directions on cake mix. Bake in three 8 inch pans. Cool. Mix: 1 frozen lemon concentrate (small size), thawed, 1 can Eagle Brand sweetened condensed milk, 8 ounce cool whip. Ice the cake with lemon mixture and refrigerate. Good to make ahead for company. You may want to garnish it with lemon slices. Makes a pretty cake!

Janice, Mrs. Jerry Ratzlaff

Magic Chocolate Frosting

2½ to 3 (1 oz.) squares
   unsweetened chocolate
1 (15 oz.) can sweetened
   condensed milk

1 tablespoon water
1 teaspoon vanilla
dash of salt

Melt chocolate over simmering water; add condensed milk and cook 5 minutes, stirring constantly. Remove from heat; add water, vanilla and salt. Stir until smooth Spread over cake. Will frost 13x9½x2 inch cake.

Deanna Giesel

Marshmallow Coconut Icing

1 cup sugar
⅓ cup water
8 large marshmallows

2 stiffly beaten egg whites
1 cup grated coconut

Mix sugar and water and cook over medium heat until it spins a thread. Add marshmallows and stir to melt them well. Fold into beaten egg whites. Spread over cooled cake layers and sprinkle with grated coconut.

Arlene Giesel Koehn

Mocha Frosting

½ cup butter, softened
1 box confectioners sugar, sifted
⅓ cup powdered instant coffee
1 slightly beaten egg
2 tablespoons milk

1 square unsweetened chocolate, melted
pinch salt
½ teaspoon vanilla

Cream butter and 1 cup sugar together well. Add next 6 ingredients and beat until smooth and creamy. Blend in remaining sugar.

Arlene Giesel Koehn

Rosie's Icing

1 pound powdered sugar
1 cup Crisco
3 tablespoons water

½ teaspoon almond extract
½ teaspoon lemon extract

Mix well. Add food coloring if desired. Good for decorating cakes. Will keep in the refrigerator for a long while.

Charmaine Wedel

Smooth and Creamy Frosting

1 package (4-serving size)
  Jell-O instant vanilla pudding,
  or other flavor

¼ cup powdered sugar
1 cup cold milk
8 oz. container Cool Whip

Combine pudding mix, sugar and milk in a bowl. Beat at lowest speed on mixer until well blended. Fold in whipped topping. Spread on cake at once. Makes about 4 cups. Note: Frosted cake should be refrigerated. For a firmer frosting let mixture stand 5 minutes before adding cool whip.

Charmaine Wedel

Speedy Caramel Frosting

½ cup butter or margarine
1 cup brown sugar, firmly packed
¼ teaspoon salt

¼ cup milk
2½ cups sifted powdered sugar
½ teaspoon vanilla

Melt butter, blend in brown sugar and salt. Cook over low heat 2 minutes, stirring constantly. Add milk; continue stirring until mixture comes to a boil. Remove from heat. Blend in powdered sugar gradually, add vanilla and mix well. Thin with small amount of cream if necessary. Add nuts if desired.

Arlene Giesel Koehn

Pie Crust

The well-to-do, the "upper crust," may find life smooth and thrilling, but it's the humble lower crust that holds in all the filling.

Cheddar Crust for Apple Pie

1¾ cups all purpose flour
⅛ teaspoon salt
4 ounces coarsely shredded sharp
   cheddar cheese (1 cup)

½ cup solid vegetable shortening
6-7 tablespoons cold water

Mix flour and salt, cut in cheese and shortening, sprinkle with water, 1 tablespoon at a time. Press lightly to form dough. Shape into 2 balls, flatten to 1 inch, wrap in plastic. Refrigerate about 1 hour until firm enough to roll. Yield: crust for one 9 inch pie.

Arlene Giesel Koehn

Low Cholesterol Pie Crust

2 cups sifted flour
1½ teaspoons salt

½ cup cooking oil
¼ cup water

Sift flour and salt together. Add oil and water. Stir with a fork until barely mixed. This is not quite as tender and flaky as regular crust and is harder to handle. Roll between two pieces of waxed paper. Put pie tin upside down on pastry- do a quick flip and you'll have the crust in your pan without tearing. Peel off paper and you're ready to go.

Mary, Mrs. Lee Giesel

Non-cholesterol Pie Crust

Note: Because of the high content of hydrogenated fat in this dough, it does not adapt itself well for baking as single crust shells.

2 cups all purpose flour	¼ cup cold water
1½ sticks, plus 2 tablespoon	
no-cholesterol margarine	

Cut margarine into flour until mealy. Add water all at once, mix quickly and lightly and gather dough together so it cleans the bowl. Divide and roll out on lightly floured surface. Yield: 10 inch double crust pie. Tender and flaky.

Edna Giesel

Pie Crust

1 cup flour	½ cup oleo
¼ cup milk	

Mix together well. Enough for 1 pie shell and a few plots.

Carol, Mrs. Gary Koehn

Pie Dough

Blend

4 cups flour	2 cups shortening

Mix together following ingredients and add to flour mixture:

¾ cup water	2 teaspoon salt
¾ cup flour	

Mix all together just until blended. Makes 4-5 single Crusts.

Reva, Mrs. Steve Yoder

Meringue

3 egg whites	¼ teaspoon cream of tartar
½ teaspoon vanilla	6 tablespoons sugar

Beat egg whites with vanilla and cream of tartar until soft peaks. Gradually add sugar, beating till peaks are stiff and glossy. Spread on pie and bake at 350 degrees for 12-15 minutes.

Mary, Mrs. Lee Giesel

Marshmallow Creme Meringue

Beat 3 egg whites with a dash of salt until soft peaks form. Gradually add 1 cup marshmallow creme, beating until stiff peaks form. Spread over pie filling, sealing to edge of crust. Bake at 350 degrees 12-15 minutes or lightly browned.

Arlene Giesel Koehn

No Fail Meringue

½ cup water   6 tablespoons sugar
1 tablespoon cornstarch

Bring to boil. Let cool while making filling. Beat 3 egg whites to frothy before they trace, add cooked mixture and beat, Beat!

Jul Nightengale

Perfect Meringue

⅓ cup water   ½ tablespoon sugar
1 tablespoon cornstarch

Boil the above until clear. Cool to lukewarm. Add 3 egg whites, stiffly beaten and 2½ tablespoon sugar and beat, beat, beat!

Jul Nightengale

Pie Meringue

2 egg whites, stiffly beaten   1 tablespoon white karo syrup
¼ teaspoon cornstarch   pinch salt
½ cup sugar   2 tablespoons water
⅛ teaspoon cream of tartar

Cook all ingredients (except egg whites) to soft ball. Pour slowly over beaten egg whites, beat with mixer on high. Add 1 teaspoon vanilla. Spread over pie filling. Serve.

Arlene Giesel Koehn

Bisquick Apple Pie

1 cup Bisquick   ⅔ cup sugar
½ cup milk   ½ cup cream
3-4 apples   cinnamon

Mix Bisquick and milk, cover bottom and sides of pie plate. Slice apples over top, cover with sugar and pour cream over all. Sprinkle with cinnamon. Bake 350 degrees for 35 minutes.

Jul Nightengale

Apple Apricot Pie Walnut Crust

2 pounds Golden Delicious
  apples, peeled, cored and sliced
1 tablespoon lemon juice
½ cup thinly-sliced dried apricots
2 teaspoon margarine, melted

1 tablespoon sugar
⅛ teaspoon ground cinnamon
1 tablespoon sugar
½ teaspoon ground cinnamon

Walnut Pastry:
¼ cup walnuts
1 tablespoon sugar
1 cup flour
⅛ teaspoon ground cinnamon

2 tablespoons margarine
1 tablespoon vegetable shortening
3-4 tablespoons ice water

Combine apples, lemon juice, 1 tablespoon sugar and ⅛ teaspoon cinnamon. Arrange in a 9 inch pie plate; top with apricots. Walnut Pastry: Combine walnuts and 1 tablespoon sugar in container of electric blender; cover and process until finely ground. Combine walnut mixture, flour and ⅛ teaspoon cinnamon. Cut in margarine and shortening with a pastry blender until mixture resembles coarse meal. Sprinkle ice water, 1 tablespoon at a time, over surface; stir with fork until dry ingredients are moistened. Shape into a ball. Wrap in waxed paper; chill 15 minutes. Yield: 1 pastry for 9 inch shell. Roll to an 11 inch circle. Place over apricots; trim edges. Flute edges of pastry, sealing to edge of pie plate. Brush pastry with margarine. Combine 1 teaspoon sugar and ½ teaspoon and cinnamon. Sprinkle over pastry. Cut slits in pastry to allow steam to escape. Bake at 350 degrees for 50 minutes or until crust is lightly brown.

Arlene Giesel Koehn   Serves 8

Hot Apple Cobbler with Cinnamon Ice Cream

½ cup butter or margarine, melted
1½ cups sugar
1 cup all purpose flour
1 tablespoon baking powder
½ teaspoon salt
1 cup milk

4 cups thinly sliced, peeled,
  and cored cooking apples
1½ cups firmly packed brown sugar
1½ teaspoons ground cinnamon
¼ teaspoon ground allspice
Cinnamon Ice Cream

Pour melted butter into a 13x9x2 inch baking dish. Combine sugar, flour, baking powder, and salt; stir in milk, mixing until smooth. Pour into prepared dish. Arrange apples evenly over batter. Combine brown sugar, cinnamon, and allspice; sprinkle over apples. Bake at 350 degrees for 1 hour or until top is golden brown. Spoon into individual serving bowls, and top each with Cinnamon Ice Cream. Yield: 8-10 servings

Cinnamon Ice Cream:
1 quart vanilla ice cream, softened
½ cup sugar

1 tablespoon ground cinnamon

Combine all ingredients in a large mixing bowl, mixing well. Freeze until firm.

Arlene Giesel Koehn   Yield: 1 quart

Sour Cream Apple Walnut Pie

Crust:

1 cup all purpose flour
¼ teaspoon salt
¼ cup cold butter or margarine,
    cut in small pieces

3-4 tablespoons cold tap water

Filling:

¾ cup sour cream
1 large egg
⅓ cup granulated sugar
1 tablespoon all purpose flour
1 teaspoon vanilla
1 teaspoon ground cinnamon

¼ teaspoon ground nutmeg
3 pounds tart apples (Pippins,
    Granny Smiths or Greenings)
    peeled, quartered, cored and
    cut in ¼ inch thick slices (10 cups)

Crumb Topping:

½ cup all purpose flour
⅓ cup packed light brown sugar
½ cup cold butter or margarine,
    cut into small pieces

1 teaspoon ground cinnamon
½ cup (2 ounces) walnut pieces,
    chopped coarse

To make crust, mix flour and salt in a medium size bowl. Cut in butter with a pastry blender until mixture resembles coarse crumbs. Sprinkle water over flour mixture, 1 tablespoon at a time, stirring lightly with a fork after each addition to distribute moisture evenly. Press lightly to form a ball. Flatten into a 1 inch thick round. Wrap in plastic; refrigerate about 1 hour until firm enough to roll. Have a 9 inch pie plate ready. Roll out dough; line pie plate.

To make Filling: whisk sour cream and egg in a large bowl until blended. Whisk in sugar, flour, vanilla, cinnamon and nutmeg; stir in apples. Spread in pie plate, mounding mixture in center.

To make Topping: mix flour, sugar and cinnamon in a medium size bowl. Cut in butter until mixture resembles coarse crumbs. Stir in walnuts. Sprinkle evenly over filling, then press down lightly. To Bake: place oven rack in center of oven; heat to 400 degrees. Bake pie 50 to 60 minutes until topping is dark brown and apples are tender when pierced. (If topping browns too quickly during baking, drape a piece of foil over pie.) Cool on wire rack. Serve warm or at room temperature.

Arlene Giesel Koehn

Makes 8 servings

Cherry Pie

3 cups cherries (partially thawed)
3 heaping tablespoons cornstarch
1 cup sugar
red food coloring (if desired)

Mix cornstarch with sugar and combine with cherries. Place in an un-baked pie shell. Dot with butter. Top with a circle of pie dough to which vents have been cut into. Crimp edges. Bake at 350 degrees until golden brown (approximately 45 minutes to 1 hour.

Crust:
2 cups flour
1 cup Crisco
½ cup milk
½ teaspoon salt

Place flour in bowl. Cut in Crisco until it is the size of peas. Add salt and milk; blend with a fork until barely mixed. Roll out on a floured pastry sheet. This makes enough for 3 single crusts or 2 double crust pies.

Janice, Mrs. Jerry Ratzlaff

Very 'Easy' Cherry Pie

Buy 2 frozen pie crusts. Place 1 can of cherry pie filling in the bottom crust. Then invert the second pie crust on top of this, until it starts to thaw. Seal the crusts together, cut some designs in the top crust, sprinkle with sugar, and put in oven and bake for 30-40 minutes at 425 degrees.

Submitted by Nathan Giesel

Fresh Fruit Pie with a Nut Crust

Nut Crust:
1 cup almonds
1 cup hazelnuts or walnuts
⅓ cup raisins
¼ cup apple juice

Filling:
2 bananas
1 tablespoon freshly squeezed
  lemon juice
2-3 kiwi fruits
1 quart fresh strawberries

Place the nuts and raisins in a blender or food processor and pulse until they are chopped well but not too fine. They should resemble small pebbles, not flour. Add the apple juice and pulse on and off for a few seconds. Pour the nut mixture into a glass pie plate and press out to shape a crust. Slice the bananas and spread them inside the bottom of the nut crust, pressing slightly. Sprinkle with the lemon juice to prevent the bananas from turning brown. Slice the kiwi fruits and add atop the bananas, pressing slightly. Slice the strawberries and add atop the Kiwis, pressing slightly. Chill the pie for at least 1 hour. Carefully slice and serve.

Arlene Giesel Koehn

Fruit Cocktail Parfait Pie

Make this pie for an elegant treat. It is as pretty as it is delicious.

1 baked 9 inch pastry shell
1 can (17 oz.) fruit cocktail
¾ cup water

1 package (3 oz.) lime gelatin
1 pint vanilla ice cream
Whipping cream

Drain fruit cocktail, reserving syrup. Pour syrup and water into a two quart saucepan. Bring to a boil, remove from heat. Add gelatin, stir until dissolved. Cut ice cream into six to eight pieces. Blend into hot gelatin until melted. Chill until partly set. Fold in fruit, pour into pastry shell. Chill to set. Serve with whipped cream.

Mornie Giesel Unruh   Makes eight servings

Freeze Ahead Peach Pie Filling

4 quarts peeled, sliced fresh peaches
3½ cups sugar
¾ cup quick-cooking tapioca

¾ teaspoon salt
¼ teaspoon lemon juice

In a large bowl, combine all ingredients. Let stand for 15 minutes. Line four 9 inch pie pans with foil. Add fruit mixture and level; place in freezer until frozen solid. When frozen, close foil, sealing well to prevent freezer burn. Remove from pans and stack in freezer until ready to use. To bake, remove peaches from foil and place in unbaked pie shell. Cover with top crust and seal. Brush with melted butter and cover crust edges with foil. Bake at 400 degrees for 50 minutes. Remove foil and bake 20 minutes or until bubbly and golden brown.

Charmaine Wedel

Peach-berry Pie

¼ cup sugar
2 tablespoons cornstarch
2 cups strawberries, washed,
  hulled, and crushed
2 tablespoons lemon juice

3 cups fresh or canned peach
  slices, drained
1 cup strawberries, washed,
  hulled, and halved
1 (9-inch) pastry shell

In saucepan, combine sugar, cornstarch, crushed strawberries and lemon juice. Cook over medium heat, stirring constantly until thickened and clear. Cool. Arrange peach slices and halved strawberries in pie shell in attractive design. Pour strawberry glaze over fruit. Chill 2 hours.

Arlene Giesel Koehn

Peaches and Cream Pie

¾ cup flour
½ cup milk
1 teaspoon baking powder
1 egg
½ cup sugar
1 small package dry vanilla pudding mix (not instant)
1 teaspoon vanilla
1 (29 oz.) can sliced peaches, drained (reserve juice)

1 (8 oz.) package cream cheese, softened
3 tablespoons reserved peach juice
½ cup sugar
1 teaspoon peach flavoring (optional)
1 tablespoon sugar
1 teaspoon cinnamon

Mix flour, milk, baking powder, egg, ½ cup sugar, pudding mix and vanilla together. Pour into a 10 inch pie plate (a smaller pan will not work). Drain peaches, reserving juice, and arrange slices on top of dough. Combine cream cheese, 3 tablespoons reserved juice, sugar and peach flavoring. Spread over peaches, but not to the edge. Combine sugar and cinnamon and sprinkle on top. Bake at 350 degrees for 35 minutes.

Charmaine Wedel

Streusel Cream Peach Pie

Pastry for one 9 inch pie crust
10 peaches
½ cup white sugar
½ teaspoon nutmeg
2 eggs

¼ cup heavy cream
¼ cup brown sugar
½ cup flour
¼ cup butter or margarine

Preheat oven to 425 degrees. Line a 9 inch pie plate with pastry. Peel, pit, and quarter peaches. Arrange in pastry-lined plate. Combine sugar and nutmeg. Sprinkle over peaches. In small bowl beat eggs and cream; pour over peaches. Blend brown sugar and flour; cut in butter or margarine until mixture resembles coarse crumbs. Sprinkle on peaches. Bake in preheated oven for 35 to 40 minutes.

Mornie Giesel Unruh

Fresh Pear Pie

Pear Filling:

1 cup sugar
1 teaspoon nutmeg

1 teaspoon cinnamon
7½ cups thinly sliced, pared pears

Combine cinnamon, nutmeg, and sugar and mix thoroughly with pears. Turn into a pastry-lined pan. Roll out remaining half of dough for top crust large enough to extend 1 inch beyond edge of pan. Make several slits near center to allow for steam to escape. Moisten edge of bottom crust with water. Place pastry over pie. Seal by pressing with fingertips; flute. Bake in 350 degrees oven for 50 minutes, until pastry is well browned.

Pastry:

2 cups all purpose flour
⅔ cup plus 2 tablespoons
    Crisco shortening
½ to 1 cup shredded sharp
    cheddar cheese

1 teaspoon salt
¼ cup ice water

In a medium bowl, mix flour and salt. Cut in shortening and cheese with a pastry blender until the particles resemble giant peas. Sprinkle with water, a little at a time, mixing lightly with a fork, until all flour is moistened. Make a ball with the dough and place on a lightly floured cloth-covered board. Divide dough in half. Roll out into 12 inch circle. Fold pastry in half and carefully transfer to 9 inch pie plate.

Arlene Giesel Koehn

French Raisin Pie

1 cup seedless raisins
1 stick butter
1½ cups sugar
3 eggs
1 cup pecans, chopped

½ teaspoon cinnamon
½ teaspoon all-spice
½ teaspoon cloves
2 tablespoons vinegar
2 pie crusts (nine inches) unbaked

Let raisins plump in boiling water until tender. Drain. Cream butter and add sugar slowly, beating constantly. Add eggs one at a time and beat just until blended. Stir in raisins and pecans. Mix spices and vinegar and add to mixture. Spoon mixture into pie crusts. Bake at 350 degrees for 30-40 minutes or until pies are set but not firm in center. Cool before serving.

Arlene Giesel Koehn   Makes 2 pies and serves 12 to 16

Mile High Pie

Almond pie shell:

1/4 cup butter
1/4 teaspoon salt
2 tablespoons sugar
1 egg yolk

3/4 cup sifted flour
1/4 cup finely chopped almonds
  or pecans

Cream butter, salt and sugar. Add egg yolk; stir in flour and nuts. Press dough into a 9 inch pie plate. Refrigerate for 30 minutes. Bake at 350 degrees for 15 minutes. Chill before pouring in filling.

Filling:

10 oz. package frozen strawberries
1 cup sugar
2 egg whites, at room temperature
1 tablespoon lemon juice

pinch of salt
1 cup whipping cream
1/2 teaspoon almond extract

Thaw strawberries and reserve a few for garnish. In mixing bowl, combine berries, sugar, egg whites, lemon juice and salt. Beat for 15 minutes or until stiff. Whip cream with almond extract. Fold into berry mixture. Mound in almond pie shell and freeze until firm. Garnish with berries.

Arlene Giesel Koehn

Pink Lady Pie

Crust:

1 1/2 cups flour
1/4 teaspoon salt
1 1/2 tablespoons sugar

1/2 cup oil
2 tablespoons milk

Filling:

2 cups diced rhubarb
1 cup sugar
1 package (3 oz.) strawberry gelatin

1 tablespoon lemon juice
2 cups whipped topping

For crust, mix flour, salt, sugar, oil and milk thoroughly. Press into 9 inch pie pan, making an edge or rim. Bake at 350 degrees 15-20 minutes. Set aside to cool. For filling; cook rhubarb and sugar slowly until tender. Add gelatin (dry). Stir gently until dissolved. Let cool. Add lemon juice. Cool to room temperature. Fold in whipped topping. Pour into cooled crust and refrigerate. This may be frozen. Top with whipped topping when served.

Mornie Giesel Unruh

Strawberry-Rhubarb Lattice Pie

Crust:

3¾ cups all purpose flour
1½ teaspoons salt
½ cup (1 stick) chilled unsalted butter, cut into pieces

½ cup chilled solid vegetable shortening, cut into pieces
½ cup plus 2 tablespoons (approx.) cold water

Filling:

1¼ pounds sliced fresh rhubarb or frozen, thawed, drained, patted dry
4 cups thickly sliced hulled strawberries (about 1 pound)

2 cups sugar
⅓ cup cornstarch
3 tablespoons butter, cut into pieces

For Crust: Combine flour and salt in large bowl. Add butter and shortening and cut in until mixture resembles coarse meal. Stir in enough water to bind dough. Divide dough in half. Flatten each piece into disk. Wrap in plastic; refrigerate 30 minutes. Preheat oven to 400 degrees. Roll out 1 dough piece on floured surface to ¼ inch thickness. Line 10 inch pie pan with dough. Place foil over crust and fill with pie weights or dried beans. Bake 10 minutes. Remove foil and weights. Bake crust until golden brown, about 15 minutes. Cool.

For Filling: Combine rhubarb and strawberries in large bowl. Mix in sugar and cornstarch. Roll out remaining dough piece on lightly floured surface to ¼ inch thickness. Cut into twelve ½ inch wide strips. Spoon filling into crust. Dot filling with butter. Place dough strips atop filling, forming lattice design. Gently pinch ends of strips to crust. Bake until dough strips are golden brown and the filling bubbles, about 55 minutes. Let cool completely before serving.

Arlene Giesel Koehn

Rhubarb Pie

3 cups rhubarb
2 tablespoons cornstarch
a little cinnamon

1½ cups sugar
salt to taste

Mix all ingredients. Place in un-baked pie shell. Dot with butter. Top with a circle of pie dough into which vents have been cut. Crimp edges. Bake at 350 degrees for approximately 45 minutes or until golden brown.

Janice, Mrs. Jerry Ratzlaff

Raspberry, Rhubarb and Pear Pie

2 (12 oz.) packages frozen
  unsweetened raspberries,
  partially thawed
1⅓ pounds fresh rhubarb, trimmed,
  cut into 1 inch pieces or one
  20 oz. package frozen rhubarb,
  partially thawed
4 cups diced, peeled, cored pears
  (about 3 medium)

2⅓ cups sugar
¾ cup plus 2 teaspoons all purpose
  flour
1 tablespoon ground cinnamon
1 egg, beaten with 2 tablespoons
  milk (for glaze)
grated peel of two oranges
sugar
vanilla ice cream or frozen yogurt

Preheat oven to 425 degrees. Combine raspberries, rhubarb, diced pears, sugar, ¾ cup all-purpose flour, grated orange peel and 1 tablespoon ground cinnamon in large bowl. Mix gently. Sprinkle each crust with 1 teaspoon flour; spread flour over. Place each crust floured side down in separate 10 inch diameter pie dishes or 9 inch diameter deep dish pie dishes. Divide fruit filling between crusts. Arrange crust atop pies. Press edges together and crimp. Cut eight 1 ½ inch long slits in each top crust, radiating from near center. Brush pies with egg glaze. Sprinkle with sugar. Bake until golden brown and filling bubbles (covering edges with foil after 30 minutes) about 1 hour. Cool pies completely. Serve pies with vanilla ice cream.

Arlene Giesel Koehn

Praline Pumpkin Pie

The crunchy pecan-brown sugar praline topping is super easy to make.

1 teaspoon all purpose flour
2 tablespoons apricot jam
1 cup plus 2 tablespoons canned
  solid pack pumpkin
¾ cup sugar
¾ cup whipping cream
6 tablespoons milk
2 large eggs, beaten to blend
1 teaspoon rum flavoring
1 unbaked pie shell

¾ teaspoon ground cinnamon
¼ teaspoon ground ginger
¼ teaspoon ground nutmeg
¼ teaspoon ground cloves
½ cup packed golden brown sugar
½ cup coarsely chopped pecans
2 tablespoons (¼ stick) unsalted
  butter, melted
whipped cream

Preheat oven to 450 degrees. Sprinkle crust with 1 teaspoon flour. Pierce crust several times with fork. Bake until set, about 10 minutes. Transfer to rack; cool completely. Brush bottom of crust with jam. Reduce oven temperature to 400 degrees. Whisk pumpkin and next 9 ingredients in large bowl to blend. Pour into prepared crust. Place pie on baking sheet. Bake 20 minutes. Reduce temperature to 350 degrees; bake until filling is completely set, cover edge of crust with foil if browning too quickly, about 45 minutes. Transfer to rack and cool completely. Preheat broiler. Mix brown sugar, pecans and butter in medium bowl. Sprinkle mixture over pie. Broil until topping bubbles, watching closely to keep pie from burning. Cool at least 1 hour. Cut pie into wedges and serve with whipped cream.

Arlene Giesel Koehn   8 servings

Pumpkin Pie

3½ cups pumpkin
1 tablespoon flour
1 teaspoon cocoa
4 eggs
½ teaspoon cinnamon
¼ teaspoon allspice

⅛ teaspoon cloves
1 teaspoon vanilla
1 cup milk
2½ or 3 cups sugar
½ teaspoon salt

Beat egg whites. Fold in last. Or mix the whole egg with the pumpkin. I got this recipe from Matilda Giesel when we were first married, and I have always liked it.

Call this Matilda's Pie, by Sophie Giesel Koehn   Makes two pies

Pumpkin Walnut Pie

1 cup flour
1 cup firmly packed brown sugar
½ cup (1 stick) butter, chilled
1 cup canned solid-pack pumpkin
2 eggs, beaten
1 cup evaporated milk

1 teaspoon ground cinnamon
¼ teaspoon ground cloves
½ cup chopped dates
⅓ cup chopped, toasted walnuts
whipped cream

Preheat oven to 350 degrees. In bowl of food processor, combine flour, ⅓ cup of the brown sugar and the ½ cup butter. Process until mixture resembles coarse meal. Press evenly onto bottom and sides of 9 inch pie plate. Prick bottom several times with fork. Bake in a 350 degree oven for 5 minutes; remove from oven. Increase oven temperature to 375 degrees. In medium bowl, combine pumpkin, eggs, milk, remaining ⅔ cup sugar, cinnamon and cloves. Stir in dates and walnuts; pour into prepared crust. Place pie on cookie sheet. Bake in a 375 degree oven for 45 to 50 minutes or until knife is inserted near center comes out clean. Cool completely. Serve topped with whipped cream.

Arlene Giesel Koehn   Makes one 9 inch pie

Sophie's Pumpkin Pie

2 eggs
1¾ cup pumpkin
¾ cup sugar
½ teaspoon salt
⅛ teaspoon all-spice
⅛ teaspoon cloves

1⅓ cup evaporated milk or
    light cream
½ tablespoon flour
1 teaspoon vanilla
1 teaspoon cocoa

Blend ingredients and pour into unbaked pie shell. Bake at 350 degrees for 55 minutes.

Nancy, Mrs. Kenneth Unruh

The Ultimate Pumpkin Pie

Crust:
1¼ cups all purpose flour
½ cup powdered sugar
3 tablespoons whipping cream

½ cup (1 stick) chilled butter,
   cut into pieces

Filling:
¾ cup sugar
1 tablespoon packed golden
  brown sugar
1 tablespoon cornstarch
2 teaspoons ground cinnamon
¾ teaspoon ground ginger

¼ teaspoon (generous) salt
16 oz. can solid pack pumpkin
¾ cup whipping cream
½ cup sour cream
3 large eggs, beaten to blend
¼ cup apricot preserves

For crust: Preheat oven to 350 degrees. Blend first 3 ingredients in processor until mixture resembles coarse meal. Add cream and process until moist clumps form. Gather dough into ball; flatten into disk. Wrap in plastic; chill 15 minutes. Roll out dough on floured surface to 14 inch round. Transfer dough to 9 inch glass pie dish. Line crust with foil, pressing firmly. Bake until sides are set, about 10 minutes. Remove foil. Bake crust until pale brown, about 10 minutes more. Reduce oven temperature to 325 degrees. For Filling: Using whisk, mix first 6 ingredients in bowl until no lumps remain. Blend in pumpkin, whipping cream, sour cream and eggs. Spread preserves over crust; pour in filling. Bake until filling puffs at edges and center is almost set, about 55 minutes. Cool on rack. Cover; chill until cold. (Can be made 1 day ahead).

Arlene Giesel Koehn

Bays Pecan Pie

1 cup white Karo syrup
¾ cup sugar
1 teaspoon vanilla
¼ teaspoon salt

1½ teaspoon lemon juice
¼ cup melted margarine
3 eggs, slightly beaten
1 cup small pecan meats

Combine syrup, sugar, salt, vanilla, margarine and lemon juice. Stir in eggs well, do not beat. Fold in pecans. Pour into pastry. Bake 425 degrees for 10 minutes. Reduce heat to 325 degrees and bake 35 to 40 minutes or until golden.

Reva, Mrs. Steve Yoder

Caramel Nut Pie

1 baked pie shell
1½ cups sugar
3 eggs, separated
5 tablespoons flour
1 cup milk

½ cup very hot water
2 tablespoons butter or margarine
1 teaspoon vanilla
1 cup nuts, walnuts or pecans

Put ½ cup sugar in heavy skillet over low heat until it melts and turns light brown. Carefully add hot water and let simmer until sugar is dissolved. Meanwhile, in heavy saucepan or double boiler, mix 1 cup sugar and flour, ½ cup milk and egg yolks. Beat well with electric mixer. Add rest of milk, mix well then add caramel mixture. Cook over medium heat until thick and creamy. Remove from heat. Add butter and vanilla and beat with mixer on low. Add nuts and pour into pie shell. Cover with meringue.

Caramel Nut Pie Meringue:
3 egg whites   3 tablespoons sugar

Beat egg whites until stiff. Fold in sugar. Spread onto pie. Brown slightly in oven.

Arlene Giesel Koehn

Date-Pecan Pie

8 oz. package chopped dates
1 cup pecans, coarsely chopped
¼ cup all purpose flour
2 cups sugar
¾ cup butter or margarine,
    softened

1½ teaspoons vanilla extract
pinch of salt
4 eggs, separated
¾ cup milk
2 unbaked, 9 inch pastry shells

Combine dates, pecans and flour; stir well and set aside. Combine sugar, butter, vanilla, and salt in a large mixing bowl; mix well. Add egg yolks and milk, mixing well. Stir in pecans and dates. Beat egg whites until stiff but not dry. Fold egg whites into creamed mixture. Pour batter evenly into pastry shells. Bake at 300 degrees for 45 minutes. Increase temperature to 325 degrees, and bake 30 additional minutes or until firm.

Arlene Giesel Koehn   Yield: two 9 inch pies

Macadamia Nut Pie

Crust:

1⅓ cups all purpose flour
½ teaspoon salt
¾ cup chopped macadamia nuts

⅓ cup Crisco shortening
4 to 5 tablespoons ice water

Filling:

1 envelope (1 tablespoon)
    unflavored gelatin
¼ cup cold water
4 eggs, separated

1 cup sugar, divided
½ teaspoon salt
¾ cup lilikoi (passion fruit) juice
1 teaspoon grated orange peel

Topping:

1½ cups whipping cream
¼ cup sugar
1½ teaspoons vanilla

½ cup whole or chopped,
    toasted macadamia nuts*

*To toast macadamia nuts, place nuts in baking pan in 350 degree oven. Stir every 2 minutes until browned. Cool before using.

Heat oven to 450 degrees. For crust, combine flour and salt in bowl. Stir in nuts. Cut in Crisco using pastry blender, until all flour is just blended in to form pea-size chunks. Sprinkle with water, one tablespoon at a time. Toss lightly with fork until dough will form a ball. Roll dough and press into pie plate. Fold edge under. Flute as desired. Prick bottom and sides thoroughly with fork (50 times) to prevent shrinkage. Bake at 450 degrees for 10 to 12 minutes or until golden brown. For Filling, sprinkle gelatin over cold water in small bowl. Set aside. Beat egg yolks lightly in small saucepan. Add ½ cup sugar, salt and lilikoi juice. Cook and stir on medium heat until mixture comes to a boil and thickens. Remove from heat. Add gelatin mixture, stirring until dissolved. Stir in orange peel when mixture begins to set. Beat egg whites until foamy. Beat in remaining ½ cup sugar, one tablespoon at a time, until stiff peaks form. Fold into partially set gelatin mixture. Pour into baked pie shell. Refrigerate until firm. For topping, beat cream until thick. Beat in sugar, one tablespoon at a time. Add vanilla. Beat until stiff. Spread over filling. Sprinkle with toasted nuts.

Arlene Giesel Koehn   One 9 inch pie

Oregon Walnut Pie

Rich and delicious. The pecan pie of the West, where walnut trees flourish. Oregon is famous for hazelnuts too, and you can also try this pie with a mixture of almonds and chopped, toasted hazelnuts.

4 large eggs	1½ teaspoons vanilla extract
1½ cups light corn syrup	⅛ teaspoon salt
1½ cups dark brown sugar, packed to measure	1½ cups broken walnuts
	1 nine inch deep dish pie shell
3 tablespoons butter or margarine, melted	

Heat oven to 400 degrees. In a medium sized bowl, beat eggs, corn syrup, sugar, butter, vanilla and salt with a fork or wire whisk until well mixed and slightly frothy. Sprinkle walnuts over bottom of pie shell and pour egg mixture over them. Place in center of oven and bake 15 minutes. Reduce heat to 350 degrees; put a baking sheet on shelf below pie to catch drips and bake 1 hour longer. Filling will rise above pie shell and drop when pie is done. When done, filling will be slightly shaky but will become very firm when cool. Remove from oven and immediately run a knife between pie pan and pie shell. Let stand 45 minutes.

Arlene Giesel Koehn   Makes 8 servings

Pecan Pie

3 eggs	1 cup brown sugar
¾ cup white Karo syrup	¼ cup sweet cream
1 tablespoon flour	¾ cup chopped pecans
salt to taste	½ teaspoon vanilla

Beat eggs, add brown sugar and syrup and beat again. Add remaining ingredients. Bake in an unbaked pie shell at 400 degrees for 10 minutes, then reduce heat to 300 degrees and bake another 30 minutes or until done. Rose Marie Boehs gave me this recipe before I was married… and I always use it! Get a lot of compliments on my pecan pie!

Janice, Mrs. Jerry Ratzlaff

Apricot Chiffon Pie

1 tablespoon gelatin	½ cup apricot juice
¼ cup cold water	2 tablespoons pineapple juice
1 cup mashed apricot	¼ teaspoon salt
½ cup sugar	¼ cup cream (whipped)

Dissolve gelatin in water. Heat fruit juices, pour over gelatin. Add sugar and salt. When slightly thickened add apricots and beat. Fold in whipped cream. Pour into baked pie shell.

Jul Nightengale

Best-ever Lemon Pie

1 baked pie shell
1¼ cup sugar
6 tablespoons corn starch
2 cups water
⅓ cup lemon juice

3 eggs, separated
3 tablespoons butter
1½ teaspoons lemon extract
(or less, to taste)
2 teaspoon vinegar

Mix sugar, cornstarch together in top of double boiler. Add the 2 cups water. Combine egg yolks with juice and beat. Add to rest of mixture. Cook until thick over boiling water for 25 minutes. Add lemon extract, butter and vinegar and stir thoroughly. Pour into deep 9 inch pie shell and let cool. Cover with meringue and brown in oven.

Valerie, Mrs. Roger Holdeman

Lemon Chiffon Pie

4 beaten eggs
½ cup lemon juice
1 envelope unflavored gelatin
1 teaspoon grated lemon peel
4 stiff-beaten egg whites
½ cup heavy cream, whipped

½ cup sugar
½ teaspoon salt
¼ cup cold water
½ cup sugar
one 9 inch baked pastry shell

Combine egg yolks, ½ cup sugar, lemon juice and salt. Cook in double boiler until thick, beating constantly with rotary beater. Add gelatin softened in cold water. Stir until gelatin dissolves. Add lemon peel and cool until partially set. Beat remaining ½ cup sugar into egg whites and fold into cooked mixture. Pour into cooled, baked shell. Chill until firm. Spread with sweetened, whipped cream before serving or cream may be folded into filling with egg whites.

Janice, Mrs. Jerry Ratzlaff

Lemon Meringue Pie

1½ cups sugar
3 tablespoons corn starch
3 tablespoons flour
dash of salt
1½ cups hot water

1 baked pastry shell
3 beaten egg yolks
2 tablespoons butter
⅓ cup lemon juice

Mix sugar, corn starch, flour and salt. Gradually add hot water, stirring constantly. Cook and stir over high heat until mixture boils. Reduce heat; cook and stir 2 minutes longer. Remove from heat. Stir small amount of hot mixture into 3 egg yolks, then return to hot mixture. Again bring to boil and cook for 2 more minutes, stirring constantly. Remove from heat and add:

2 tablespoons butter

⅓ cup lemon juice

Mix well. Pour into baked shell and cover with meringue. Bake at 350 degrees 12-15 minutes.

Mary, Mrs. Lee Giesel

Egg Custard Pie

Who remembers the egg pies? My Mom used to make them thin. I believe she would make 2 pies with this recipe.

2 cups milk, scalded
3 tablespoons butter
4 eggs, beat well
¾ cup sugar

1½ teaspoon vanilla
⅛ teaspoon salt
⅛ teaspoon nutmeg

Add sugar, vanilla and salt to beaten eggs. Stir scalded milk, and butter into egg mixture and mix thoroughly. Pour into pie shell. Sprinkle in nutmeg and bake at 425 degrees for 25 minutes or until set.

Carolyn, Mrs. Wayne Holdeman

Squash Custard Pie

1 cup mashed, cooked winter
   squash or pumpkin
1 cup whipping or heavy cream
1 cup sugar
3 eggs

1 teaspoon ground ginger
1 teaspoon cinnamon
½ teaspoon nutmeg
dash salt
1 unbaked pie shell

In mixing bowl combine all ingredients except pie shell. Pour into the pie shell. Bake at 375 degrees for 10 minutes. Reduce heat to 350 degrees. Bake for 45 minutes or until set. Cool.

Charmaine Wedel

Almond Cream Pie

1 baked pie shell
¾ cups sugar
⅓ cup flour or 3 tablespoons
   cornstarch
¼ teaspoon salt

3 slightly beaten egg yolks
2 tablespoons butter
1 teaspoon vanilla
2 cups milk

Mix all dry ingredients. Add egg yolks and enough milk to make a paste. Add remaining milk. Bring to boiling, stirring constantly. Cook 2 minutes; add butter and vanilla. Cool. Add:

½ cup roasted chopped almonds   ½ cup Cool Whip

Pour into shell. Top with whipped topping and a few almonds on top.

Jane Giesel

Butterscotch Cream Pie

Mix 1 cup brown sugar and ½ cup flour; set aside. In saucepan, beat 3 large egg yolks with a fork. Add 2½ cups cold milk. Heat, then add brown sugar mixture. Cook until thickened. Remove from heat and add 3 tablespoons oleo and 1 teaspoon vanilla. Pour in baked crust and top with cool whip or meringue.

Kathy Wedel.

Date Cream Pie

1 cup dates, cut up	1 tablespoon flour
1 cup cream	2 egg yolks
¾ cup sugar	

Stew dates in water until tender. Drain, add cream, mix sugar and flour together. Add to cream mixture. Cook five minutes. Add the egg yolks and cook until filling thickens. Add vanilla. Pour into baked pie shell and top with meringue or whipped cream.

Arlene Giesel Koehn

Easy Milky Way Pie

1 unbaked pie shell	4 (1.5 oz.) Milky Way candy bars
1 (21 oz.) can cherry pie filling	⅓ cup chopped nuts
2 teaspoons lemon juice	

Add lemon juice to pie filling. Put in pie shell. Slice candy bars over filling. Sprinkle with nuts. Bake at 450 degrees for 10 minutes, then 375 degrees for 10-15 minutes. Cool. Serve with ice cream or topping.

LeAnne Nichols

Grandma's (Mary Giesel) Peanut Butter Pie

1 baked pie shell

Topping:

¼ cup crunchy peanut butter	⅓ unsifted powdered sugar

Mix together till crumbly and spread ½ mixture on bottom of pie shell. Save the remainder for garnish on top of pie.

Filling:

1 box instant French vanilla pudding mix	1 package Dream Whip
	1¾ cups cold milk

Blend 3 minutes on high speed with electric mixer. Pour pudding over peanut butter mixture. Top with remaining crumb mixture. Grandma often served this pie to us for Sunday dinner. We enjoyed it the last time we were invited to her home for a meal, just shortly before she suffered from a stroke. What wouldn't I give for another bite of Grandma's Peanut Butter Pie!

Finette Giesel Koehn

Sawdust Pie

1 9-inch pie shell, unbaked	1½ cups finely chopped nuts
1½ cups graham cracker crumbs	1½ cups sugar, divided
1½ cups flaked coconut	1 cup egg whites (about 7)

Press a double fold of aluminum foil into pie shell and bake at 400 degrees for 8 minutes. Remove foil and bake 5 minutes more; remove from oven and reduce oven temperature to 350 degrees. In a large mixing bowl, combine crumbs, coconut, nuts and 1 cup sugar. In a separate bowl, beat egg whites with remaining ½ cup sugar. Fold egg whites into crumb mixture. Pour into pie shell. Bake at 350 degrees for 30-35 minutes.

LeAnne Nichols

Walnut Cream Pie

1¾ cup milk	⅛ teaspoon salt
½ cup brown sugar	¼ cup Half and Half
¼ white sugar	1 teaspoon vanilla
5 tablespoons flour	2 egg yolks

Stir enough Half and Half into sugar till smooth and thick. Add 2 egg yolks to above mixture and rest of ingredients, except milk. Bring milk to boiling, add a little to mixture to thin, then mix all together and boil until thick. Add ½ cup chopped nuts. Works best to cook in double boiler. Pour into baked pie shell and chill. Top with whipped cream.

Coreen Holdeman

Chocolate Ice Cream Pie

2 cups vanilla ice cream	1 box instant chocolate pudding
1 cup milk	

Mix well and pour into a graham cracker crust. Freeze till serving time. This is a quick dessert I got from my Aunt Mornie.

Carol, Mrs. Gary Koehn

Cocoa Pie

1 cup sugar	small lump of margarine
4 tablespoons (rounded) flour	(size of walnut)
4 tablespoons (level) cocoa	2 teaspoons vanilla
½ teaspoon salt	1 baked pie shell
2½ cups boiling water	

Mix sugar, flour, cocoa and salt together in saucepan. Add boiling water, stir well and put over heat and cook until thickened. Add margarine and vanilla. Cool a few minutes and pour into pie shell. Refrigerate. Serve with whipped topping or whipped cream.

Mornie Giesel Unruh

Chocolate Marshmallow Pie

Pastry for single-crust pie
16 large marshmallows
½ cup milk

1 cup whipping cream
1 (8 oz.) milk chocolate candy bar
with almonds, broken into chunks

Prepare and roll out pastry. Line a 9 inch pie plate. Prick bottom and sides of pastry. Bake at 450 degrees for 10 to 12 minutes or till golden. Cool on wire rack. Melt marshmallows in milk. Add chocolate bar; stir till smooth. Cool to room temperature. Whip cream; fold into marshmallow mixture. Turn into baked pastry shell. Cover with waxed paper or clear plastic wrap. Refrigerate 6 hours or overnight.

Arlene Giesel Koehn

Chocolate Mint Pie

1 cup crushed chocolate covered
mint flavored cookies
3 tablespoons hot water
1 prepared graham cracker crumb
crust (6 ounces)
4 ounces cream cheese, softened

⅓ cup sugar
2 tablespoons milk
¼ teaspoon peppermint extract
8 ounces Cool Whip, thawed
8-10 drops green food coloring

Mix cookies and hot water in small bowl. Spread evenly in bottom of crust. Beat cream cheese and sugar in large bowl with electric mixer on medium speed until smooth. Gently stir in whipped topping and food coloring. Spoon mixture into pie crust. Refrigerate 3 hours or until set. Garnish with a dollop of whipped topping and maraschino cherry before serving. Store any leftovers in refrigerator.

Jolene Unruh

Chocolate Nut Pie

9-inch pie shell
1 cup semi-sweet chocolate morsels
(one 6 ounce package)
2 cups assorted unsalted nuts
(cashews, pecans, macadamia,
peanuts, etc.)

3 eggs, slightly beaten
½ cup Dixie Crystals light brown
sugar, firmly packed
½ cup light corn syrup
2 tablespoons melted butter
1 teaspoon vanilla extract

Sprinkle chocolate morsels evenly over bottom of unbaked pie shell. Top with nuts. Lightly whisk eggs with light brown sugar, corn syrup, butter and vanilla. Pour mixture slowly over the nuts, position nuts as desired. Bake in preheated 375 degree oven for 40-50 minutes or until golden. Cool at least 30 minutes before slicing.

Arlene Giesel Koehn

Recipe yields one 9 inch pie

Chocolate Town Pie

9 inch unbaked pie shell	1 cup sugar
½ cup margarine, softened	½ cup flour
2 eggs	1 cup semi-sweet chocolate chips
2 teaspoons vanilla	1 cup chopped pecans

Prepare pastry shell; set aside. Heat oven to 350 degrees. In small mixing bowl, cream butter, add eggs and vanilla. Combine sugar and flour. Add to creamed mixture. Stir in chocolate chips and nuts, pour into unbaked pie shell. Bake 45-50 minutes or until golden.

Charmaine Wedel

French Chocolate Pie

Cream ½ cup oleo with ¾ cup sugar. Stir in 2 squares cooled melted unsweetened chocolate. Add 2 eggs, one at a time, beating at high speed for 5 minutes after each egg. Fold in 2 cups thawed cool whip. Pour into a cooled, baked pie shell. Chill till firm, about 2 hours or you can freeze.

Louise Wedel

Frozen Chocolate Pie

Melt 20 marshmallows and ⅓ cup milk in double boiler. Add 3 Hershey candy bars and melt. Cool mixture. Add 1 cup cream (whipped) to above mixture and pour into graham cracker crust and freeze several hours before serving.

Jul Nightengale

German Chocolate Pie

9-inch unbaked pie shell	3 tablespoons cornstarch
4-ounce package German sweet chocolate	⅛ teaspoon salt
¼ cup butter	2 eggs
1 can evaporated milk	1 teaspoon vanilla
1½ cup sugar	1 cup coconut
	¾ cup chopped pecans

Melt chocolate and butter over low heat. Remove from heat and blend in milk. Set aside. Mix sugar, cornstarch and salt together. Beat in eggs and vanilla. Blend in chocolate mixture. Pour into pie shell. Combine coconut and nuts. Sprinkle on top of chocolate mixture. Bake at 375 degrees for 45 minutes.

Charmaine Wedel

Marbled Brownie Fudge Pie

Cream Cheese Filling:

1 package (8 ounces) cream
   cheese, softened
5 tablespoons butter, softened
⅓ cup sugar

3 eggs
½ cup all purpose flour
¾ teaspoon vanilla extract

Brownie Crust:

1 cup butter or margarine, softened
1½ cups sugar
4 eggs
½ cup unsweetened cocoa

1 cup all purpose flour
1 teaspoon vanilla extract
dash salt

Fudge Frosting:

1 cup sugar
¼ cup unsweetened cocoa
4 tablespoons butter or margarine
½ cup milk
2 tablespoons dark corn syrup

dash salt
1¾ cups confectioners sugar
1 teaspoon vanilla extract
¾ cup chopped toasted pecans

In a mixing bowl, beat cream cheese with butter; add sugar, eggs (one at a time), flour and vanilla. Beat until smooth; set aside. For crust, cream butter and sugar. Beat in eggs (one at a time), cocoa, flour, vanilla and salt. Lightly grease two 9 inch pie pans. Spread ¼ of batter in bottom of each pan. Pour half of filling into each pan, spreading almost to edges. Dollop remaining batter over filling; swirl with knife to "marble". Bake at 335 degrees for 25 to 30 minutes or until toothpick inserted in middle comes out clean. Cool on racks at least 15 minutes. For frosting, combine sugar and cocoa in a saucepan. Add butter, milk, corn syrup and salt and bring to a boil, stirring frequently. Boil vigorously 3 minutes, stirring occasionally. Remove from heat. Beat in confectioners sugar and vanilla. Stir in nuts. Cool 10 minutes; pour onto warm pies, spreading to cover. Serve warm.

Charmaine Wedel

Baked Rice Pudding

Mix:

½ cup rice
½ to 1 cup sugar (to taste)

1 teaspoon vanilla
1 quart skim milk (or regular milk)

Bake at 350 degrees until rice is tender.

Connie Martens Koehn

Blueberry Pudding

This satisfying dessert has a moist, cake-like texture and lots of berry flavor.

16 oz. package frozen unsweetened blueberries (about 4 cups)
¾ cup firmly packed golden brown sugar
1 tablespoon plus 1 cup all purpose flour
½ cup (1 stick) chilled unsalted butter, diced
1 cup milk
1 egg
2 teaspoons grated lemon peel
½ teaspoon vanilla extract

Preheat oven to 350 degrees. Grease 9 inch glass pie dish. Place frozen berries in bowl. Add ¼ cup brown sugar and 1 tablespoon flour; toss to coat berries. Spoon mixture into prepared pie dish. In medium bowl, rub remaining 1 cup flour and butter together with fingertips until coarse meal forms. Mix in remaining ½ cup brown sugar. Add milk, egg, lemon peel and vanilla; stir to blend. Pour batter over berry mixture. Bake pudding until firm in center and top is golden brown, about 55 minutes. Let cool 10 minutes. Spoon into deep dessert bowls; top with ice cream.

Arlene Giesel Koehn   4 servings

Bread Pudding

2 eggs
¾ cup sugar
dash of salt
4 cups loosely cut pieces of bread
1 teaspoon vanilla
2 cups milk

Beat eggs well. Add sugar, salt and vanilla. Then add milk and bread crumbs. Bake 1 hour at 350 degrees. If you like, put cinnamon on top before baking. This is a recipe from my mom.

Carol, Mrs. Gary Koehn

Date-rice Pudding

½ cup chopped sugar-coated dates
⅔ cup diluted evaporated milk
¾ cup cooked rice
¼ cup maple syrup
1 egg, separated
⅛ teaspoon salt
1 teaspoon vanilla
1 tablespoon sugar
cinnamon sugar

Place the dates, milk and rice in top of a double boiler. Beat syrup into egg yolk and add salt and vanilla. Stir into rice mixture. Cook over boiling water for 5 to 6 minutes or until thickened, stirring frequently. Place over cold water until cool. Beat egg white with sugar until stiff and fold into pudding. Sprinkle cinnamon sugar over pudding and serve with ice cream, if desired.

Arlene Giesel Koehn

Hot Fudge Pudding

1 cup flour	4 tablespoons cocoa
2 teaspoons baking powder	½ cup milk
½ teaspoon salt	2 tablespoons melted butter
¾ cup sugar	½ cup nuts

Measure dry ingredients into 9x9 pan. Stir in milk and butter. Add nuts. Smooth batter and sprinkle with ½ cup sugar and ½ cup brown sugar. Pour 1 cup cold water over top. Bake at 350 degrees for 40 minutes. Serve with ice cream. This is a family favorite that dates way back! I made this a lot in my early cooking days and still make it regularly. Very simple and goes well with an oven meal.

LeAnne Nichols

Pantry Pudding

Company's coming and there is no time to make a dessert—so what to do? Keep your cool, desserts need not always be elaborate, elegant or unusual. Take a look around the kitchen and chances are you have most of the ingredients on hand to make a Pantry Pudding Surprise. You'll need vanilla flavored instant pudding pie filling, corn flakes, brown sugar, cinnamon, milk and butter. It's so simple, so delicious, and so easy.

4 cups corn flakes	⅓ cup margarine, melted
⅓ cup firmly packed brown sugar	1 package (4 serving size) instant
½ teaspoon cinnamon	pudding and pie filling

Combine cereal with sugar, cinnamon and margarine; reserve ½ cup. Press in 8 inch square pan. Prepare pudding mix as directed. Pour into pan over cereal; top with ½ cup reserved cereal mix. Chill at least 1 hour. Cut into rectangles.

Mornie Giesel Unruh   Makes 6 to 8 servings

Vanilla Pudding

⅓ cup sugar	2½ cups milk
3 tablespoons cornstarch	1½ teaspoons vanilla
¼ teaspoon salt	

Mix sugar, cornstarch and salt; gradually blend in milk. Cook over medium heat, stirring constantly, until mixture thickens. Cook 2 or 3 minutes more. Add vanilla.

Chocolate Pudding:

Follow directions for vanilla pudding, but increase sugar to ½ cup and 1 tablespoon. Mix ⅓ cup cocoa (I use 3 tablespoons) with sugar and cornstarch. Jennie, (Mother), Mrs. Calvin Unruh gave this recipe to me. It can be made in the microwave.

Elaine, Mrs. David Unruh

Angel Food Dessert

1 package Knox gelatin dissolved in ½ cup cold water. Let stand 5 minutes. Add ½ cup boiling water, ¾ cup sugar and 1 cup crushed pineapple. Let stand in refrigerator until it starts to jell. Add 1 pint of cream that has been whipped (or one 16 ounce container of cool whip). Break 1 Angel Food cake in bite size pieces and put in 9x13 pan. Cover with above mixture and put in refrigerator to chill.

Carolyn. Mrs Wayne Holdeman.

Apple Berry Breakfast Crisp

1 cup quick or old-fashioned
   oatmeal, uncooked
½ cup firmly packed brown sugar

⅓ cup margarine or butter, melted
2 tablespoons all-purpose flour

Filling:

4 cups thinly sliced and peeled
   apples, about 4 medium
2 cups fresh or frozen blueberries
   or sliced strawberries
¼ cup frozen orange juice
   concentrate, thawed

2 tablespoons all-purpose flour
1 teaspoon ground cinnamon
¼ cup firmly packed brown sugar

Heat oven to 350 degrees. In a medium bowl, combine topping ingredients; set aside. In a large bowl, combine filling ingredients; stir until fruit is evenly coated. Spoon filling into 8 inch square glass baking dish. Sprinkle topping evenly over fruit. Bake in a 350 degree oven 30 to 35 minutes or until apples are tender. Serve warm with yogurt, if desired.

Arlene Giesel Koehn

Makes 9 servings

Apple Crisp

3 cups apples (sliced)

½ cup sugar—cinnamon

Mix together and put in bottom of pan.

Topping:
1 cup flour
¼ teaspoon salt

½ cup brown sugar
Crumble with ½ cup oleo

Bake at 350 degrees for 35-40 minutes.

Jul Nightengale

Apple Crisp

1 cup quick oat meal
1 cup flour
½ cup melted butter

1 cup brown sugar
1 teaspoon soda

Mix dry ingredients and stir in melted butter. Place 1 quart canned sliced apples (may use pears or peaches in place of apples) in 8x8 inch baking pan. Spread crumb mixture over apples. Sprinkle with cinnamon. Bake at 350 degrees until golden brown.

Arlene Giesel Koehn

Blueberry Yum-Yum

2 cups blueberries
2 cup sugar (divided)
1 cup water
¼ cup cornstarch
3 tablespoons water

8 ounces cream cheese
8 ounces whipped topping
1 cup flour
½ cup soft oleo
1 cup nuts

Combine berries, 1 cup sugar and 1 cup water. Boil. Combine cornstarch and 3 tablespoons water in small bowl. Add to berries, stirring till thickened. Set aside to cool. Mix oleo, flour and nuts well. Press into 9x13 inch pan. Bake at 350 degrees till slightly brown, 10-15 minutes. Cool. Combine cream cheese and 1 cup sugar until smooth. Fold in whipped topping. Spread over cooled crust. Pour blueberry mixture evenly over top. Refrigerate. Cut into squares. Garnish with topping, blueberries or nuts if desired. This has been a family favorite for many years.

Jana, Mrs. Robert Nichols

Buster Bar Delight

2½ cups Oreo cookie crumbs,
    (divided)
½ cup butter or margarine (melted)
½ cup sugar

Chocolate Sauce:
2 cups powdered sugar
⅔ cup semi-sweet chocolate chips
1 can (12 ounce) evaporated milk

½ gallon chocolate, coffee, or
    vanilla ice cream, (softened)
1½ cups salted peanuts
8 oz. carton whipped topping

½ cup butter or margarine
1 teaspoon vanilla

Combine 2 cups crumbs with butter and sugar. Press into the bottom of a 13x9 inch pan. Freeze for 15 minutes. Spread ice cream over crumbs; freeze until firm, about 3 hours. Meanwhile, combine first 4 sauce ingredients in a saucepan, bring to boil. Boil for 8 minutes. Remove from heat and stir in vanilla. Allow to cool to room temperature. Spoon sauce over ice cream. Sprinkle with nuts. Freeze until firm. Spread whipped topping over nuts and sprinkle with remaining cookie crumbs. Freeze at least 3 hours before serving. Can be stored in freezer up to a week.

Jana, Mrs. Robert Nichols   12-16 servings

Butter Pecan Torte

Crust:

30 Ritz crackers, crushed ½ cup margarine, melted

Mix crackers and margarine, put into 8x11 inch pan and bake at 350 degrees for 10 minutes.

Filling:

2 packages instant butter pecan   1½ cups milk
   pudding mix   1 quart vanilla ice cream

Blend pudding and milk. Fold in softened ice cream and spread over cooled crust.

Top with:

1 carton Cool Whip   Heath bars, grated

Refrigerate until ready to serve.

Mary, Mrs. Lee Giesel

Caramel Dumplings

Bring to boil in a medium sized kettle:

1¼ cup brown sugar   1½ tablespoons margarine
1½ cups water

Let simmer while you make dumplings:

¼ cup sugar   ¾ cup flour
¼ teaspoon salt   2 tablespoons margarine
1½ teaspoon baking powder   ¼ cup milk

Cream butter, salt and sugar. Add rest of ingredients to make a stiff dough. Drop by tablespoon into simmering sauce. Cover and simmer for 15 minutes while you eat supper. Do not lift lid! Quick and Yummy! Serve with ice cream.

Deanna Giesel

Chocolate Angel Food Dessert

Mix 1 package chocolate instant pudding with 1½ cups milk. Chill. Fold in ½ cup cream, whipped, 2 cups miniature marshmallows, ⅓ cup walnuts. Slice 1 Angel Food cake into 2 layers. Spread filling between layers and on top. Chill until serving.

Jul Nightengale

Chocolate Desserts

1 German Chocolate cake mix   1 large carton of Cool Whip
2 package chocolate pudding (instant)   8 Heath or Skor Candy Bars

Bake cake according to directions on box. When cool, break into pieces in a 13x9 inch pan. Mix pudding according to package directions. Spread over cake. Spread cool whip over the pudding. Crush candy bars and sprinkle over the Cool Whip. (I put candy bars in freezer until frozen, then crush.)

Mae Unruh

Chocolate Dessert

1 Jiffy Brownie Mix
No-Bake Jell-O Mousse Mix

Cool Whip
3 Skor candy bars

Bake the Jiffy mix according to directions. When cool crumble in a 9x13 inch pan. Mix mousse according to directions and spread over brownies. Spread cool whip on top. Crush candy bars and sprinkle on top. Store in refrigerator.

Holly Koehn

Coffee Bavarian

Press into bottom of an 8 inch square pan a mixture of 1 cup fine graham cracker crumbs and ¼ cup melted butter or margarine. Chill. In a 1 quart saucepan soften 1 envelope unflavored gelatin in ½ cup cold water. Add ½ cup sugar, 1 tablespoon instant coffee, and ¼ teaspoon salt. Stir over medium heat until gelatin and sugar are dissolved. Stir in 1 cup evaporated milk. Chill in electric mixer bowl until firm. Beat with mixer at low speed until mixture is broken up. Beat in ⅔ cup evaporated milk. Beat at high speed until mixture fills bowl. Pour over crumbs in pan. Sprinkle with shaved chocolate. Chill for 1 hour. This recipe is quite a bit of work, but very delicious! It is one of my husband Jeff's favorites.

Deanna Giesel

Cool Springtime Treat

⅓ cup peanut butter
⅓ cup corn syrup
2 cups Rice Krispies cereal

1 quart vanilla ice cream,
   slightly softened

Measure peanut butter and syrup into mixing bowl. Mix until thoroughly combined. Add Rice Krispies, stir until well coated. With back of tablespoon, press mixture evenly and firmly in bottom and around sides of lightly buttered 9 inch pie pan to form crust. Chill until firm. Spread ice cream evenly in chilled crust. Freeze until firm. Garnish with fruit, toppings, or make tarts in muffin tins.

Wilma Giesel

Death by Chocolate

1 family size fudge brownie mix
3 boxes instant chocolate pudding

8 Skor or Heath candy bars
12-ounce container Cool Whip

Bake brownies according to directions. Cool. Whip up pudding according to directions. Break candy bars into small pieces. Break up brownies. Layer in bowl in the order given. This makes a big bowl full. Delicious.

Arlene, Mrs. Randy Giesel

Dirt Cups

Children find these "cups of dirt" fun to make, fun to look at, and fun to eat!

1 package (16 oz.) chocolate
   sandwich cookies (Oreos or
   similar kind)
2 cups milk

1 package (4 serving size)
   instant chocolate pudding
8 oz. Cool Whip, thawed
8-10 clear plastic cups (7-9 oz. size)

Decorations:

gummy worms
gummy frogs or turtles

candy flowers
chopped peanuts or granola

Crush cookies in plastic bag with rolling pin or use food processor. Pour milk into medium-large bowl. Add pudding mix. Beat with wire whisk until well blended, 1 or 2 minutes. Divide crushed cookies into 2 small bowls. Stir Cool Whip and one bowl of cookies into pudding. Place 1 tablespoon crushed cookies into cups. Spoon pudding mixture evenly into cups. Top with remaining crushed cookies and refrigerate one hour. Decorate just before serving. (Gummy snacks are hard to chew when refrigerated). Could also decorate with Teddy Grahams, gummy bears, M&M's, or fruit shaped snacks.

Jolene Unruh   Makes 8-10 servings

Easy Cake Dessert

1 yellow cake mix made according to directions on box. Spread sugar, cinnamon and nuts on top before you bake. Bake as directed on box. Cool. Top with 1 box instant butter pecan pudding as directed on box. Add 1 package dream whip or cool whip and fold together and frost the cake and chill.

Louise Wedel

Four Layer Delicious Dessert

Layer 1:
1 cup flour   ½ cup oleo
½ cup nuts, chopped

Mix and press into ungreased 9x13 inch pan. Bake at 325 degrees for 15 minutes.

Layer 2:
1 cup powdered sugar   1 cup Cool Whip
8 oz. package cream cheese

Cream together sugar and cream cheese. Fold in cool whip and spread over cooled crust.

Layer 3:
2 small packages butterscotch instant pudding mix (or use chocolate)

Prepare according to package directions. Spread over layer 2.

Layer 4:
Spread cool whip over layer 3 and sprinkle with nuts. An elegant, but easy dessert.

Charmaine Wedel

241

Frozen Mocha Cheesecake

24 striped fudge cookies
   (crushed)
¼ cup sugar
¼ cup margarine (melted)
8 oz. package cream cheese
   (softened)

14 oz. can Eagle Brand
   Sweetened condensed milk
⅔ cup chocolate flavored syrup
1½ tablespoons instant coffee
1 teaspoon hot water
16 oz. Cool Whip

In small bowl, combine cookie crumbs, sugar and margarine. In 9 inch spring form pan or 9x13 inch baking pan, pat crumb mixture firmly on bottom of pan. Chill. In large mixer bowl, beat cream cheese, Eagle Brand and chocolate syrup. In small bowl, dissolve coffee in water; add to Eagle Brand mixture. Mix well. Fold in about ¾ of the Cool Whip. Pour into pan. Cover. Freeze 6 hours or until firm. Top with remaining Cool Whip and garnish with chocolate shavings from a Hershey's candy bar or crushed semi-sweet chocolate chips if desired. Freeze. Return leftovers to freezer. Very delightful!

Gayla, Mrs. Duane Martens   Yield: 10 to 12 servings

Fruit Pizza

1½ cups margarine or butter
1 cup powdered sugar
3 cups flour
1 (8 oz.) package cream
   cheese, softened
½ cup sugar

1 teaspoon vanilla
1 teaspoon lemon juice
1 cup pineapple juice or
   other fruit juice
2 tablespoons cornstarch
¾ cup sugar

Desired Fruit: blueberries, sliced pineapple, oranges, kiwi, peaches, apples, bananas, halved strawberries or seedless grapes (about 3 cups total)

Step one: In a large mixing bowl, beat margarine on medium speed of an electric mixer until softened. Beat in powdered sugar. Slowly beat in the flour until well combined. Step two: Spread or pat the dough into the bottom of a 12 inch pizza pan. Bake in a 325 degree oven for about 30 minutes or until edges are lightly brown. Cool. Step three: In a small mixing bowl, beat together cream cheese, ½ cup sugar, vanilla and lemon juice until creamy. Spread over cooled crust. Step four: In a small saucepan, combine juice, cornstarch and remaining ¾ cup sugar. Cook and stir over medium heat till thickened and bubbly. Cook and stir 1 minute more. Remove from heat and cool slightly. Step five: Top pizza with desired fruit. (I start from the outside edge and go to the center. Then fill in spaces with smaller fruit.) Spoon glaze over fruit. Refrigerate until well chilled.

Betty, Mrs. Gordon Unruh

Ice Cream Dessert

2 cups flour
1 cup oleo
1 cup nuts

½ cup brown sugar
½ cup oatmeal (quick)

Mix the above and spread in 9x13 inch pan. Bake 20 minutes at 350 degrees. When cool, crumble; spread ½ mixture in pan and reserve the other ½. Drizzle 1 jar of caramel topping over crumbs and then put a layer of ice cream. Cover with remaining crumbs and freeze.

Arlene Giesel Koehn

Ice Cream Roll

4 eggs

1 teaspoon vanilla

Beat until thick

Add:
1 cup sugar

Sift together:
1 cup flour
¾ teaspoon baking powder

½ teaspoon salt

Fold into egg mixture. Pour into jelly roll pan lined with wax paper. Bake 12-15 minutes at 350 degrees. Remove from pan onto damp, clean towel. Roll up and then unroll again and spread with softened ice cream. Roll again without towel. This is delicious served with fresh strawberries or peaches.

Deanna Giesel

Jiffy Dessert

Prepare 1 chocolate jiffy cake mix. Bake in a 9x13 pan. Beat together:
8 ounces cream cheese

½ cup powdered sugar

Mix:
1 large box vanilla instant pudding

2½ cups milk

Mix pudding and cream cheese with:
4 ounces Cool Whip

Put on cooled cake. Top with remaining 4 ounces Cool Whip.

Crush:
3-4 Skor candy bars

Sprinkle on top

Beulah, Mrs. Dennis Unruh

Kansas Dirt Cake

1 large package Oreo cookies
8 ounces cream cheese
½ cup oleo
1 cup powdered sugar
1 small tub Cool Whip

2 (3 oz.) boxes instant
  vanilla pudding
3 cups milk
1 teaspoon vanilla

Crush cookies and put ½ in 9x13 inch pan. Mix cream cheese and butter till smooth. Mix in powdered sugar. Fold in Cool Whip. In separate bowl mix pudding, milk and vanilla. Fold two mixtures together and pour into pan on crumbs. Spread on remaining crumbs. Can be chilled or frozen. We like it chilled.

Arlene, Mrs. Randy Giesel

Lemon Crunch

½ cup sugar
2½ tablespoons cornstarch
¼ teaspoon salt
1⅓ cups milk

1 beaten egg
¼ cup lemon juice
1 tablespoon butter
few drops vanilla

Combine sugar, cornstarch and salt. Stir in milk. Cook until thick, stirring constantly. Mix egg and lemon juice, stir in a little of hot mixture, return to pan. Cook and stir over low heat 2 minutes. Add butter and vanilla. Pour into coconut crust.

Coconut Crust:

Mix:
1¼ cups shredded coconut
¾ cups fine cracker crumbs
  (soda or club)

½ cup sugar
½ cup flour
½ cup margarine

Put half of crumbs in 8x8 inch pan. Pour in filling, top with remaining crumbs. Bake in hot 400 degree oven 25 minutes or till top is browned. Cut into squares.

Mary, Mrs. Lee Giesel

Lo-Cal Punch Bowl Cake

1 Angel Food cake
1 large package instant vanilla
  pudding mix (sugar-free)
1 large container frozen
  unsweetened strawberries

1 large container light non-dairy
  whipped topping (Cool Whip
  Lite recommended)

Cut cake into pieces, place in bottom of large bowl. Make pudding and pour over cake. Add layer of strawberries. Finish with whipped topping. Chill for several hours.

Louise Wedel

Luscious Layered Blueberry Delight

14 whole graham crackers
1 large box instant vanilla pudding

1 cup Cool Whip
1 can blueberry pie filling

Line a 9 inch square pan with whole graham crackers. Prepare pudding as directed on box. Let stand 5 minutes then fold in cool whip. Spread half the pudding over crackers. Add another layer of crackers, the rest of the pudding, more crackers, then top it all with pie filling. Chill 3 hours. Makes 9 servings.

Charmaine Wedel

Mae's Dessert

1 can carnation milk
1 large can pumpkin
4 eggs, beaten

1½ cups sugar
2 teaspoons pumpkin spice

Mix ingredients together; place in greased 9x13 inch pan. Sprinkle with:

1 package yellow cake

1 cup chopped nuts

Melt:

1 stick oleo, pour over all

Bake at 350 degrees for 1½ hours. Cut in squares, garnish with whipped cream and maraschino cherries or serve with ice cream.

Mae Unruh

Peach and Pecan Crumble

⅓ cup light brown sugar,
  firmly packed
2 tablespoons flour
¼ teaspoon freshly grated
  nutmeg, or more to taste

2 tablespoons fresh lemon juice
3 pounds ripe peaches, peeled,
  pitted and sliced

Topping:
1½ cups flour
1 cup granulated sugar, more or
  less, depending on sweetness
  of peaches
pinch salt

¾ cup cold butter, cut into
  ½ inch cubes
2 cups chopped pecans
Heavy cream, whipped cream,
  or ice cream for garnish

Lightly butter a 9 inch square baking pan. Preheat oven to 375 degrees. In a large bowl, combine brown sugar, 2 tablespoons flour, and nutmeg. Add lemon juice and peaches, toss and pour into prepared baking pan. To make topping, combine 1 ½ cups flour, granulated sugar, salt and butter. Using your fingers, quickly blend mixture until it resembles coarse crumbs. Mix in chopped pecans and spread topping evenly over peach mixture. Bake crumble in preheated oven for 30 minutes, or until juices are bubbling and top is golden. Garnish with cream or ice cream.

Arlene Giesel Koehn

Serves 6 to 8

Peanut Chocolate Parfait Dessert

Base:

1 package Devil's Food cake mix	1 egg
½ cup margarine, melted	¾ cup peanuts
¼ cup milk	

Filling:

¾ cup peanut butter	8 oz. Cool Whip
1½ cups powdered sugar	5¼ oz. package instant vanilla
8 ounces cream cheese	pudding mix
2½ cups milk	

Topping:

½ cup peanuts	1.45 oz. bar milk chocolate, grated

Heat oven to 350 degrees. Grease and flour bottom of 13x9 inch pan. In large bowl, combine all base ingredients at medium speed until well blended. Spread evenly in pan. Bake at 350 degrees for 20-25 minutes. Do not over bake. Cool. In small bowl, combine peanut butter and powdered sugar until crumbly; set aside. In large bowl, beat cream cheese until smooth. Add milk, whipped topping and pudding mix, beat 2 minutes at low speed until well blended. Pour half of cream cheese mixture over base. Sprinkle with half of peanut butter mixture. Repeat with remaining cream cheese and peanut butter mixtures. Sprinkle with ½ cup peanuts, press gently into filling. Sprinkle with grated chocolate. Cover. Refrigerate until serving time.

Mary, Mrs. Lee Giesel

Pistachio Dessert Delight

1½ cups flour	2 tablespoons sugar
1 stick oleo	¼ cup nuts

Bake at 350 degrees for 12 minutes.

Second Layer:

8 oz. package cream cheese	½ large carton cool whip
⅔ cup powdered sugar	

Cream cheese and sugar together. Add cool whip and spread on crust.

Third Layer:

2 packages instant pistachio pudding	2½ cups milk

Beat until thick and spread on dessert. Then spread rest of Cool Whip on top. Has a refreshing taste and a pretty appearance!

Donna, Mrs. Donavon Nikkel

Punch Bowl Cake

1 (18.5 oz.) box white or
  yellow cake mix
1 (6 oz.) box vanilla instant
  pudding
1 (3 oz.) box vanilla instant
  pudding
2½ cups milk

2 (20 oz.) cans crushed pineapple,
  well drained and chilled
2 (21 oz.) cans apple, cherry or
  strawberry pie filling, chilled
1 (12 oz.) carton whipped topping
  coconut and nuts (optional)

Bake cake according to directions and cool. Using large punch bowl crumble ½ inch layer of cooled cake in the bottom. Mix both packages of pudding with milk. Pour half of the pudding mix over cake. Spoon ½ can drained pineapple over pudding. Cover with 1 can pie filling and layer with half of the whipped topping, coconut, and nuts. Repeat layers. Chill and refrigerate.

Arlene Giesel Koehn

Rhubarb Custard Kuchen

1¾ cups flour
½ teaspoon baking powder
⅛ teaspoon salt

¾ cup shortening
1 egg
1 tablespoon milk

Sift together flour, baking powder and salt into mixing bowl. Cut in shortening until coarse crumbs. Combine egg and milk and stir into crumb mixture. Pat into bottom and sides of 13x9 inch pan.

Fill crust with:
4 cups cubed rhubarb

Combine:
1½ cups sugar
2 tablespoons flour
1 teaspoon cinnamon

1 egg
¾ cup milk
1 teaspoon vanilla

Pour over all. Bake at 425 degrees 20 minutes. Reduce heat to 350 degrees and bake an additional 15 minutes.

Mary, Mrs. Lee Giesel

Rhubarb Dream Dessert

Mix:

1 cup flour   ½ cup butter or oleo
5 tablespoons powdered sugar

Bake at 350 degrees in a 7x11 inch pan for 15 minutes.

Sift together:

1½ cup sugar   ¾ teaspoon salt
¼ cup flour

Add:

2 beaten eggs   2 cups fresh chopped rhubarb

Pour over baked crust. Bake 30-35 minutes longer. Serves 6-8. Good served with ice cream.

Betty Giesel Martens

Rhubarb Torte

Crust:

1 cup margarine   2 cups flour
1 tablespoon sugar

Mix as for pie crust. Pat into 9x13 inch pan. Bake 15 minutes at 350 degrees.

Filling:

6 egg yolks, beaten   4 tablespoons flour
2 cups sugar   ½ teaspoon salt
1 cup cream or evaporated milk   5 cups rhubarb, cut up

Mix together and pour over baked crust. Bake at 350 degrees 40 minutes.

Meringue:

6 egg whites   1 teaspoon vanilla
¾ cup sugar   ¼ teaspoon salt

Spread over rhubarb and return to oven until brown.

Mary, Mrs. Lee Giesel

Strawberry Swirl

1 Angel Food cake, torn
    into pieces
2 egg yolks
1 cup sugar
2 cups milk

1 (3 oz.) package strawberry Jell-O
2 egg whites, beaten
1 cup whipping cream
1 cup frozen strawberries, drained

Arrange cake pieces over bottom of 10x14 inch pan. Stir egg yolks and sugar together. Add milk. Stir constantly over medium heat until thick. Add Jell-O to hot mixture and allow to cool until it begins to congeal. Fold in egg whites, whipped cream and strawberries. Pour over cake pieces. Refrigerate several hours or overnight.

LeAnne Nichols

Strawberry Trifle

1 yellow cake mix, baked as directed

Break into bite size pieces in 9x13 inch pan. Sprinkle on cake:
4 cups sliced, sweetened, strawberries

Combine and spread on strawberries:
1 large box French vanilla
    pudding mix (instant)

1 (8 oz.) Cool Whip

Mix pudding as directed. Attractive when layered in large glass bowl. May be made the day before.

Carolyn, Mrs. Wayne Holdeman

Serves 15

Striped Delight

1½ cup cookie crumbs*
¼ cup sugar
⅓ cup melted butter
1 (8 oz.) package cream
    cheese (softened)
¼ cup sugar

2 tablespoons milk
1 (8 oz.) container whipped
    topping, thawed
2 small boxes instant pudding*
3½ cups cold milk

Combine crumbs, sugar and melted butter. Press firmly into bottom of 13x9 inch pan; chill 5 minutes. Or for firmer crust, bake at 375 degrees for 8 minutes; cool. Beat cream cheese with sugar and milk until smooth. Fold in half of the whipped topping. Spread over crust. Prepare pudding as directed on package using 3½ cups milk; pour over cream cheese layer. Chill several hours or overnight. Spread remaining whipped topping over pudding.

*Suggested flavors: chocolate pudding with graham cracker crumbs. Butterscotch or lemon pudding with ginger snap crumbs.

Charmaine Wedel

Gingerbread

½ cup Crisco oil
½ cup sugar
1 egg
2½ cups sifted flour
1½ teaspoon baking soda
1 teaspoon cinnamon

1 teaspoon ginger
½ teaspoon cloves
½ teaspoon salt
1 cup pure Sorghum Molasses
1 cup hot water

Mix oil, sugar and egg; beat well. Sift together flour, soda, salt and spices. Combine water and Sorghum; add alternately with flour to first mixture. Pour into greased and floured 13x10 inch pan. Bake 350 degrees for 50-60 minutes. We like a white frosting sprinkled with coconut.

Arlene Giesel Koehn

Strawberry Shortcake

1 cup flour
½ cup (scant) sugar

1 teaspoon baking powder
pinch of salt

Mix together. Work in:
3 tablespoons butter

Save ½ cup crumbs. Add ½ cup milk to the remaining mixture. Put in 9 inch pan, sprinkle crumbs on top. Bake at 350 degrees for 20 minutes.

Coreen Holdeman

Shortcake

1 cup sugar
1 egg
1 cup cream
1 cup flour

1 teaspoon baking powder
½ teaspoon salt
1 teaspoon vanilla

Mix together and put on top of your favorite fruit and bake. Rhubarb is very good.

Jul Nightengale

Shortcake

1 cup flour
½ cup milk
1 tablespoon sugar
¼ teaspoon cream of tartar

¼ cup Crisco
2 teaspoons baking powder
½ teaspoon salt

Cut Crisco into the flour. Then add the other ingredients and stir well. Put in an 8 inch cake pan and bake 10 minutes at 400 degrees. This is the recipe my mother used when we had fresh strawberries or peaches. Top the cake with fresh fruit (which has been sweetened) and then pour cold cream over it. Delicious! Of course, you can use whipped topping...but it wouldn't be the same.

Janice, Mrs. Jerry Ratzlaff

Shortcake

4 cups flour
2 cups sugar

1 cup margarine
pinch of salt

Mix and reserve 1½ cups crumbs for top.

Add to remaining crumbs:
2 cups milk

4 teaspoons baking powder

Spread in a 10x15 inch pan. (Sheet cake). Put reserved crumbs on top and bake at 350 degrees for 15 minutes. Very good with fresh strawberries.

Connie Martens Koehn

A Good Cookie Recipe

½ cup butter
½ cup shortening
½ cup brown sugar
½ cup white sugar
2⅛ cups flour
1 egg

1 teaspoon vanilla
⅓ teaspoon salt
1 teaspoon cream tartar
1 teaspoon soda
½ cup nuts (optional)
Chocolate chips (optional)

Roll in ball size of walnut. Dip in water or milk and then in sugar. Put on greased cookie sheet and bake at 350 degrees.

Sophie (Giesel) Koehn

Amish Cookies

½ cup powdered sugar
½ cup white sugar
½ cup oil
½ cup oleo
1 egg

2¼ cups flour
½ teaspoon vanilla
½ teaspoon soda
2½ teaspoons cream of tarter

Mix first 4 ingredients, add egg and vanilla, mix cream of tarter, soda with flour, add with above. Make into balls and flatten with fork. Bake 12 minutes at 325 degrees.

Mable (Giesel) Ratzlaff

Makes 4 dozen

Anise Cookies

3 cups all-purpose flour
1½ teaspoons aniseed, crushed
1 teaspoon baking powder
1¼ cups butter-flavored shortening
1 egg
½ cup sugar

3 tablespoons frozen orange
 juice concentrate, thawed
1 teaspoon vanilla
cinnamon-sugar (optional)
Crushed aniseed (optional)

Stir together flour, 1½ teaspoons aniseed, baking powder, and ½ teaspoon salt; set aside. In a large mixing bowl beat shortening with an electric mixer on medium speed till fluffy. Add egg, sugar orange juice, and vanilla, beating till mixture is light. Beat or stir in the flour mixture (dough will be stiff). Divide dough into 2 portions. On a lightly floured surface, use a floured rolling pin to roll dough to ¼" thickness. Using a cookie cutter, cut in 2½" rounds. If desired, sprinkle cutouts with cinnamon-sugar and additional crushed aniseed. Arrange on greased cookie sheets; bake in a 350 degree oven about 9 minutes or till golden on bottom. Remove from cookie sheets; cool on wire racks.

Arlene Giesel Koehn   Makes about 3 dozen

Brad's Cookies

Cream together:
2 cups brown sugar
2 cups white sugar

1 pound butter

Add:
1 teaspoon vanilla

4 eggs, one at a time, beating well

Sift, then add:
6 cups flour
2 teaspoons soda
Add:
1½ cups oatmeal

2 teaspoons baking powder

1¼ cups coconut

Makes a stiff dough. Drop by tablespoonfuls on greased pan. Bake at 350 degrees until golden brown, 8-10 minutes. Makes a soft cookie if you use butter. This is a recipe brought home from school by Jerry's nephew, Brad. We really like them... makes a big batch!

Janice, Mrs. Jerry Ratzlaff

Brown Butter Pecan Cookies

Melt 1 cup butter to a golden brown, stirring all the time. Then add 2 cups brown sugar. Remove from stove. In a bowl beat 2 eggs, and 1 teaspoon vanilla. Add sugar and butter mixture, 3 cups flour, 1 teaspoon baking soda, 1 teaspoon cream tartar, ¼ teaspoon salt, and 1 cup chopped pecans. Dough will be sticky. Roll into balls and store in refrigerator over night. You can use ½ cup butter and ½ cup Crisco as a substitute for 1 cup butter, if you like.

Sophie (Giesel) Koehn   Makes 70 to 75 cookies

Brown Sugar Drops

1 cup soft shortening
2 cups brown sugar, unpacked

2 eggs

Cream together till fluffy. Stir in:

1 cup very coarsely chopped
   English walnuts

½ cup milk

Sift together:

3½ cups sifted flour
1 teaspoon soda

1 teaspoon salt

Thoroughly mix sifted ingredients into creamed mixture. Drop onto cookie sheet. Bake in 400 degree oven for 8 to 10 minutes. "My Dad sometimes made these when I was a little girl. They are soft and chewy, plump and delicious! That is, if you have 'the touch'. Somehow mine never are as good as Dad's were. According to him, the secret to success is using your fingers instead of a teaspoon to drop the cookies onto the cookie sheet, dipping your thumb and forefinger into a glass of water after each cookie is dropped."

Finette Giesel Koehn

Cake Mix Cookies

1 cake mix (any kind, but I like
   lemon or cherry chip)
1½ cups Cool Whip

1 egg
Powdered sugar

Beat egg with a whisk. Beat Cool Whip. Add cake mix and mix well. Chill. Roll in small balls and roll in powdered sugar. Bake on ungreased cookie sheets 10 minutes at 350 degrees. My Aunt got this recipe when she was a nurse aide at a hospital. We call them "hospital cookies"!

Michele, Mrs. Richard Ensz

Cashew Cookies

½ cup butter or margarine, softened
1 cup firmly packed brown sugar
1 egg
½ teaspoon vanilla extract
2 cups all-purpose flour
¾ teaspoon baking powder
¾ teaspoon baking soda
¼ teaspoon salt
½ cup commercial sour cream
2 cups chopped cashews
Coffee Icing

Cream butter; gradually add brown sugar, beating well at medium speed of an electric mixer. Add egg and vanilla; beat well. Combine flour, baking powder, soda, and salt. Gradually add to creamed mixture, mixing well. Add sour cream, mixing until smooth. Stir in cashews. Drop by teaspoonfuls onto greased cookies sheets. Bake at 400 degrees for 6 to 8 minutes or until golden brown. Cool on wire racks. Frost with Coffee Icing. Yield: 7 dozen.

Coffee Icing:
¼ cup butter or margarine
3 tablespoons hot coffee
¼ teaspoon vanilla extract
2 cups sifted powdered sugar

Melt butter in a medium saucepan; add coffee and vanilla; stir well. Remove from heat; stir in powdered sugar and until mixture is smooth. Yield: 1¼ cups.

Arlene Giesel Koehn

Cherry Winks

Sift together:
2¼ cups flour
1 teaspoon baking powder
½ teaspoon soda
½ teaspoon salt

Cream:
¾ cup butter
1 cup sugar

Add:
2 eggs, unbeaten
2 tablespoons milk
1 teaspoon vanilla

Beat well. Add and blend in the dry ingredients, gradually. Mix thoroughly. Add:
1 cup pecans (chopped)
1 cup dates (chopped) and ⅓ cup Maraschino cherries drained and chopped

Mix well. If desired, chill dough before shaping. Drop by rounded teaspoonfuls into:
2½ cup cornflakes, coarsely crushed

Toss lightly to coat. Shape into balls. Place on greased baking sheets. Top each with ¼ cherry. Bake in 375 degree oven, for 12 to 15 minutes.

Carolyn, Mrs. Wayne Holdeman   Makes 5 dozen

Cheese Cookies

2 cups flour
2 sticks margarine, melted
2 cups Rice Krispies

1 package (12 ounces) grated
  Cheddar cheese
salt and pepper

Mix all ingredients, form into balls. Bake at 350 degrees until crisp, 10-12 minutes.

Jana, Mrs. Robert Nichols

Chewy Brownie Cookies

⅔ cups Crisco shortening
1½ cups brown sugar
1 tablespoon water
1 teaspoon vanilla
2 eggs

1½ cups flour
⅓ cup cocoa
¼ teaspoon soda
½ teaspoon salt
2 cups chocolate chips

Combine Crisco, sugar, water, and vanilla. Beat until well blended. Beat eggs into creamed mixture, Combine dry ingredients. Stir into creamed mixture, add chocolate chips. Drop rounded tablespoonfuls 2" apart onto ungreased baking sheet. Bake 7-9 minutes at 375 degrees. Cookies will appear soft and moist. Do not overbake!

LeAnne Nichols   Yield: 3 dozen cookies

Chocolate-Caramel Cookies

1 cup butter or margarine,
  softened
1 cup sugar
1 cup firmly packed brown sugar
2 large eggs
2¼ cups flour

¾ cup cocoa
1 teaspoon baking soda
2 teaspoons vanilla
1 cup chopped pecans, divided
1 tablespoon sugar
1 (9 dozen) package Rolo's

Beat butter at medium speed until creamy; add sugars, beating well. Add eggs, beating well. Combine flour, cocoa, and soda; add to butter mixture. Stir in vanilla and ½ cup chopped pecans. Chill dough for 1 hour. Combine remaining nuts and 1 tablespoon sugar; set aside, Gently press 1 tablespoon cookie dough around each candy, forming a ball. Press or dip one side of ball into nut mixture place pecan side up, 2 inches apart on ungreased cookie sheet. Bake at 375 degrees for 8 minutes (Cookies will look soft.) Let cool 1 minutes on cookie sheet. Remove to rack to cool.

Connie, Mrs. Marlon Giesel   Yields: 4 dozen

Chocolate Chip Cookies at Their Best

1 cup butter or margarine, softened
½ cup solid vegetable shortening
1⅓ cups granulated sugar
1 cup firmly packed brown sugar
4 eggs
1 tablespoon vanilla
1 teaspoon lemon juice
3 cups all-purpose flour

2 teaspoons baking soda
1½ teaspoons salt
1 teaspoon cinnamon (optional)
½ cup rolled oats
2 large packages (12 ounces each)
  semisweet chocolate chips
2 cups walnuts

In large bowl of an electric mixer, beat butter, shortening, and sugars on high speed until very light and fluffy (about 5 minutes). Add eggs, one at a time, beating well after each addition. Beat in vanilla and lemon juice. In another bowl, stir together flour, baking soda, salt, cinnamon, and oats. Gradually add to butter mixture, blending thoroughly. Stir in chocolate chips and walnuts. Use a scant ¼ cup of dough for each cookie. Drop dough onto lightly greased baking sheets, spacing cookies about 3 inches apart. For soft dough cookies bake in a 325 degree oven for 17 to 19 minutes or until light golden brown, for crisp cookies, bake in a 350 degree oven for 16 to 18 minutes or until golden brown. Transfer to racks and let cool. Store airtight.

Melissa, Mrs. Jason Koehn   Makes about 3 dozen

Chocolate Chip Cookies

1 cup shortening
¾ cup brown sugar
¾ cup white sugar
2 eggs
1 teaspoon vanilla
2½ cups flour

1 teaspoon salt
1 teaspoon soda (in one
  teaspoon hot water)
6 ounces chocolate chips
1 small box Instant Vanilla Pudding

Cream sugars and shortening. Add eggs and vanilla and beat. Mix together flour, salt, and soda and add. Add the pudding mix and beat well. Add chips and bake at 325 degrees till brown.

Elaine, Mrs. Bruce Unruh   Makes 3 dozen

Chocolate Chip Cookies

1 cup shortening
½ cup sugar
½ cup brown sugar
1 teaspoon vanilla
1 egg

2 cups flour
½ teaspoon salt
1 teaspoon cream of tarter
1 teaspoon soda
chocolate chips

Cream shortening and sugars together. Add egg and vanilla and mix well. Stir in flour, salt, cream of tarter and soda. Add the chocolate chips. Bake at 350 degrees until light brown for 10 to 12 minutes.

Marisa Giesel Wedel

Chocolate Crunch Cookies

1 cup soft shortening
½ cup chunky peanut butter
1 cup firmly packed brown sugar
1 cup granulated sugar
2 eggs
1 teaspoon vanilla

½ cup flaked coconut
½ cup chopped nuts
2½ cups all purpose flour
½ teaspoon soda
½ teaspoon salt
⅓ cup cocoa

In mixing bowl, cream together shortening, peanut butter, brown sugar, granulated sugar, eggs and vanilla until fluffy. Stir in coconut and nuts. Sift together flour, soda, salt and cocoa. Mix into creamed mixture. Form dough into one inch balls. Flatten with fork dipped in sugar. Bake 7 to 9 minutes in 350 degree oven. Do not over bake.

Edna Giesel   Yield: 3½ dozen cookies

Chocolate Cookies

1 cup flour
½ teaspoon baking powder
½ teaspoon baking soda
½ teaspoon salt
½ cup butter or margarine
    (softened)
½ cup sugar

½ cup brown sugar
1 egg
1½ ounces unsweetened
    chocolate
½ cup quick cooking oats
½ cup nuts

In small bowl, mix flour, baking powder, baking soda and salt; set aside. Melt chocolate over very low heat, stirring constantly; remove from heat. In large mixer bowl, beat butter, sugar, brown sugar, and egg until creamy. Blend in melted chocolate. Stir in flour mixture, oats and nuts. Drop dough by slightly rounded tablespoonfuls onto ungreased cookie sheet. Bake 8 to 10 minutes at 350 degrees.

Pat, Mrs. Mitchell Unruh

Chocolate Filled Bon Bons

¾ cup shortening
½ cup sugar
¼ cup firmly packed brown sugar
1 egg
2 teaspoons vanilla
½ teaspoon almond extract

1¾ cups all purpose flour
½ teaspoon baking powder
½ teaspoon salt
½ cup finely chopped pecans
4 dozen milk chocolate kisses

Preheat oven to 350 degrees. In large mixer bowl cream shortening and sugars until light and fluffy. Add egg and extracts. Beat well. Add flour, baking powder, salt and nuts; mix until blended. Roll dough into 1 inch balls. Press each ball around a candy kiss, completely enclosing the kiss like a chocolate covered cherry. Bake 12 to 15 minutes on ungreased cookie sheets. Remove to wire racks to cool.

Jul Nightingale   Makes 4 dozen

Chocolate Freezer Cookies

1 cup brown sugar	½ cup shortening
1 cup white sugar	2 eggs
½ cup oleo	

Blend first five ingredients. Add:

½ cup milk	1 teaspoon vanilla

Mix in:

4 cups flour	8 level tablespoons cocoa
¼ teaspoon salt	Nuts (if desired)
2 teaspoons soda	

Chill in refrigerator, then roll onto floured wax paper and make into 4 rolls. Put in freezer until ready to bake. Bake at 350 degrees for 11 to 12 minutes. This has been a favorite ever since I was a little girl.

Bev, Mrs. Lonnie Unruh

Chocolate Oatmeal Drops

1½ cups sugar	3 cups quick-cooking oats
½ cup margarine or butter, softened	1 cup flour
½ cup shortening	⅓ cup cocoa
¼ cup water	½ teaspoon baking soda
1 egg	½ teaspoon salt
1 teaspoon vanilla	1 package (6 oz.) semisweet chocolate chips

Mix sugar, margarine, shortening, water, egg, and vanilla. Stir in remaining ingredients Drop by rounded teaspoonfuls about 1 inch apart onto ungreased cookie sheet. Bake 10 to 12 minutes at 350 degrees. A favorite at our house!

Pat, Mrs. Mitchell Unruh

Christmas Cookies

1½ cups powder sugar	½ teaspoon almond flavoring
1 cup butter (½ oleo)	2½ cups flour
1 egg	1 teaspoon soda
1 teaspoon vanilla	1 teaspoon cream of tartar

Mix and refrigerate 2 to 3 hours. Roll out on floured board and cut in desired shapes. Bake at 375 degrees for 7 to 8 minutes.

Icing:

Powdered sugar	vanilla
soft oleo	food coloring if desired

Jul Nightingale

Cocoa Drop Cookies

½ cup shortening (part butter)
1 cup sugar
1 egg
¾ cup buttermilk or sour milk
1 teaspoon vanilla

1¾ cups flour
½ teaspoon soda
1 teaspoon salt
½ cup cocoa
½ cup nutmeats

Mix first 3 ingredients, add buttermilk and vanilla. Sift together next four ingredients and stir in. Add nutmeats if desired. Chill for one hour. Bake in 400 degree oven for 8 to 10 minutes. Frost with powdered sugar icing, if desired.

Jul Nightingale

Coffee Shop Oatmeal Cookies

1 cup brown sugar
½ cup white sugar
1 cup margarine
2 eggs
¼ cup milk or butter milk
1 teaspoon vanilla
2 cups quick oatmeal
2 cups flour

½ teaspoon cinnamon
½ teaspoon salt
1 teaspoon soda
2 teaspoons baking powder
1 cup raisins (optional)
1 cup chocolate chip (optional)
1 cup nutmeats

Cream sugars and margarine, add eggs one at a time, beating after each addition. Stir in milk, vanilla, and oatmeal. Add dry ingredients, sifting together. Mix thoroughly. Add raisins, chips and nutmeats, Drop by spoonfuls unto greased cookie sheet and bake at 350 degrees 10 to 12 minutes or until golden brown.

Mornie Giesel Unruh   Yields 60 cookies

Cookie Recipe

2 cups butter
2 cups sugar
2 cups brown sugar
4 eggs
2 teaspoons vanilla
4 cups flour
5 cups blended oatmeal*

1 teaspoon salt
2 teaspoons baking powder
2 teaspoons baking soda
24 oz. chocolate chips
1 (8 oz.) Hershey bars (grated)
3 cups chopped nuts

Cream butter and sugars. Add eggs and vanilla. Mix flour, oatmeal, salt, baking powder and soda. Add chocolate and nuts. Roll into balls and place 2 inches apart on cookie sheet. Bake 10 minutes at 350 degrees. Makes 112 cookies. *Measure oatmeal and blend in a blender to a fine powder.

Charmaine Wedel

Corn Flake Cookies

2 cups corn flakes (crushed)
½ cup sugar
2 cups sifted flour
1 cup finely chopped pecans

1½ cups sifted powdered sugar
1 cup oleo
2 teaspoons vanilla
1 teaspoon cinnamon

Crush corn flakes. Blend oleo, sugar and vanilla. Sift together flour and cinnamon. Add cornflakes and nuts to oleo mixture. Then add flour mixture. Roll in balls the size of a walnut. Place on greased cookie sheet and bake for 30 minutes at 350 degrees. When done and still hot, roll in powdered sugar. Makes 30 big cookies.

Carol, Mrs. Gary Koehn

Cow Chip Cookies

Melt:
1 cup oleo

1 cup shortening

Blend in:
2 cups packed brown sugar
2 teaspoons vanilla

2 cups white sugar
4 eggs

Add:
4 cups flour
2 teaspoons baking powder

2 teaspoons baking soda

Mix:
2 cups oatmeal
2 cups cornflakes
1 cup chopped nuts

1 cup coconut
2 cups chocolate chips

Drop 6 very big spoonfuls onto a lightly greased cookie sheet and "mash" them out 3 to 4 inches across with a fork. Bake at 350 degrees for 15 minutes. It works just as good to make them regular size.

Reneé Koehn

Cry Baby Cookies

1 cup sugar (or ½ cup honey)
1 cup molasses
1 cup shortening or oil
1 egg
2 teaspoons cinnamon

2 teaspoons ginger
2 teaspoons soda in 1 cup
    hot water
1 teaspoon baking powder
5 cups sifted flour

Place all ingredients in large mixing bowl, blend well. Drop by teaspoon on greased cookie sheet. Bake at 350 degrees for 12 minutes.

Bernice Lorenzen

Date Filled Cookies

Date Filling:

2 cups dates, finely cut up
¾ cup sugar

¾ cup water
½ cup chopped nuts

Cook together slowly, stirring constantly until thickened. Add nuts and cool.

Cookie Dough:

1 cup soft shortening
2 cups brown sugar
2 eggs
½ cup water or buttermilk
⅛ teaspoon cinnamon

1 teaspoon vanilla
3½ cups flour
½ teaspoon salt
1 teaspoon soda

Heat oven to 400 degrees. Mix shortening, brown sugar and eggs thoroughly. Stir in water and vanilla. Sift together flour, salt, soda, and cinnamon and stir into sugar egg mixture. Drop by the teaspoon on ungreased baking sheet and place ½ teaspoon date filling on dough. Bake until lightly browned, 10 to 12 minutes.

Jul Nightingale

Date Pinwheels

Cream:

½ cup butter
½ cup white sugar

½ cup brown sugar

Add:

1 beaten egg
2 cups sifted flour
½ teaspoon baking soda

½ teaspoon salt
½ teaspoon cinnamon

Mix and chill.

Mix:

1 (6 oz.) package dates
⅓ cup sugar

½ cup water

Cook like jam, cool, and add:

½ cup nuts

Roll dough and spread with this date mixture. Roll up like a jelly roll, then cool and slice. Bake at 375 degrees.

Sophie (Giesel) Koehn

Delicious Cookies

2 sticks oleo	3½ cups flour
1 cup corn oil	1 teaspoon salt
¾ cup brown sugar	1 teaspoon soda
¾ cup white sugar	1 teaspoon cream of tartar
1 egg	1 cup oatmeal
2 teaspoons vanilla	1 cup coconut
1 teaspoon coconut flavoring	1 cup Rice Krispies
½ teaspoon butter flavoring	1 cup chopped pecans

Blend oleo, oil, and sugar., Add egg and flavoring, and beat well. Sift together flour, soda, cream of tartar, and salt, and mix well. Stir in oatmeal, coconut, Rice Krispies, and pecans. Use a rounded teaspoon of dough per cookie and press with fork. (I roll mine in a ball.) Bake approximately 12 minutes at 350 degrees. Enjoy! These come out of freezer just as crisp as they are when baked. No thawing.

Sophie (Giesel) Koehn

Easy Chocolate Crackles

1 box devil's food cake mix	powdered sugar
½ cup shortening	1 tablespoon water
2 eggs slightly beaten	

Stir together cake mix, eggs, water, and shortening until well blended. Shape dough into balls, roll in powdered sugar. Place on greased cookie sheet. Bake at 375 degrees for 10 minutes.

Charmaine Wedel   Makes 3 dozen

Easy Color Cookies

Blend and beat:

2 cups shortening	1 teaspoon water
2 cups brown sugar	4 eggs
2 teaspoons vanilla	

Sift and add to mixture above:

4 cups plus 8 tablespoons flour	2 teaspoons salt
2 teaspoons soda	

Add:

3 cups M & M Plain chocolate candies

Drop by teaspoons onto ungreased cookie sheet. Bake at 375 degrees for 10-12 minutes.

JoEtta Koehn

French Cream Peanut Butter Cookies

½ cup butter
½ cup solid shortening
½ cup peanut butter
1 ½ cups confectioner's sugar
  (sifted, then measured)
1 teaspoon vanilla

1 egg (beaten)
2 cups sifted flour
1 teaspoon baking soda
¼ teaspoon salt
1 teaspoon cream of tartar

Cream butter, shortening, and peanut butter. Add sugar, beating until mixture is fluffy. Blend in vanilla and egg until creamy. Combine flour, baking soda, salt, and cream of tartar; add to creamed mixture, blending well. Chill slightly for easier handling. Roll into 1-inch balls, place on cookie sheet; flatten with fork. Bake at 350 degrees for 12 minutes. These are good frosted with chocolate.

Kristin Giesel

Fudge Puddles

½ cup margarine (softened)
½ cup creamy peanut butter
½ cup sugar
½ cup packed brown sugar
1 egg

½ teaspoon vanilla
1¼ cups flour
¾ teaspoon baking soda
½ teaspoon salt

Fudge Filling:
1 cup milk chocolate chips
1 cup semisweet chocolate chips
1 can (14 oz.) sweetened
  condensed milk

1 teaspoon vanilla
chopped peanuts

Cream butter, peanut butter and sugars: add eggs and vanilla. Stir together flour, soda, and salt; add to creamed mixture. Shape into 48 balls, 1 inch each. Place in lightly greased mini muffin pans. Bake at 325 degrees for 14-16 minutes or until lightly browned. Remove from oven and immediately make wells in the center of each by lightly pressing with a melon baller. Cool in pans 5 minutes, then carefully remove to wire racks. For filling, melt chocolate over low heat. Stir in milk and vanilla. Fill each shell with filling. Sprinkle with peanuts. Leftover filling may be store in refrigerator and served warm over ice cream.

Charmaine Wedel

Makes 4 dozen

Giant Gingerbread People

½ cup shortening
2½ cups flour
½ cup sugar
½ cup molasses
1 egg
1 tablespoon vinegar

1 teaspoon baking power
1 teaspoon ground ginger
½ teaspoon baking soda
½ teaspoon ground cinnamon
½ teaspoon ground cloves

In medium mixing bowl beat shortening with an electric mixer on medium-high speed for about 30 seconds or until softened. Add about half of the flour, the sugar, molasses, egg, vinegar, baking powder, ginger, baking soda, cinnamon, and cloves. Beat until well combined, scraping sides of bowl occasionally. Stir in remaining flour. Refrigerate for 2 to 3 hours or until easy to handle. Divide dough in half. On lightly floured counter roll each half to slightly less than ¼ inch thickness. Using cookie cutters, cut into people shapes. Place 1 inch apart on greased cookie sheets. Bake in a 375 degree oven for 6 to 8 minutes or until edges are firm and bottoms are lightly browned. Cool on cookie sheets for 1 minute. Remove and cool completely on wire racks. (I like to decorate with white frosting in a decorating tube. These are favorites with Andrew and Joseph).

Melissa, Mrs. Jason Koehn

Gingersnaps — a Favorite!

1 cup sugar
2 cups flour
½ teaspoon salt
1 teaspoon soda
1 teaspoon cinnamon
1 teaspoon ground ginger

½ teaspoon ground cloves
¾ cup shortening
¼ cup molasses or dark corn syrup
1 egg, slightly beaten
sugar

Combine 1 cup sugar, flour, salt, soda, and spices; stir lightly. Cut in shortening to resemble coarse crumbs. Stir in molasses and egg. Shape dough into 1 inch balls, roll in sugar, and place on ungreased cookie sheet; flatten slightly. Bake at 350 degrees for about 10 minutes.

Valerie, Mrs. Roger Holdeman

Gingersnaps

¼ cup shortening
1 cup sugar
¼ cup light molasses
1 egg
¼ teaspoon salt

2 cups flour
2 teaspoons soda
1 teaspoon cinnamon
1 teaspoon ginger
1 teaspoon cloves

Cream shortening and sugar. Add molasses and egg. Beat well. Roll into balls, dip in sugar. Bake 10-12 minutes at 350 degrees. This is a recipe I got from Grandma Mornie. They are the good coffee dunking kind.

LeAnne Nichols

Grandma Carrie Giesel's Sugar Cookies

3 eggs
2 cups sugar

1 cup lard

Mix together well.

Add:

1 cup sour cream
½ teaspoon baking soda
a little salt

2 teaspoons vanilla
3 teaspoons baking powder
5½ cups flour

Make a soft dough and chill before rolling out. Cut in shapes. Bake 350 degrees for 10-12 minutes. I remember getting these good cookies out of Grandma's cookie jar!! (By the way, I'm the lucky one who has Grandma's cookie jar.)

Carol, Mrs. Gary Koehn, Louise Wedel

Grandmother's Ginger Cookies

⅔ cup cooking oil
1 cup sugar
1 large egg
4 teaspoons molasses
2 cups flour

2 teaspoons soda
½ teaspoon salt
1 teaspoon ginger
1 teaspoon cinnamon
2 teaspoons vanilla

Beat together oil, sugar, and egg and vanilla. Add dry ingredients. Mix well. Roll into balls. Dip in sugar. Bake on greased cookie sheet at 250 degrees 7-10 minutes.

Monica Koehn, Valetta, Mrs. John Koehn

Irresistible Peanut Butter Cookies

¾ cup creamy peanut butter
½ cup Crisco shortening
1¼ cups brown sugar
3 tablespoons milk
1 tablespoon vanilla

1 egg
1¾ cups flour
¾ teaspoon salt
¾ teaspoon baking soda

Combine peanut butter, Crisco, brown sugar, and milk in large bowl. Beat at medium speed. Add egg and vanilla. Beat until blended. Add dry ingredients. Drop by heaping teaspoonfuls. Flatten slightly in crisscross pattern with fork tines. Bake 7-8 minutes at 375 degrees or until set and just beginning to brown.

LeAnne Nichols

3 dozen cookies

Miniature Peanut Butter Treats

Cookie:

½ cup butter (softened)
½ cup brown sugar (packed)
½ cup granulated sugar
1 egg
½ cup creamy-style peanut butter

½ teaspoon vanilla
1¼ cups all-purpose flour
¾ teaspoon baking soda
½ teaspoon salt

Filling: about 42 miniature peanut butter-chocolate cups

Combine butter, sugars, egg, peanut butter, and vanilla in mixing bowl; beat until smooth. In separate bowl, combine flour, baking soda, and salt; add to creamed mixture. Cover dough and chill. When cold enough to handle easily, roll in small (walnut-sized) balls; place each ball in greased miniature muffin tin. Bake at 375 degrees for 8-9 minutes. Remove from oven; gently press 1 peanut butter cup into each cookie to make depression. Cool in pan 10 minutes; remove from pan and cool on rack. Store in cool place until serving time.

Monica Koehn   Yield: about 3½ dozen cookies

New Year's Cookies

2½ cups milk
½ cup cream
2 tablespoons yeast
¼ cup water (warm)
⅔ cup sugar
1 tablespoon butter

6 eggs (beaten)
1 tablespoon vinegar
7 cups flour
5 teaspoons salt
2 pounds raisins

Scald milk and cream and set aside to cool. Dissolve yeast in warm water. Put raisins in pan and cover with water. Bring to boil; set aside. Mix milk and yeast mixture together. Then add the rest of the ingredients. (Drain water from raisins.) Let dough rise until double in bulk. Drop by spoonfuls into hot deep fat. Fry. Roll in sugar, powdered sugar, or glaze. Very good!

Ronda, Mrs. Kenny Giesel

No Bake Summer Snack

2 cups sugar
¼ cup cocoa
½ cup milk
1 stick oleo

1 teaspoon vanilla
3 cups quick-cooking oatmeal
½ cup peanut butter

Mix first four ingredients in a saucepan. Bring to a boil, remove from heat, and cool 1 minute. Add peanut butter, vanilla, and oatmeal. Stir well. Drop by teaspoonfuls on waxed paper.

Charmaine Wedel

Oatmeal Cookies

1 cup sugar
1 cup brown sugar
1 cup Crisco
1 cup self-rising flour

2 eggs
2 teaspoons vanilla flavoring
2 teaspoons almond flavoring
3-4 cups oats

Mix all. Spoon on cookie sheet. Bake 12 minutes at 350 degrees.

Jana, Mrs. Robert Nichols

Oatmeal Cookies

3 cups flour
3 cups oatmeal
2 cups sugar
1 teaspoon soda

1 cup shortening
½ cup sour milk
2 eggs
pinch of salt

Mix all dry ingredients, cut in shortening, then mix in eggs and milk.

Filling:
2 cups chopped dates
⅔ cup sugar

⅔ cup water

Cook 6 minutes. Add:
1 tablespoon butter

1 tablespoon lemon juice

Cool. Roll dough very thin or make balls size of walnuts and press down with cup dipped in sugar. Bake 350 degrees until very light brown. Spread filling between cookies.

Wilma Giesel

Oatmeal, Date, Pecan, and Chocolate Chip Cookies

1½ cups old-fashioned oatmeal
½ cup all purpose flour
1 teaspoon baking soda
1 teaspoon baking powder
½ cup (a stick) unsalted butter
    at room temperature
⅔ cup firmly packed dark
    brown sugar

½ cup sugar
1 egg
1 teaspoon vanilla
¾ cup chopped pitted dates
    (about 5 ounces)
¾ cup chopped pecans
    (about 3 ounces)
⅔ cup semisweet chocolate chips

Preheat oven to 375 degrees. Grease 2 heavy large cookie sheets. Mix first 4 ingredients together in medium bowl. Using electric mixer, cream butter and both sugars in large bowl until light and fluffy. Beat in egg and vanilla. Mix in oatmeal mixture. Stir in remaining ingredients. Drop rounded tablespoons of dough about 2 inches apart onto pans. Bake until golden brown.

Arlene Giesel Koehn

Makes about 2 dozen

Oatmeal Pudding Cookies

1¼ cups unsifted flour
1 teaspoon baking soda
1 cup butter of margarine, softened
¼ cup granulated sugar
¾ cup brown sugar firmly packed

1 package Instant Vanilla Pudding
2 eggs
3½ cups quick cooking rolled oats
1 cup raisins (optional)

Mix flour with baking soda. Combine butter, sugars, and pudding mix in large bowl; beat until smooth and creamy. Beat in eggs. Gradually add flour mixture; then stir in oats and raisins. (Batter will be stiff). Drop by rounded teaspoonfuls onto ungreased baking sheets, about 2 inches apart. Bake at 375 degrees for 10 to 12 minutes.

Serena Amoth   Makes about 5 dozen

Orange Candy Cookies

1½ cups brown sugar
½ teaspoon salt
½ cup shortening
1 pound orange slice candy
2 eggs

½ cup flour
2 cups sifted flour
½ cup coconut or nutmeats
1 teaspoon soda
½ cup rolled oats

Cream sugar and shortening until light and fluffy. Beat in eggs. Sift two cups flour with soda and salt and blend into creamed mixture. Dice orange slices and mix with half cup of flour. Fold into creamed mixture with coconut or nuts and oatmeal. Mix well. Roll into balls about an inch in diameter. Place on greased cookie sheet and press down with a fork. Bake in slow oven at 325 degrees for 12 minutes. Yield: six dozen cookies.

Sophie (Giesel) Koehn, Betty, Mrs. Gordon Unruh

Outrageous Chocolate Chip Cookies

½ cup granulated sugar
⅓ cup packed brown sugar
½ cup margarine or butter,
   softened
½ cup peanut butter
½ teaspoon vanilla

1 egg
1 cup flour
½ cup oatmeal
1 teaspoon baking soda
¼ teaspoon salt
6 ounces chocolate chips

Beat sugars, margarine, peanut butter, vanilla, and egg in medium bowl with wooden spoon until creamy and well blended. Mix in flour, oats, baking soda, and salt. Stir in chocolate chips. Drop dough by rounded tablespoonfuls about 2 inches apart on ungreased cookie sheet. Bake 10-12 minutes at 350 degrees.

Elaine, Mrs. Bruce Unruh   About 2 dozen cookies

Pancake Cookies

½ cup melted oleo
¾ cup sugar
1 teaspoon vanilla

2 beaten eggs
6 tablespoons cocoa
1 cup flour

Stir together. Dough will be very thick. You will have to spread it on griddle with a spoon. Fry on a pancake griddle until done.

Charmaine Wedel

Peanut Butter Cookies

1 cup peanut butter
1 cup brown sugar
1 cup white sugar
2 teaspoons soda

½ cup shortening
2 cups flour
2 eggs
1 teaspoon vanilla

Cream peanut butter, shortening. Add sugars and eggs gradually. Cream until light in color. Sift flour and soda. Add and mix well. Shape in balls and flatten with fork. Bake 10 to 13 minutes at 350 degrees.

Mable (Giesel) Ratzlaff, Jolene Unruh   Yield: 4½ dozen

Peanut Butter Jumbos

1 cup margarine
1 cup peanut butter
1 cup granulated sugar
1 cup brown sugar firmly packed

2 eggs
2 cups flour
1 teaspoon soda
1½ cups peanut M&M's

Beat together first 4 ingredients; blend in eggs. Gradually add flour and soda. Mix well. Add candies. Drop by ¼ cup full on greased cookie sheet about 3" apart. Press 3 or 4 M&M's into cookies. Bake at 350 degrees for 14 to 16 minutes or until golden brown. Cool on cookie sheet 3 minutes. Variation: For 2½" cookies, drop by rounded teaspoonfuls. Bake 11 to 13 minutes.

Serena Amoth   Makes 2 dozen 4" cookies

Pecan Crispies

½ cup shortening
½ cup butter or margarine
2½ cups brown sugar
2 eggs well beaten

2½ cups sifted flour
½ teaspoon soda
1 cup chopped pecans

Thoroughly cream together, butter, shortening, and sugars; add eggs and beat well. Sift dry ingredients and add to creamed mixture. Add nuts. Drop by teaspoonfuls and press thin onto greased cookie sheet 2 inches apart. Bake at 350 degrees for 12 to 15 minutes.

Serena Amoth   Makes about 5 dozen

Peppernuts

1 cup butter	1 tablespoon hot water
4 cups brown sugar	1 teaspoon cloves
4 eggs	1 teaspoon nutmeg
6 cups flour	1 teaspoon cinnamon
1½ teaspoons anise oil	1 teaspoon cream of tartar
3 cups nuts, chopped fine	1 teaspoon mace
1 tablespoon soda	

Make into balls, roll, and chill. Bake 350 degrees for 6 minutes.

Coreen Holdeman

Peppernuts

2 cups brown sugar	1 cup butter or Crisco
2 cups white sugar	

(You can use 4 cups brown sugar instead of the brown and white)

Beat, then add:

4 eggs

Beat some more. Add:

1 tablespoon baking soda in	1 teaspoon anise oil (not extract)
1 tablespoon hot water	

Beat. Add:

1½ cups chopped pecans.

Sift together:

6½ cups flour	1 teaspoon cinnamon
1 teaspoon cream of tartar	1 teaspoon mace
1 teaspoon nutmeg	

Mix all together. If using mixer you may have to finish by hand. I line two good sized cookie pans with wax paper and put in freezer. Bake when convenient. Cut into strips and little squares. Bake for 8 minutes in 300 to 350 degrees oven. They still look white on top but let them set in pan a few minutes after taking out of oven. One year I sold hundreds of ,dollars of these. It was hard to keep up with the demand. Now I make them to eat and give away.

Sophie (Giesel) Koehn

Zella Fay's Peppernuts

3 cups white sugar
1 cup white syrup
1 teaspoon nutmeg
1 teaspoon allspice
1 teaspoon pepper
1 teaspoon salt
1 teaspoon vanilla

3 eggs
1 cup sour cream
1 teaspoon cinnamon
2 teaspoons anise oil
1½ cups oleo, melted
1½ teaspoons soda
8-10 cups flour

Mix all ingredients, and add enough flour to make a very stiff dough. Knead until well blended and smooth. Let stand overnight in a cool place. Make into small logs and slice. Bake at 350 degrees until done!

Janice, Mrs. Jerry Ratzlaff

Raisin Bran Chewies

1 cup shortening
1 cup brown sugar
½ cup sugar
2 eggs
2 tablespoons honey
2 teaspoons vanilla

2 ¼ cups flour
½ teaspoon soda
¼ teaspoon salt
3 cups Raisin Bran cereal
¾ cups raisins
½ cup chopped walnuts

In mixing bowl, cream shortening and sugars. Add eggs, honey, and vanilla. Add dry ingredients. Stir in cereal, raisins, and walnuts. Bake at 350 degrees on greased baking sheet 12 to 14 minutes.

LeAnne Nichols

4 dozen

Reese's Peanut Butter Specials

1 package refrigerated peanut butter cookies
40 Reese's miniature chocolate peanut butter cups

Coat miniature muffin tins with nonstick spray

Cut cookies into 10 slices. Quarter each slice and place one quarter in each. Bake according to package directions (about 8 minutes). Take out of oven and immediately place one miniature peanut butter cup in center. Allow to cool before removing.

Louise Wedel

Makes 40 cookies

Refrigerator Date Cookies

2 cups brown sugar
1 cup butter
3 eggs
4 cups flour
1 teaspoon soda

½ teaspoon salt
1 teaspoon cinnamon
2 cups dates or prunes
½ cup sugar
½ cup water

(One cup of white sugar may be used instead of all brown.) Cream butter until soft. Add sugar gradually. Cream until fluffy. Add the well beaten eggs and beat vigorously. Add the sifted dry ingredients. Roll dough into a sheet ½ inch thick. Cook dates or prunes, sugar, and water over a slow fire until paste forms. Spread filling on dough, and roll like jelly roll. Wrap in waxed paper and put in refrigerator overnight. Cut in thin slices and bake at 400 degrees for 10 or 12 minutes. I used greased pans, and I use a 350 degree oven. This is my family's favorite cookie!

Nancy, Mrs. Kenneth Unruh

Rich Sugar Cookies

1 cup sugar
1 cup powdered sugar
1 cup margarine (2 sticks)
1 cup cooking oil
½ teaspoon salt

1 teaspoon vanilla
2 eggs
4½ cups flour
1 teaspoon soda
1 teaspoon cream of tartar

Roll in balls (size wanted). Dip in sugars, put in pan, and flatten with fork on glass. Bake until golden at 350 degrees. This was Grandma Mornie's last sugar cookie recipe that she used. She always dipped the dough in the colored balls before they were baked. They always went over well with children. She would quite often give us one of these when we stopped in.

Elaine, Mrs. David Unruh

Saucepan Peanut Cookies

1 cup light corn syrup
1 cup granulated sugar

1½ cups peanut butter
4 cups corn flakes

Mix the corn syrup and sugar together in a medium sized saucepan. Bring mixture to a full boil. Remove from heat and stir in the peanut butter. Add corn flakes and mix well. Drop by heaping teaspoons onto buttered baking pan. (This recipe is very special to me because of the memories it recalls. They were the very first cookies I learned to make, and my Dad helped me stir them up the first few times I tried it. Added to that, they are delicious and always go over well at basket dinners!)

Finette Giesel Koehn

Sensibly Delicious Chocolate Chip Cookies

1¼ cups brown sugar
½ cup granulated sugar
½ cup margarine
1 teaspoon vanilla
2 egg whites
⅓ cup water

3 cups flour
1½ teaspoon soda
1 teaspoon salt
2 cups chocolate chips
⅓ cup nuts

Cream brown sugar, sugar, margarine, and vanilla. Add eggs white. Gradually add dry ingredients alternately with water. Stir in chocolate chips and nuts. Bake 10-12 minutes at 350 degrees. (Yields approximately 5 dozen.) Each cookie contains 4 grams fat versus 7 grams in traditional recipe.)

LeAnne Nichols

Snowballs (Christmas cookie)

1 cup butter (stick margarine
   can be used)
2 cups sifted unbleached flour

1 to 2 cups ground pecans
¼ cup powdered or granulated sugar
1 teaspoon vanilla

Cream butter until soft, add other ingredients. Chill dough. Shape 1 tablespoon batter into ball. Bake on ungreased baking sheet about 45 minutes in slow (300-325 degree oven. Cool, then roll in powdered sugar.

Bernice Lorenzen   Makes approximately 4 dozen

Soft Molasses Cookies

½ cup margarine
½ cup shortening
1½ cups sugar
½ cup molasses
2 eggs slightly beaten
4 cups flour leveled

½ teaspoon salt
2¼ teaspoons baking powder
2¼ teaspoons ginger
1½ teaspoons cloves
1½ teaspoons cinnamon

Cream together margarine, shortening, and sugar until light colored and fluffy. Beat in molasses and eggs; set aside. In a large bowl combine flour, salt, soda, and spices. Blend thoroughly. Gradually mix with creamed mixture, on low, until dough is smooth. Roll into 1 ½" balls, dip in sugar. Line on greased cookie sheet 1 ½ inches apart. Bake at 350 degrees for 11 minutes. DO NOT OVERBAKE! Store in a tight container to keep soft. My boys love these!

Serena Amoth

Soft Sugar Cookies

2 eggs
1 cup lard
1 teaspoon vanilla
2 teaspoons baking powder
2 teaspoons soda (scant)

1½ cups sugar
1 cup milk (sweet)
4 cups flour
1 teaspoon cream of tartar

Beat eggs 1 minute. Add sugar and shortening and beat one minute. Add vanilla and milk. Sift dry ingredients and combine with first mixture. Drop by spoon onto cookie sheet and bake. When cool spread icing on top.

Icing:
1 teaspoon vanilla
⅛ teaspoon salt

1 pound powdered sugar
4-5 tablespoons milk

Put all ingredients in bowl and beat at high speed for 1 minute. Divide icing into several parts and color each with food coloring. Make variety out of one batch of cookies. I remember these soft sugar cookies being in Grandma Mornie's cookie jar at times. The cookie jar that says $C,OOK,IES!

Jana, Mrs. Robert Nichols

Sour Cream Cookies

1 stick oleo (soft)
1 cup sugar
¼ teaspoon salt
1 teaspoon vanilla
1 egg

1 cup sour cream
3 cups flour
1 teaspoon baking powder
½ teaspoon soda

Mix oleo and sugar and then add in order given. Pat out on floured surface and cut out with cookie cutter. Bake at 350 degrees 7-12 minutes. Frost with powdered sugar frosting.

Barbara, Mrs. Ervin Koehn

Toasted Oatmeal Cookies

¾ cup butter or margarine
2 ½ cups rolled oats
¾ cup all-purpose flour
1 teaspoon baking soda
1 cup packed brown sugar

2 eggs, well beaten
1 teaspoon vanilla extract
½ cup salted peanuts
   (coarsely chopped)

In a large skillet over medium heat, melt butter until lightly browned. Add oats, stirring constantly until golden, about 8-10 minutes. Remove from the heat; cool. Combine flour and baking soda; set aside. In a large mixing bowl, beat brown sugar, eggs, and vanilla until light. Stir in dry ingredients and peanuts until well blended. Let stand for 15 minutes. Drop by rounded teaspoonfuls onto greased cookie sheets. Bake at 375 degrees for 10 minutes or until golden. Remove to wire rack and cool. These cookies keep well when stored in airtight containers.

Betty, Mrs. Gordon Unruh   Yield: 3½ dozen

Walnut Refrigerator Cookies

3¼ cups flour
1 teaspoon baking power
¼ teaspoon baking soda
1 teaspoon salt
⅔ cup granulated sugar

1 cup brown sugar
1¼ cup shortening (part butter)
2 eggs
1½ teaspoons vanilla
1 cup chopped walnuts

Sift flour, add baking powder, soda, and salt. Cream shortening. Gradually add both sugars. Cream until fluffy. Add eggs and vanilla and beat at high speed until mixed. Then add flour and nuts and mix until thoroughly blended. Press and shape dough into 3 loaves 2" square and 5" long on sheets of waxed paper. Wrap them tightly and chill 4 hours, or dough may be kept chilled for 2 weeks. To bake, cut chilled loaf into thin slices ⅛-¼ inch thick with sharp knife. Place slices 1" apart on ungreased baking sheet and bake at 400 degrees for 5-8 minutes.

Carolyn, Mrs. Wayne Holdeman

6 dozen cookies

White Chocolate and Macadamia Nut Cookies

1 cup all purpose flour
¾ teaspoon baking powder
⅛ teaspoon salt
⅛ teaspoon baking soda
½ cup plus 2 tablespoons
  (1¼ sticks) unsalted butter
  (room temperature)
¾ cup packed golden brown sugar

1 teaspoon vanilla extract
1 large egg
1½ cups vanilla milk
  (white chocolate) chips
¾ cup coarsely chopped
  macadamia nuts
¾ cup coarsely chopped pecans

Preheat oven to 350 degrees F. Grease 2 heavy large cookies sheets. Mix first 4 ingredients in small bowl. Using electric mixer, beat butter, sugar and vanilla in large bowl until light and fluffy. Beat in egg. Stir in dry ingredients, then vanilla milk chips and nuts. Drop cookie dough by scant ¼ cupfuls onto prepared cookie sheets, spacing evenly. (makes about 18) Bake until golden brown, about 15 minutes. Cool cookies on sheets 5 minutes. Transfer cookies to rack and cool. (Cookies can be made 1 day ahead. Store in airtight container at room temperature.)

Arlene Giesel Koehn

Bars

½ cup light corn syrup
½ cup sugar
dash of salt
1 cup of peanut butter
1 teaspoon vanilla

2 cups Rice Krispies
1 cup cornflakes-crushed
1 cup chocolate chips
  (semi-sweet or milk chocolate)

Combine sugar, syrup, and salt. Bring to full boil. Add peanut butter and ½ cup chocolate chips. Stir in vanilla and cereal. Chill one hour. Topping: Melt ½ cup chocolate chips and 2 tablespoons butter. Then add 3 tablespoons milk and ½ teaspoon vanilla. Add enough powdered sugar to spread. Frost bars.

Bev, Mrs. Lonnie Unruh

Cherry Bars

1 cup oleo or butter
1½ cups sugar
4 eggs beaten
1 can Wilderness cherry pie filling

2 cups flour
1 teaspoon vanilla
1 teaspoon almond flavoring

Cream together oleo, sugar, eggs and add flour. Stir in vanilla and almond flavoring. Spread on greased 1" deep cookie sheet. Mark into 24 squares. Spoon cherry filling into the center of each square. Bake 350 degrees for 25 minutes or until golden brown. Sprinkle with powdered sugar or frost after cooling 5 minutes.

Deloris, Mrs. Isaac Unruh, Jr.

Chocolate Swirled Peanut Butter Squares

2 cups unsifted flour
1 cup packed brown sugar
½ cup butter or margarine
1 cup peanut butter
3 (8 oz.) packages cream cheese
1½ cups granulated sugar

¾ cup peanut butter
6 eggs
1 tablespoon vanilla
3 cups heavy cream (whipped)
1 cup chocolate sauce

In bowl stir together flour and brown sugar. Using pastry blender cut butter and 1 cup peanut butter in till coarse crumbs form. Press crumb mixture into bottoms of 2 (15½" x 10½") jelly-roll pans. Bake in 350 degree oven 12 to 15 minutes or until browned. Cool on racks. In large bowl using mixer on medium speed, beat together cream cheese, sugar, and ¾ cup peanut butter. Add eggs and vanilla. Beat until smooth. Fold in whipped cream. Spread cream cheese mixture over each cooled crust. Drizzle chocolate sauce evenly over each cream cheese layer. Swirl with metal spatula to create a marbled effect. Cover and freeze 6 hours or until firm. Serve frozen or partially thawed. Cut each panful into 18 squares.

Kristin Giesel   Makes 36 servings

Choco-Walnut Bars

Crumb Base:

¾ cup oleo
2 cups oatmeal
1¼ cups flour

¾ cup brown sugar (packed)
½ teaspoon salt
½ teaspoon baking soda

Topping:

1 cup chopped walnuts
1½ cups chocolate chips

1 (14 oz.) can sweetened
   condensed milk

For crumb base, add oleo to dry ingredients. Beat on low speed of electric mixture till mixture resembles coarse crumbs. Press into bottom of a well greased 13 x 9" pan. For topping, sprinkle walnuts over base, pour condensed milk over, and then sprinkle chocolate chips. Bake at 350 degrees for 25 minutes or until light golden brown. Cool. Easy and good!

Arlene, Mrs. Randy Giesel

Delicious Bars

(These are so easy to make and oh so good. MINUTE FOOD. Just takes a minute to make.)

1 cup white corn syrup

1 cup white sugar

Bring to a boil, then add:

1¼ cup extra crunchy
   peanut butter

¼ cup butter or oleo

Mix well and add

4-5 cups Cocoa Pebbles
1 cup coconut

¾ cup salted peanuts

Pour into greased pan, cool and cut into bars.

Valetta, Mrs. John Koehn

Frank Burns Bars

Graham crackers-enough to line the bottom of 10x15 or 12x17 cookie sheet

1 stick oleo
1 cup brown sugar

⅔ cup chocolate chips
nuts

Line cookie sheet with foil. Lay graham crackers in bottom of pan on foil. Cook oleo and brown sugar 2 minutes, stirring constantly. Pour and spread on crackers. Bake at 400 degrees 5-6 minutes. Sprinkle on chocolate chips. Let chips melt enough to spread around. Sprinkle on nuts. (A quick, easy, and delicious bar.)

Dawn Giesel Dyck

Frosted Fruit Bars

1 cup white syrup
¼ cup mild-flavored molasses
½ cup soft shortening
1 egg
½ cup each of raisins, cut-up dates, and chopped, raw unpeeled apple

1 cup coarsely broken English walnuts
2½ cups all-purpose flour
1 teaspoon soda
1 teaspoon salt

With mixer, beat together syrup, molasses, shortening, and egg until creamy. Stir in fruits and nuts. In small bowl blend flour, soda, and salt. Add dry ingredients to creamed mixture, mixing thoroughly. Smooth batter into a well greased, 15½x 10½x1 inch jelly roll pan. Bake in a 350 degree oven, 15-20 minutes. Frost while still warm.

Cinnamon Icing:
2½ cups confectioners' sugar (measured, then sifted)
4 to 5 tablespoons milk

2 tablespoons soft margarine
1 teaspoon cinnamon
½ teaspoon vanilla

Beat together all ingredients until smooth.

Edna Giesel

Mildred's Bars

1 yellow cake mix
1 egg, beaten

⅓ cup melted oleo

Mix together above ingredients with a spoon and press mixture into lightly greased 9"x13" pan. Mixture will be sticky.

1½ cups unpacked brown sugar
2 tablespoons flour
¼ teaspoon baking powder
½ teaspoon salt

¾ cup chopped nuts
½ cup coconut(optional)
2 eggs slightly beaten
1 teaspoon vanilla

Mix together and spread onto cake mix layer. Bake at 350 degree oven for 20 to 30 minutes, or until filling doesn't jiggle when you gently shake the pan. Cool slightly, then frost.

Frosting:
1½ cups powdered sugar
2 tablespoons melted oleo

3 tablespoons light cream
¼ teaspoons vanilla

(My mother revised this recipe from one that a friend named Mildred gave her. Even though these bars only faintly resemble those Mildred brought to our home,the name "Mildred's Bars" has stuck. I often take these to sewing and basket dinners.)

Finette Giesel Koehn

Nutty O's

½ cup brown sugar (packed)
½ cup dark corn syrup
¼ cup butter
½ teaspoon salt

6 cups Cheerios
1 cup walnuts, pecans, peanuts, or
  a mix of nuts
½ cup slivered almonds

Heat oven to 325 degrees. Butter cookie sheet. Heat sugar, syrup, butter, and salt in 3 quart sauce pan over medium heat until sugar is dissolved, about 5 minutes. Remove from heat and stir in cereal and nuts until well coated. Put in pan and bake for 15 minutes. Cool 10 minutes and loosen with metal spatula. Let stand one hour. Break up and store in tightly closed container. Happy Eating!

Sophie (Giesel) Koehn

Oatmeal Scotchies

1 cup flour
1 teaspoon baking soda
½ teaspoon salt
½ teaspoon cinnamon
1 cup butter (softened)
¾ cup sugar

¾ cup brown sugar
2 eggs
1 teaspoon vanilla
3 cups oats
12 oz. package butterscotch morsels

Preheat oven to 375 degrees. In a small bowl combine flour, baking soda, salt, and cinnamon, set aside. In a large bowl combine butter, sugar, brown sugar, eggs, and vanilla. Beat until light and fluffy. Gradually add flour mixture. Stir in oats and butterscotch morsels. Spread dough into greased 15x10x1" baking pan. Bake 20-25 minutes. Can also be made into cookies, if you choose.

Fonda, Mrs. Gareth Eicher

Orange Slice Bars

1 pound orange slice candy
6 tablespoons boiling water
1 stick oleo
2 cups sugar
4 eggs

2½ cups flour
1 teaspoon vanilla
2 teaspoons baking powder
½ teaspoon salt
½ cup nuts

Cut up candy into eighths, add boiling water and let set 2 hours or overnight. Cream oleo, sugar, and eggs, beat well, add dry ingredients, vanilla and nuts. Stir in orange slices. Pour into 10" by 15" jelly roll pan. Bake in 325 degrees oven for 20 minutes.

Jul Nightengale

Peanut Butter Bars

Cream:

1 cup butter	2 eggs
1 cup sugar	⅔ cup peanut butter
1 cup brown sugar	1 teaspoon vanilla

Add:

2 cups flour	½ teaspoon salt
1 teaspoon soda	2 cups oatmeal

Beat at 350 degrees for 20 minutes. Sprinkle with 2 cups chocolate chips. Spread, then frost with: 1 cup powdered sugar, ½ cup peanut butter, 6 tablespoons milk.

Amy Giesel

Peanut Butter Cups

This recipe tastes just like the candy peanut butter cups sold under a brand name. We just love 'em and this recipe makes a whole panful at a fraction of the cost.

⅓ pound graham cracker crumbs	1 pound powdered sugar
½ pound butter or margarine	2 cups chocolate chips
1 cup peanut butter	

Combine crumbs, butter, peanut butter, and sugar. Work together until smooth. Press this mixture into a 9 by 9-inch buttered pan (or a larger pan if you want thinner bars). Melt chocolate chips over hot water. Spread over cracker mixture. Refrigerate until firm. Cut into squares.

Carolyn, Mrs. Wayne Holdeman

Pumpkin-Raisin Squares

⅓ cup raisins	3 tablespoons vegetable oil
1 cup plus ¼ teaspoon all-purpose flour divided	1 teaspoon baking powder
⅔ cup firmly packed light brown sugar	½ teaspoon ground cinnamon
½ cup cooked mashed pumpkin	½ teaspoon ground allspice
1 egg	¼ teaspoon salt
1 egg white	vegetable cooking spray
	½ teaspoon powdered sugar

Toss raisins with ¼ teaspoon flour, and set aside. Combine brown sugar and next 4 ingredients in a medium bowl; beat at medium speed with an electric mixer until well blended. Combine remaining cup flour, baking powder, and next 3 ingredients. Add to pumpkin mixture, and beat at low speed until smooth; stir in raisins. Pour batter into an 8-inch square baking pan coated with cooking spray. Bake at 350 degrees for 25 minutes. Cool completely in pan on a wire rack; sprinkle with powdered sugar.

Arlene Giesel Koehn   Yield: 16 servings

Quick N Easy Bars

42 soda crackers
1 cup butter
1 cup brown sugar

1 (6 oz.) package chocolate chips
1 (6 oz.) package butterscotch chips
chopped nuts

Place crackers in bottom of 10½ x 15 x 12" jelly roll pan. Heat butter and brown sugar, stirring constantly; boil 3 minutes. Pour over crackers. Bake at 400 degrees for 5 minutes. Cool slightly. Sprinkle with chips while still warm; spread lightly. Sprinkle with nuts and cut into squares immediately.

Mary, Mrs. Lee Giesel

Rocky Road Nut Bars

1¾ cups sugar
4 eggs
1¾ cups chopped walnuts
1½ cups flour

½ teaspoon baking powder
¾ cup oleo (melted)
½ teaspoon salt
1 teaspoon vanilla

Blend together sugar, flour, salt, eggs, baking powder and vanilla. Add nuts and oleo. Mix well. Put in a jelly roll pan and bake at 350 degrees for 25-30 minutes. Remove from oven and put on enough miniature marshmallows to cover the bars. Cover at once with tin foil so marshmallows melt. Drizzle or spread icing over bars. Icing: Combine in saucepan: 1 cup packed brown sugar, ⅓ cup milk, ½ cup oleo, ¼ teaspoon salt. Boil 2 to 3 minutes. Add 1 cup powdered sugar. Beat well. Pour on bars.

Carol, Mrs. Gary Koehn

Trio Bars

10 (2½" square) Honey Grahams
½ cup creamy peanut butter
½ cup margarine
⅔ cup sugar
1 egg

1 teaspoon vanilla extract
1 cup all-purpose flour
⅓ cup cocoa
½ teaspoon baking soda
1 cup raisins

Spread grahams with peanut butter. Place grahams, peanut butter-side up, in an 11 x 7 x 1½" baking pan, cutting to fit; set aside. In small bowl, with electric mixer at high speed, beat margarine, sugar, egg, and vanilla until light and fluffy. Mix flour, cocoa, and baking soda; blend into margarine mixture. Stir in raisins. Spread batter over peanut butter layer. Bake at 350 degrees F for 20 minutes. Cool completely. Cut into 24 bars. Note: To make in a 8x8x2-inch baking pan, prepare as above using 9 grahams, overlapping slightly to fit. Bake at 350 degrees F for 25-30 minutes; cool.

LeAnne Nichols

Salted Peanut Chew

Base:

1 package Pillsbury Plus Yellow
    Cake Mix
⅓ cup margarine or butter (softened)

1 egg
3 cups miniature marshmallows

Topping:

⅔ cup corn syrup
¼ cup margarine or butter
2 teaspoons vanilla
12 oz. package (2 cups) peanut
    butter chips

2 cups crisp rice cereal
2 cups salted peanuts

Heat oven to 350 degrees F. In large bowl, combine all base ingredients except marshmallows at low speed until crumbly. Press in bottom of ungreased 13 x 9-inch pan. Bake at 350 degrees F. for 12 to 18 minutes or until light golden brown.

Remove from oven and immediately sprinkle with marshmallows. Return to oven 1 to 2 minutes or until marshmallows just begin to puff. Cool while preparing topping. In large saucepan, heat corn syrup, margarine, vanilla, and chips just until chips are melted and mixture is smooth, stirring constantly. Remove from heat; stir in cereal and nuts. Immediately spoon warm topping over marshmallows; spread to cover. Chill; cut into bars. Store covered.

Arlene Giesel Koehn   36 bars

Batter up Brownies

1 cup flour
½ teaspoon baking powder
½ teaspoon salt
½ cup shortening
1½ cups sugar

3 eggs
½ cup peanut butter
1 teaspoon vanilla
1 cup chopped nuts
1 cup chocolate chips

Mix well, put in greased 9x13 pan. Bake 25-30 minutes at 350 degrees. Pour on powdered sugar glaze while hot. Easy and delicious!

Ronda, Mrs. Kenny Giesel

Brownies

4 eggs
2 cups sugar
1 cup melted oleo
1 teaspoon vanilla

5 tablespoons cocoa
2 cups flour
1 cup chopped nuts

Preheat oven to 350 degrees. Grease 15x9 pan. Beat eggs. Add sugar and beat some more. Add remaining ingredients. Pour into pan and bake 20 minutes at 350 degrees.

Donna, Mrs. Quinn Schmidt; Valerie Holdeman; Cherylyn Unruh

Butterscotch Brownies

¼ cup oleo
1 cup brown sugar
1 egg
¾ cup flour

1 teaspoon baking powder
½ teaspoon salt
½ teaspoon vanilla
½ cup nuts

Melt oleo. Stir in sugar, then egg. Add dry ingredients, then vanilla and nuts. Bake in 12x8 pan, 20 minutes at 350 degrees. (For variety, chocolate chips can be sprinkled on before baking.)

LeAnne Nichols, Jul Nightengale

Cake Mix Brownies

1 package Devils food cake mix
1 egg

¼ cup water
chopped nuts

Mix well, batter will be very thick. Spoon into greased 9x13 pan and press down. Bake at 350 for 20 minutes for chewy brownies, longer for cake-type brownies.

Mary, Mrs. Lee Giesel

Double Fudge Saucepan Brownies

⅔ cup flour
¼ teaspoon baking soda
¼ teaspoon salt
2 tablespoons butter or margarine
2 tablespoons water

2 cups chocolate chips (divided)
2 eggs slightly beaten
1 teaspoon vanilla
½ cup chopped nuts (optional)
½ cup sugar

In bowl, stir together flour, baking soda and salt. In medium saucepan combine sugar, butter, and water. Cook over low heat, stirring constantly until mixture comes to a boil. Remove from heat; immediately add 1 cup chocolate chips, stirring until melted. Stir in eggs and vanilla until blended. Gradually add flour mixture, blending well. Stir in remaining 1 cup chips and nuts if desired. Pour batter into greased 9 inch square baking dish. Bake 25-30 minutes at 325 degrees.

Elaine, Mrs. Bruce Unruh

About 1½ dozen

Easy "Toffee" Candy

1¼ cup butter (not margarine), divided
35-40 soda crackers
1 cup dark brown sugar

1 (14 oz.) can sweetened condensed milk
1½ cup semi-sweet chocolate morsels
¾ cup nuts, finely chopped

Heat oven to 425 degrees. In medium pan melt ¼ cup butter. Pour into foil lined 15" by 10" jelly roll pan. Arrange crackers over butter; cut crackers to fill empty spaces. Melt remaining butter; stir in sugar. Bring to boil and cook for two minutes, stirring occasionally. Remove from heat, stir in sweetened condensed milk. Spread over crackers. Bake 10 to 12 minutes until mixture is bubbly and slightly darkened. Carefully remove from oven; cool 1 minute. Sprinkle with chocolate chips; let stand 5 minutes until melted. Spread chocolate. Sprinkle with nuts, press into chocolate. Cool, chill until chocolate is set. Invert cookie sheet and dislodge candy. Remove foil; cut candy into pieces. Store in airtight container.

LeAnne Nichols

English Buttercreams

½ cup salted butter, NO SUBSTITUTE
1 tablespoon shortening

1 tablespoon milk
1 (16 oz.) box powdered sugar, sifted
1½ teaspoons peppermint extract

Cream butter, shortening, and milk together until light and fluffy. Gradually add sifted sugar, beating each addition in fully. Stir in extract. Continue until all sugar is mixed well and you are not able to feel any grains of sugar when you test a tiny bit with your tongue. Roll out onto aluminum foil in ¾ inch diameter ropes. Slice each rope into ¼ inch slices. Cover lightly and store overnight to set. Note: Mixture may be divided and tinted with food color. Easier when made in a food processor.

Arlene Giesel Koehn

Fudgesicle Cubes

1 can Hershey chocolate syrup
1 can evaporated milk

½ cup sugar
2⅓ cup milk

Mix all together and stir until sugar is dissolved. Pour into 2 ice cube trays. Freeze at least 6 hours.

Arlene, Mrs. Randy Giesel

Maple Almond Brittle

1½ cups maple syrup
¼ cup lite corn syrup
½ teaspoon salt

1½ cups sugar
2 cups sliced unblanched almonds
toasted lightly

In heavy sauce pan, combine maple syrup, corn syrup, salt and sugar. Bring to boil, stirring and washing down any sugar crystals clinging to side with a brush dipped in cold water. Boil mixture undisturbed until it registers 300 degrees Fahrenheit on candy thermometer. Stir in almonds quickly and pour mixture onto oiled marble slab or a baking sheet lined with foil. Spread thin with metal spatula. Let cool. Break into pieces.

Arlene Giesel Koehn

Makes 1½ pounds

Marla's Mints

1 (8 oz.) package cream cheese
   at room temperature
1 bag powdered sugar (C & H only)

¼ to ½ teaspoon peppermint
   flavoring (or to taste)

Mix cheese and sugar in large bowl. Knead and knead. When thoroughly kneaded add flavoring and color. Pinch off dab, roll in sugar and mold. Dry several hours on each side.

Carol, Mrs. Gary Koehn
Jackie Koehn

Makes approximately 250 roses

Maple Taffy

1 cup maple syrup
½ cup water
½ cup sugar

1 tablespoon butter
⅛ teaspoon cream of tartar

Mix all ingredients and boil until the hard ball stage. Pour onto a large buttered dish. As the edges of the taffy cool, fold forward toward the center until totally cooled (enough to retain a thumbprint). Butter your hands and pull taffy until very pale in color. Twist and cut with scissors. Wrap each piece in waxed paper. Keep refrigerated.

Arlene Giesel Koehn

Marshmallow Pecan Fudge

¼ pound butter
1 can evaporated milk
5 cups sugar
pinch of salt

1½ cups chocolate chips
2 cups small marshmallows
1 teaspoon vanilla
1½ cup chopped pecans

Combine butter, sugar, and salt in stainless steel saucepan and cook over low heat, stirring constantly, until sugar is dissolved and butter melted. Increase heat to medium low and boil 8 minutes without stirring. Meanwhile combine chocolate chips and marshmallows in a greased bowl. When syrup is done, pour immediately over chocolate chip mixture. Do not scrape pan. Stir until chocolate is dissolved. Add vanilla and pecans. Spread in buttered 13 inch by 9 inch pan and cool completely. Cut into squares. This is the fudge Randy likes to make — delicious!

Arlene, Mrs. Randy Giesel

Millionaires

2 (14 oz.) packages caramels   3 or 4 tablespoons milk

Melt in double boiler.

Add:

2 cups pecans (toasted is better)

Drop by spoonfuls onto buttered wax paper. Put into refrigerator or freezer until firm. Melt 10 Hershey bars and ⅓ sheet of paraffin wax in double boiler or microwave. Take candies out of refrigerator and place on wire rack. Pour melted chocolate over candies, turn candies over and pour on other side. The chocolate that runs off can be re-used.

Kathy Wedel

Mint Wafers

1 egg white
2½ powdered sugar

2 teaspoons butter
½ teaspoon peppermint flavoring

Knead with hands, shape into small balls. Place on waxed paper, flatten with fork. Let set for 2 or 3 hours. Coat with chocolate: 1 package semi-sweet chocolate chips, ¼ bar of wax, and 4 ounces sweet chocolate melted together.

Coreen Holdeman

Never Fail Divinity

½ cup water
2 cups sugar
pinch of salt

1 pint of marshmallow cream
1 cup chopped pecans
1 teaspoon vanilla

Combine water, sugar and salt in saucepan. Bring to rolling boil and boil for 3 minutes. Place marshmallow cream in large bowl and pour hot syrup into it all at once. Stir until candy loses its gloss. Add chopped nuts and vanilla and drop by spoonfuls onto waxed paper.

Arlene Giesel Koehn

Peanut Brittle

1 cup raw peanuts
1 cup granulated sugar
½ cup white corn syrup
⅛ teaspoon salt

1 teaspoon butter
1 teaspoon vanilla
1 teaspoon baking soda

In a 1½ quart casserole mix peanuts, sugar, salt and corn syrup. Microwave on HIGH for 7-8 minutes, stirring well after 4 minutes. Add butter and vanilla and microwave 1-2 minutes more. Peanuts will be lightly browned and syrup very hot. Add baking soda, stir gently until foamy. Pour onto lightly buttered cookie sheet; let cool ½ hour, break into pieces and store in airtight container.

Arlene Giesel Koehn

Peanut Brittle

½ cup hot water
1 cup corn syrup

2 cups sugar

Cook to soft crack. Add 1 bag of peanuts and cook until brown (325 degrees). Remove from heat and add 2 teaspoons soda and 1 teaspoon vanilla. Spoon out in cookie sheets and stretch as soon as possible.

Jul Nightengale

Peanut Butter Bon Bons

2 cups crunchy peanut butter
4 cups powdered sugar
1 stick oleo

1 teaspoon vanilla
3 cups Rice Krispies

Mix together and form into walnut-sized balls. Let bon bons set overnight or several hours in fridge. Melt 2 to 4 ounces paraffin and 6 Hershey candy bars (equal to about 4 - 6 ounces milk chocolate chips). Melt slowly in double boiler. Dip bon bons in chocolate and place on wax paper to cool. Store in closed container. This recipe comes from sister Mable (Giesel) Ratzlaff.

Sophie Giesel Koehn

Peanut Clusters

1 pound white almond bark   12 oz. semi-sweet chocolate chips

Melt in double boiler.

Add:

13 oz. peanuts

Drop by teaspoonfuls onto greased cookie sheet.

Serena Amoth

Pecan Clusters

1 (7 oz.) jar marshmallow creme   1 (13 oz.) can evaporated milk
1½ pounds milk chocolate kisses   ½ cup butter
5 cups sugar   6 cups pecan halves

Place marshmallow creme and kisses in a large bowl; set aside. Combine sugar, milk, and butter in a saucepan. Bring mixture to a boil, then cook for 8 minutes. Pour over marshmallow creme and kisses, stirring until well blended. Stir in pecans. Drop by teaspoonfuls onto waxed paper.

Arlene Giesel Koehn   Yield: about 12 dozen

Peppermint Mints

Melt one package Almond Bark. Crush 5 candy canes. Mix well together and pour into different shapes. Cool; pop out. A good Christmas treat!

Carol, Mrs. Gary Koehn

Perfect White Fudge

2 cups sugar   ¼ teaspoon salt
½ cup dairy sour cream   2 teaspoons vanilla
⅓ cup white corn syrup   1 cup chopped nuts
2 tablespoons butter

In 2 quart saucepan, combine sugar, sour cream, white corn syrup, butter, and salt. Bring to boil, stirring until sugar dissolves. Boil, without stirring, over medium heat to 236 degrees or soft ball stage. Remove from heat. Let stand for 15 minutes. Add vanilla. Beat until candy begins to lose gloss. Add nuts and pour in buttered pan.

Mary, Mrs. Lee Giesel

Sponge Candy

1 cup sugar	1 tablespoon distilled white vinegar
1 cup dark corn syrup	1 tablespoon baking soda, sifted

Line 9-inch square cake pan (2" deep) with foil, extending foil over sides. Generously butter foil. Combine sugar, corn syrup and vinegar in heavy large deep saucepan. Stir over medium heat until sugar dissolves. Continue cooking without stirring (swirl pan occasionally) until clip-on candy thermometer registers 300 degrees Fahrenheit, (about 18 minutes). Remove from heat. Immediately add baking soda and stir until well combined (mixture will foam vigorously). Immediately pour mixture into prepared pan. Cool completely.

Arlene Giesel Koehn   Makes about 6 cups

Taffy

2 cups white syrup	3 cups white sugar
butter size of egg, less 1 tablespoon, dash of salt	1 tablespoon vinegar

Boil all together to 256 degrees. Then add 2 teaspoons vanilla and any other flavoring and coloring. Bring back up to 260. Pour into buttered pan. Cool. Pull until it gets bubbles. Twist and cool again. Cut and wrap.

Carol, Mrs. Gary Koehn

Turtles

Melt in double boiler or microwave: 48 caramels and 2 tablespoons evaporated milk. Then add 1 cup peanuts. Spoon onto buttered cookie sheet and let cool. Then dip in chocolate [1 (12 oz.) Hershey's chocolate bar and ¼ bar paraffin melted together].

Coreen Holdeman

Waldorf Fudge

Boil for 5 minutes:

4 cups sugar	1 large can Pet Milk
¼ pound oleo	

Add:

4 or 5 (½ pound) Hershey bars	1½ cup pecans
1 pint marshmallow cream	1 teaspoon vanilla

Mix and pour in buttered pan, 7½" x 11" or larger. Dr. Waldorf's recipe. In 1986, 1 Hershey bar cost $1.57.

Jennie, Mrs. Calvin Unruh   Makes about 5 pounds candy

Coffee Nut Ice Cream - Dr. Waldorf's

Beat 10 minutes:

6 eggs   2 cups sugar

Add:

1 pint of heavy cream   1 cup chopped pecans,
1 tablespoon vanilla   browned in butter
3 tablespoons instant coffee

Add enough milk to fill freezer to desired level.

Arlene Giesel Koehn   Yield: 1 gallon

Freezer Ice Cream

1 gallon:

4 eggs   2 tablespoons vanilla
6 cups milk   ½ teaspoon salt
4 cups light cream   fruit of your choice
2½ cups sugar

Beat eggs until light. Add sugar and beat until thick. Add milk and cream, vanilla and salt. Stir well. Pour in freezer and start cranking.

Mary, Mrs. Lee Giesel

Home-made Strawberry Ice Cream

2 boxes frozen strawberries   1 pint whipping cream
   (10 oz. size)   1½ cups milk
1 scant cup sugar mixed with   2 cans strawberry pop, pour in
   thawing strawberries   just before freezing
1 can Eagle Brand sweetened
   condensed milk

Add enough milk to make 1 gallon.

Nathan Giesel's daughter-in-law, LeWanda Giesel

Ice Cream

1 quart cream   ½ teaspoon salt
2 cups sugar   2 teaspoons vanilla
1 package junket mix   7 eggs

Add enough milk to fill freezer. Freeze.

Jolene, Mrs. Dennis Koehn

Ice Cream

Cream together 3 eggs, beaten, and 1 cup sugar. Add 2 boxes ice cream powder, 3 pints cream, 2 tablespoons vanilla and finish with milk. For Butterfinger Ice Cream, add 4 large crushed Butterfinger candy bars.

Louise Wedel

Incredible Fried Ice Cream

1 quart vanilla ice cream	oil enough for deep frying
4 cups fine Cornflakes crumbs	whipping cream (optional)
2 teaspoons cinnamon	honey (optional)
4 egg whites	maraschino cherries (optional)

Scoop ice cream into 8 balls about ½ cup each. Freeze 1½ hours or until firm. In a small shallow bowl mix cinnamon and Cornflakes crumbs. In another shallow bowl, beat egg whites with fork until foamy. Dip ice cream in egg bowl and then into crumb mixture. If balls are not completely covered, roll into mixtures a second time. Freeze 3 to 4 hours. Deep fat fry 2 or 3 balls at a time at 375 degrees for 10 to 15 seconds. Drain on paper towel. Serve as frying or freeze. Put whipped cream with cherry on top or use honey.

Monica Koehn   Yield: 8 balls

Peanut Butter Ice Cream Balls

1 cup graham cracker crumbs	2 tablespoons sugar
¼ cup peanut butter	1 quart vanilla ice cream

Blend graham cracker crumbs, peanut butter and sugar. Scoop ice cream into large balls and roll in crumb mixture until well-coated. Freeze until serving time. Serve with chocolate syrup.

LeAnne Nichols   6-8 servings

Snow Ice Cream

½ cup powdered sugar	½ teaspoon vanilla
1⅓ cups cream	4-6 cups clean snow
1 egg	

Put all ingredients in blender, except snow. Blend on medium, then high. Blend well. Pour slowly over snow, using whip to stir.

Elaine, Mrs. David Unruh

Blackberry Topping

4 cups well-drained blackberries   **1 cup sugar**

Cook, mashing berries for 5 minutes. Add sugar and cook for 6-8 minutes, stirring frequently until slightly thickened. Remove from heat, let cool. Topping keeps for 1 month covered in refrigerator. Serve over ice cream, cheese cake, or pudding.

Arlene Giesel Koehn   Makes 1 pint

Praline Ice Cream Sauce

1½ cup chopped pecans   **¾ cup corn syrup**
¼ cup butter   **3 tablespoons flour**
1¼ cup brown sugar   **1 (5.33 oz.) can evaporated milk**

Bake pecans at 300 degrees for 15 minutes, set aside. Melt butter in medium sauce pan, add sugar, corn syrup and flour, stirring well. Bring to a boil, reduce heat and simmer, stirring constantly for 5 minutes. Remove from heat and let cool to luke-warm; gradually stir in milk and pecans. Serve warm over ice cream.

Coreen Holdeman   Yield: 3 cups

Quick and Easy Chocolate Sauce

Boil together until slightly thickened: 1 can evaporated milk and ½ cup sugar. Add 1 cup (more or less) chocolate chips. Stir until chips are melted.

Mary, Mrs. Lee Giesel

Toasted Pecan Sauce

½ cup sugar   **1 egg, slightly beaten**
⅓ cup Land-O-Lakes sweet   **1 tablespoon vanilla**
  cream butter   **1 cup pecan halves, toasted**
1 cup light corn syrup

In 2-quart saucepan, combine all ingredients except pecans. Cook over medium heat, stirring constantly, until mixture comes to a full boil (6 to 8 minutes). Just before serving, stir in pecans. Serve warm or cool over ice cream, cake, pancakes or waffles. Yield: 2 cups. Microwave directions: In 2-quart casserole, combine sugar, butter and corn syrup. Microwave on high 2 minutes; mix well. Stir 1 tablespoon hot sugar mixture into beaten egg. Slowly stir egg mixture into hot sugar mixture. Microwave on high, stirring every minute, until mixture comes to a full boil (3 to 4 minutes). Microwave on high 1 minute. Just before serving, stir in pecans. Serve warm or cool over ice cream, cake, pancakes or waffles.

Arlene Giesel Koehn

Vanilla Sauce

1 cup sugar
½ cup canned milk (or 1 cup cream)
½ cup margarine

1 tablespoon flour
1 teaspoon vanilla

Mix sugar and flour together, add milk and oleo, bring to boil and boil 5 minutes. Add vanilla. Good on ice cream or as icing for a cake. Add 2-3 teaspoons Quick Chocolate for chocolate sauce.

Jul Nightengale

PRESERVES & PICKLES

Carrot Jam

5 pounds carrots
6 cups sugar

juice of 6 lemons

Wash, pare and grate carrots, add lemon juice and sugar. Cook slowly until thick.
Pour into Kerr canning jars and seal.

Louise Wedel

Corn Cob Jelly

Serve this with soft candlelight.

14 large red corn cobs
1 (1¾ oz) package Sure Jell

3 cups cob water
3 cups sugar

Run water over cobs to rinse off the last of the chaff. In large saucepan cover cobs
with water (plenty water must be used as cobs absorb liquid. Boil gently for 30 minutes; strain cob water through cloth and measure 3 cups liquid, add Sure Jell and
bring to a boil over high heat. Quickly stir in sugar, allow to return to a fast boil and
cook 1 minute. Remove from heat, skim foam from top. Pour into glass jelly jars.

Give as a novelty gift!

Edna Giesel

Yield: 4½ pint jars

Better-than-Smuckers Grape Jelly

1 (12 oz.) can frozen concentrated
    sweetened grape juice
2 juice cans cold water

1 (1¾ oz.) package Sure Jell
6 cups sugar

Thaw juice; mix with water and SureJell. Bring mixture to a full boil over high heat,
stirring constantly. Quickly add 6 cups sugar, mix and return to full boil for 1
minute, stirring constantly. Remove from heat, skim foam from top and pour into
glass jelly jars. Refrigerate.

Edna Giesel

Yield: 4 pints

Freezer Jam

3½ cups prepared fruit pulp
¼ cup lemon juice

1 package Sure Jell

Mix together, and let set for 30 minutes, stirring every 5 minutes. Add 4½ cups
sugar, 1 cup corn syrup. Bring to 100 degrees (no hotter!). Pour into jars. Freeze.

Valerie Koehn

Grape Jam

In large saucepan, measure 4 quarts washed and stemmed purple grapes (Concord). Crush, and stir in ½ cup water. Cover and bring to simmer for 10 minutes; put grapes through a fine sieve or food processor to remove seeds and skins. Make jam while pulp is hot. Mix 2 cups grape pulp and 3 cups sugar, place over medium heat, cook, stirring constantly, until sugar is completely dissolved. Simmer a few minutes longer. Skim and pour into hot jars. Cover with paraffin and seal. This yields about 10 pints jam. Cook only one batch at a time (2 cups pulp, 3 cups sugar).

Mary, Mrs. Lee Giesel

Peach Seed Jelly

Cover seeds with water and simmer. Strain juice. Mix 3½ cups juice, 4½ cups sugar, 1 box Sure Jell. Cook according to package directions.

Sophie Giesel Koehn

Rhubarb-Pineapple Jam

Chop 7 pounds rhubarb and 2 medium pineapples into small pieces. Add 2½ pounds sugar, and cook 15 minutes; add an additional 2 ½ pounds sugar and simmer, stirring frequently, until rich and thick. Pour into jars and seal.

Louise Wedel

Strawberry Syrup

A must for ice cream, sodas, pancakes and french toast.

4 cups ripe strawberries, rinsed and hulled
1¾ cups water

2 teaspoons finely grated lemon zest
1¼ cups sugar

Crush berries in a heavy saucepan, add 1 cup water and lemon zest. Bring to a boil, reduce heat slightly and simmer over medium heat for 5 minutes, skimming foam off the top. Set aside to cool. Place sugar and the remaining ¾ cup water in a small heavy saucepan. Bring to a boil and cook until syrup reaches 260 degrees on a candy thermometer. Set aside. Strain cooled strawberry mixture through a double thickness of cheese cloth. Squeeze well until all juice and pulp are extracted and seeds are left behind. Discard cheese cloth and contents. Pour the clear strained liquid into saucepan with the sugar syrup. Bring to boil and cook for 8 minutes. Pack in 2 half-pint jars, leaving a ¼ inch head space. Process in a boiling water bath for 10 minutes.

Arlene Giesel Koehn

Catsup Recipe

8 cups tomato juice	1½ cups sugar
1 cup vinegar	¼ teaspoon dry mustard
½ teaspoon cinnamon	4-5 small onions, chopped
cloves to taste	1 tablespoon salt
⅓ teaspoon pepper	1 tablespoon paprika

Cook tomatoes and onions until tender, about 1 hour. Press through colander. Bring to boil; add sugar, vinegar, and salt. Continue to cook until thick; add spices. Fill jars and seal.

From Elma, Mrs. Alfred Koehn's recipes; submitted by daughter, Louise Wedel

Frozen Corn

4 cups corn, cut from cob, raw	3 teaspoons sugar
1 cup ice water	1 teaspoon salt

Mix together and freeze. Retains "fresh from garden taste."

Finette Giesel

Spectacular Frozen Corn

20 cups freshly husked corn, cut from cob, raw	1 pint half and half
1 pound butter, melted, (do not substitute)	

Place corn into a large roaster. Mix melted butter and half and half, pour over corn, stir well. Bake in 325 degree oven for 1 hour, covered. Stir every 15 minutes. Remove from oven and cool. Spoon corn into freezer bags, seal and freeze. To serve add salt and a pinch of sugar. This corn is delicious!

Finette Giesel

Baked Apples, Canned

7 quarts apples, quartered, peel if you like	2 teaspoons cinnamon, or 2 cups red hot candies, dissolved in hot water
8 cups water	
4 cups sugar	⅔ cup plus 1 tablespoon cornstarch

Place apples in jar, mix sugar, cinnamon and cornstarch with 4 cups water. Stir until smooth. Add remaining water and bring to boil, stirring frequently. Pour over apples in jar. Process in hot water bath 30 minutes. Use as needed, baking 45-60 minutes in a 350 degree oven.

Sophie Giesel Koehn

Canning Pinto Beans

Soak beans over night. Cover beans with fresh water and bring to a boil, cook for 30 minutes. Drain and place in jars, cover with fresh hot water, leaving a 1" head space. Add 1 teaspoon salt to each quart jar. Process for 20 minutes at 10 pounds pressure.

Sophie Giesel Koehn

Beet Pickles

1 cup vinegar	3 cups water
2 cups sugar	1 tablespoon mixed spices

Prepare fresh whole beets for cooking, leaving 1-2 inches of tops and all the roots. Cook beets until done. Remove skins and cut as desired. Combine vinegar, sugar, water, and spices and heat while stirring until sugar is dissolved. Place beets into hot pickle mixture and simmer for 10-15 minutes. Pack in jars, cover with pickle liquid and seal.

Sophie Giesel Koehn

Crisp Cucumber Slices

16 thinly sliced unpeeled cucumbers	1 green pepper, cut into thin strips
6 onions	⅓ cup salt
1 red pepper cut into thin strips	pimiento

Mix salt into vegetables and cover with ice cubes. Let stand 4 hours, drain. Heat to boiling 1½ teaspoons mustard seed, 1½ teaspoons celery seed, 1½ teaspoons tumeric, 3 cups vinegar, 5 cups sugar and green food coloring. Add drained vegetables and bring to a boil. Place into jars and seal.

Jul Nightengale   Yield: 6 pints

Cucumber Cinnamon Rings

Peel and slice cucumbers (cut centers out to make rings) 2 gallons large cucumbers, about 15. Put rings in lime water, let set 24 hours. Drain. Wash in cool water. Pour cold water over rings—soak for 3 hours and drain. Add 1 cup vinegar, 1 teaspoon alum, and water to cover. Simmer for 2 hours and drain. Make syrup as follows: 2 cups sugar, 2 cups water, 10 cups sugar, 8 sticks cinnamon, 2 teaspoons red food coloring, 1 package Brach's Imperials red hots. Add cucumber rings and bring to boil. Place in jars and seal.

Jul Nightengale

Pickled Green Beans

In bottom of each pint jar, place the following; ¼ teaspoon crushed red pepper, 2 cloves garlic, 1 head fresh dill. Pack long uncut beans in jars. Make a brine of the following: 2 cups vinegar, 2 cups water, ¼ cup salt. Heat to boiling and pour over beans and seal. Hot water bath just till color changes. Not too long or they will not stay crisp. My mother- in-law makes these, and they are a favorite with us.

Janice, Mrs Jerry Ratzlaff

Dill Pickles

16 cups water
1 cup salt

1 cup vinegar
¼ teaspoon alum, to each quart

To each quart, add dill and garlic (enough for 6 quarts) Bring water and vinegar to boil, add salt and boil. Pour over cucumbers and seal.

Jul Nightengale

Dill Pickles

Cucumbers
2 quarts water
½ cup pickling salt
1 cup vinegar

dill
garlic
horseradish leaf (optional)

Make brine of water, salt and vinegar, bring to a boil; place cucumbers, dill, garlic, and horseradish leaf in each jar. Pour hot brine to cover, seal; place in pressure canner. Add 2 quarts water, heat on high till steam can be seen coming from vent. Set timer for 10 minutes, lower heat to medium. Remove from canner end of 10 minutes.

Jolene Unruh

Dill Pickles

Put dill, garlic, grape leaves, tumeric, alum, onion, hot pepper and cucumbers in jars. Heat 1 quart water, ¼ cup salt, and ½ cup vinegar. Pour over cucumbers and seal.

Deanna Giesel   Makes 4 pints

Fresh Dills

1 quart water
¼ cup pickling salt

1 tablespoon vinegar

Slice cucumbers crosswise in ½-1 inch pieces. Pack in jars with 1 head dill, a clove of garlic, and a horseradish leaf. Pour cool brine over cucumbers and place jars in refrigerator for 2 days. Pickles are crisp and ready to eat.

Jolene Unruh   Yield: 2 quarts

Sweet Dill Pickles

1 gallon sliced dill pickles

(make your own dill pickles and leave set for 2 days before using in this recipe)

Brine:

10 cups sugar   2 teaspoons celery seed
4 teaspoons mustard seed   2 cups vinegar

Drain dill pickles and put cold sweet brine over pickles. Let set for 6-8 hours in this brine. Stir and mix several times. Drain and heat brine to boiling. Place pickles in jars and cover with brine to fill and seal.

Jul Nightengale   Yield 4-5 pints

Sweet Pickles

No need to can, keep in refrigerator; 10 pounds pickles, soak in brine, 1 cup salt to each 2 quarts water, for 3 weeks; drain and cover with cold vinegar, let stand for 10 days. Drain and cut in chunks. Add 9 cups sugar, 2 tablespoons whole cloves, 2 tablespoons whole allspice and 1 box stick cinnamon. Refrigerate, stir occasionally, will keep for several years. This is my favorite recipe.

Mary, Mrs. Lee Giesel

Frozen Pickles

2 quarts sliced cucumbers   1½ cups sugar
2 tablespoons salt   ½ cups white vinegar
1 large onion

Prepare first 3 ingredients, cover and refrigerate for 24 hours. Drain and add sugar and vinegar, refrigerate for another 24 hours. Freeze.

Deanna Giesel

Refrigerator Pickles

(From Grandma Mornie)

2 cups sugar   1½ teaspoons celery seeds
1 cup vinegar   1 teaspoon mustard seeds

Heat to dissolve. Cool.

Mix:

1 cup thinly sliced onions   ¼ cup salt
4 cups thinly sliced cucumbers

Let stand 30 minutes, drain and wash. Place cucumber and onion slices in jars. Pour syrup over and keep in refrigerator.

Elaine, Mrs. David Unruh   Makes 1½ pints

Relish From Aunt Carolyn

2 gallons, washed and sliced cucumbers

Brine:

1 gallon water   1 cup salt

Pour over cucumbers, weight down to keep cucumbers covered. Soak in this brine for 3 days. Drain. Add boiling water, let stand 1 day. Drain. Next day add onion, and green pepper slices, add 1 gallon boiling water adding 2 tablespoons alum. Next day drain and grind. Mix 8 cups sugar, 4 cups vinegar. Add 2 tablespoons pickling spices, (tied in cotton cloth) bring to boil, stirring until sugar is dissolved. Pour over relish. Let stand for a day, drain and reheat brine and pour over relish. The next day drain and reheat brine. Put relish in jars and pour hot brine to fill jars. Seal. Water bath to seal.

Elaine, Mrs. David Unruh

Pickled Okra

Make brine by boiling following:

3 cups vinegar

6 tablespoons salt

3 cups water

In bottom of each quart jar place ½ teaspoon mustard seed and 3 hot pepper pods or ½ teaspoon crushed pepper. Pack washed okra in jars, seal and hot water bath 5 minutes.

Janice, Mrs. Jerry Ratzlaff

Pepper Relish

12 sweet peppers (use some red
    for color)
24 sweet banana peppers
3 hot peppers
7 medium onions

3 cups vinegar
2 cups sugar
2 tablespoons mustard seed
2 tablespoons salt

Chop or grind peppers and onions. Combine with other ingredients and boil 30 minutes. Pack in jars and seal. Meat and vegetable dishes will take on a special flavor with a spoonful of pepper relish.

Arlene Giesel Koehn

Zucchini Relish

7-8 medium sized zucchini
(unpeeled)

4 large onions
3 large stalks celery, diced

Mix together and sprinkle with ½ cup salt. Let stand over night. Drain and rinse.
Make brine:

3 cups cider vinegar
3 cups sugar
2½ teaspoons celery seed

2 teaspoons mustard seed
2 teaspoons turmeric

Combine and boil for 2 minutes; pour over vegetables and let stand 2 hours. Pack in jars and water bath 5 minutes to seal.

Arlene Giesel Koehn

Garden Tomato Hint

Wash tomatoes, cut out area around stem and freeze. Later, place frozen tomatoes in a bowl of hot tap water till skin slips off easily. Thaw tomatoes and use as desired. They can be used in soups, canned or made into other tomato products.

Jolene Unruh

Homemade Tomato Soup

14 quarts tomatoes
7 onions
1 bunch celery
3 bay leaves
14 sprigs parsley

14 tablespoons flour
14 tablespoons oleo
3 tablespoons salt
8 tablespoons sugar
2 teaspoons pepper

Make tomatao juice. Chop onions, celery, bay leaves, parsley in blender, add flour and some juice. Mix all ingredients together and bring to boil. Place in jars and process 45 minutes in water bath, or at 10 pounds pressure for 15 minutes in pressure canner.

Jolene Unruh

Enchilada Sauce

1 pound oleo
2 cups flour
4 pints tomato juice
3 quarts water

4 teaspoons salt
¾ cup chili powder
pepper

Melt oleo, stir in flour. Add other ingredients, heat until thickened. Put in jars in pressure canner. Process at 10 pounds pressure for 15 minutes.

Jolene Unruh

Yield: 12 pints

Pizza Sauce

2 gallons tomato juice
2 green peppers, chopped
3 hot peppers, chopped

3 onions, chopped
2-3 cloves garlic, chopped

Blend all above ingredients; cook 1 hour. Then add:

1 pint oil
¼ cup sugar
½ cup pickling salt
2 tablespoons oregano

2 tablespoons basil
2 tablespoons parsley flakes
6 bay leaves
4 (6 oz.) cans tomato paste

Cook 1 hour longer. Put in jars and pressure 5 minutes at 10 pounds pressure. Yield: 20 pints. Makes pizza-making a snap!

Michele, Mrs. Richard Ensz

Canning Beef Roast

Cut roast in serving pieces, place in roaster, sprinkle with tenderizer. Bake until juice forms. Pack meat in jars, add 1 teaspoon salt to each quart. Strain broth and add dry onion soup mix and dry minced onion; pour over meat in jars. Process at 10 pounds pressure for 90 minutes. Use as roast beef , or flour meat and fry until crispy brown.

Sophie Giesel Koehn

Pork Sausage

30 pounds ground pork
½ cup salt

3 handfuls Watkins pepper
1½ bottle Wright's liquid smoke

Mix well. Make into link sausage or bulk. Pressure can or freeze. Uncle Ervin's recipe.

Arlene Giesel Koehn

Pressure Pan Sausage

Place 2 cups water in small pressure cooker with rack. Add 2 pounds frozen link sausage on rack. Start on high heat, when regulator begins rocking, reduce heat and cook 30 minutes. Let pressure drop of its own accord. Cut sausage into serving pieces and brown in ungreased pan.

Jolene Unruh

POTPOURRI

Make your own brown sugar.

To each cup of white sugar add 2 teaspoons molasses. Mix well. I prefer this brown sugar to regular packaged brown sugar. I mix it with my mixer and add the amount of molasses according to whether I want dark or light brown sugar. I like to mix as much as my canister holds. This mixture never gets hard or lumpy for me.

Betty Giesel Martens

Fruit Flavor Popsicles

1 package (3 oz) Jell-O	2 cups boiling water
½ cup sugar	2 cups cold water

Dissolve Jell-O and sugar in boiling water. Add cold water. Pour into popsicle molds. Freeze until almost firm, about 2 hours. Insert popsicle sticks. Freeze until firm, at least 8 hours or overnight. Makes about 4 cups or 8 large popsicles.

Charmaine Wedel

TIP: For perfectly shaped round cookies, pack homemade refrigerator cookie dough into clean 6-ounce juice cans (don't remove bottoms) and freeze. Thaw about 15 minutes, open bottom and push up, using the top edge as a cutting guide.

TIP: Use muffin pans to make extra large ice cubes for punch.

TIP: A contour twin sheet fits on most picnic tables nicely. If you like, decorate the sheet with appliques.

Depression Garden

(A childhood memory)

Place 3 or 4 pieces of any kind of coal in an open glass dish. Pour 2 tablespoons water, 2 tablespoons bluing, and 2 tablespoons salt over the coal. Let stand 24 hours. Then add 2 more tablespoons salt. On the third day, add 2 tablespoons each of salt and water. Then let it stand, and the chemical reaction will soon create a beautiful bowl of "flowers" or "coral."

Arlene Giesel Koehn

Bubble Solution

1 cup water	2 tablespoons light corn syrup
⅓ cup Joy dishwashing liquid	

Mix well and allow to sit for 1 hour before using. Cover and store any leftovers in the refrigerator. Use wire loops, empty thread spools or straws to make bubbles.

Charmaine Wedel

Play Dough

1 cup flour
½ cup salt
2 teaspoons cream of tartar
1 tablespoon vegetable oil

1 cup water
Food coloring, optional
¼ teaspoon peppermint extract,
  optional

Mix ingredients in saucepan. If colored play dough is desired, add color to water before mixing. If scented play dough is desired, add peppermint extract. Heat over medium heat, stirring until mixture comes away from side of pan. Let cool and have children knead until smooth. Add a little more flour while kneading if it is sticky. Store in airtight container.

Arlene Giesel Koehn

Mud Pies

4 cups dirt
1½ cups water

1 cup sand
½ cup crushed leaves

Blend dirt and water with hands. Stir briskly until thick. Gradually mix in sand. Put in leaves and shape pies. Bake in sun until crisp. Put in shade to cool.

Valerie Koehn

Homemade Paint

On days when the children are stuck indoors, keep them happy with harmless homemade paint. Pour a can of evaporated milk into several small containers, then mix a different food coloring into each one. This works great with either finger painting or brushes.

Charmaine Wedel

Pre-Wash

½ cup household ammonia
½ cup dish detergent

¼ cup all-purpose degreaser
1½ cups water

Mix together and put in squirt bottle. This is especially good for scrubbing men's shirt collars. Just apply to soiled garment and rub. Then toss into machine and wash as usual.

Edna Giesel

Grandpa Ike's Cooked Soap Formula

From his diary.

10 pounds grease
2 cans lye

3 or 4 gallons of water

Cook for 2 hours, add 1 pint of salt. Cook for 30 more minutes. Hope you never need to make it. He made soap soon after we were married. His diary says he cooked some for Elma a few times.

Mornie Giesel Unruh

Silver Cleaner

1 cup boiling water
1 teaspoon salt

1 teaspoon baking soda
1 piece, 4" by 5" tin foil

Dissolve salt and soda in boiling water, add crumpled foil. Add silver. Leave set until clean. Wash in soapy water.

Arlene, Mrs. Randy Giesel

Stain Treatment

1 gallon hot water
1 cup Cascade dishwasher soap

¼ cup Clorox bleach

Soak stained items such as tablecloths in this mixture. Do not use boiling water, just hot.

Jolene Unruh

Tupperware Cleaner

To clean yellowed and sticky Tupperware. Coat entire container with an all-purpose kitchen degreaser. Then spray with WD-40, and allow to rest 10 to 15 minutes. Vigorously rub all surfaces with a plastic chore girl. Wash in hot sudsy water, rinse and dry.

Edna Giesel

INDEX

Index

Index

DESSERTS

Index

Index

PRESERVES AND PICKLES

POTPOURRI

This Cookbook is the perfect gift for Weddings, Anniversaries, Birthdays and Holidays.

To order extra copies as gifts for your family and friends, please use the order blanks provided below..

You may order as many copies of *Golden Moments* as you wish for the regular price of $17.95, plus $3.05 for shipping and handling. Mail the order form below with your check or money order to:

Golden Moments Publishing
P.O. Box 1531
West Point, MS 39773

Please send _____ copies of *Golden Moments* @ $17.95 each, plus $3.05 S&H per book ordered.

Name _____

Address _____

City _____ State_____ Zip _____

You may order as many copies of *Golden Moments* as you wish for the regular price of $17.95, plus $3.05 for shipping and handling Mail the order form below with your check or money order to:

Golden Moments Publishing
P.O. Box 1531
West Point, MS 39773

Please send _____ copies of *Golden Moments* @ $17.95 each, plus $3.05 S&H per book ordered.

Name _____

Address _____

City _____ State_____ Zip _____

This Cookbook is the perfect gift for Weddings, Anniversaries, Birthdays and Holidays.

To order extra copies as gifts for your family and friends, please use the order blanks provided below..

You may order as many copies of *Golden Moments* as you wish for the regular price of $17.95, plus $3.05 for shipping and handling. Mail the order form below with your check or money order to:

Golden Moments Publishing
P.O. Box 1531
West Point, MS 39773

Please send _____ copies of *Golden Moments* @ $17.95 each, plus $3.05 S&H per book ordered.

Name _____

Address _____

City _____ State_____ Zip _____

You may order as many copies of *Golden Moments* as you wish for the regular price of $17.95, plus $3.05 for shipping and handling Mail the order form below with your check or money order to:

Golden Moments Publishing
P.O. Box 1531
West Point, MS 39773

Please send _____ copies of *Golden Moments* @ $17.95 each, plus $3.05 S&H per book ordered.

Name _____

Address _____

City _____ State_____ Zip _____